WILD
guide

Scandinavia
Norway, Sweden, Denmark and Iceland

Swim, camp, canoe and explore
Europe's greatest wilderness

Ben Love

WILD
THINGS
PUBLISHING

WILD
guide

Contents

Overview of the region

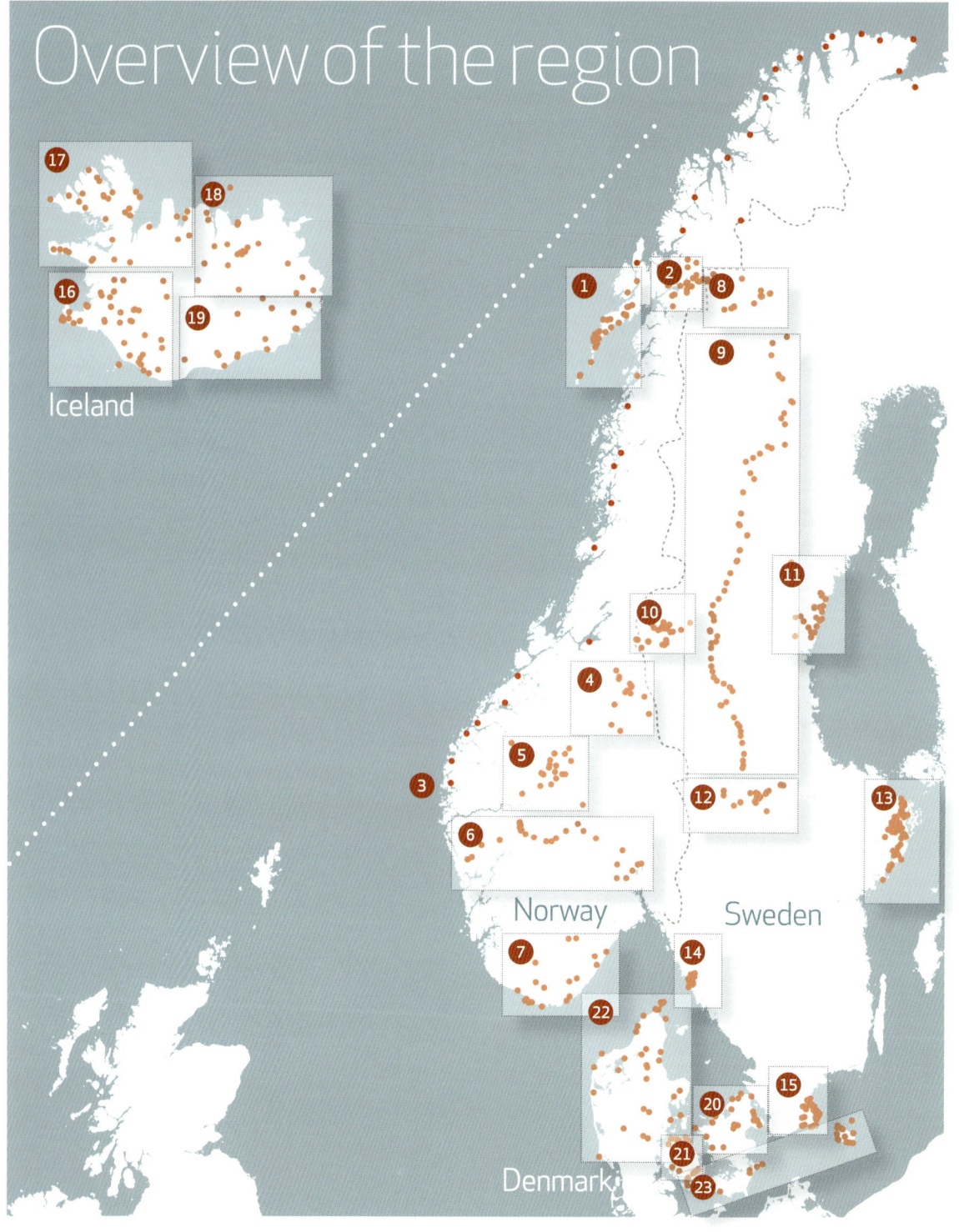

Iceland

Norway

Sweden

Denmark

Norway

④ Røros   p72

High in the mountains bordering Sweden is Røros, a small UNESCO world heritage mining town with a rich culture and surrounded by pristine wilderness. Visit a national park and stay in one of the many mountain huts, or step back in time by visiting the charming 16th- and 17th-century wooden villages and taking a tour in a horse-drawn cart.

① Lofoten   p4

Above the Arctic Circle are a chain of islands defined by their dramatic cliffs, breathtaking mountain vistas and secluded white-sand beaches lapped by azure seas. Celebrate the often warm summer weather with a sea swim under the midnight sun followed by a driftwood fire.

② Narvik   p50

Nestled deep in the stunning Ofotfjord and framed by spectacular high mountains, the iron ore port town of Narvik is the springboard from which to hike, swim, paddle and explore the wilds of the surrounding landscape. See Sami tending their reindeer in mountain farms, learn birch bark weaving and stay in a turf-roofed eco-lodge on the coast.

③ Hurtigruten   p60

Historic sea route that wends its way along the breathtakingly beautiful coast of Norway from Bergen up to the Russian border. Stopping frequently at many remote ports, you can choose whether to live on-board and rent a cabin, or use your ticket to hop on and off and explore the stunning coastal landscapes at your own pace.

⑤ Jotunheimen   p80

With 29 of the highest peaks in Norway, the 'Land of Giants' borrows its name from Norse mythology. Extraordinary waterfalls, glaciers, fjords and mountain passes command breathtaking views. Stay on a traditional mountain farm and sample their organic cheese or visit one of the many fairytale wooden stave churches.

⑥ Mountain Railway   p88

A spectacular railway line that whisks you from central Oslo, up into the Scandinavian Mountains and across a high and remote plateau before descending into Bergen. There's the option to make a more dramatic descent on a breathtaking branch line or rent a bicycle and enjoy a downhill, car-free ride on the Rallarvegen, wild camping on route.

⑦ Sørlandets Kysten   p100

Also known as the Norwegian Riviera, a mixture of waterfalls, beaches, rugged coastline and an unusual geology that includes Brufjell, a completely natural water park with slides and plunge pools makes this a great summer destination. Cross the Gjeveden lake by wooden raft Huckleberry Finn-style or stay in a secluded lighthouse.

Sweden

8 Kiruna Lapland p110

Some call this Europe's last true wilderness – a vast and incredibly beautiful landscape. Wild swim under the midnight sun, climb Sweden's highest mountain, watch the aurora borealis, canoe camp on the lakeshore, and enjoy a wood-fired sauna. You will also meet the reindeer-herding Sami people famous for their folk crafts.

9 Inlandsbanan p120

Discover remote villages and landscapes on this inland train journey from the forests of mid-Sweden to the Arctic tundra. Not exactly an express train, the driver frequently stops to point out wildlife such as moose and bears. Taste smoked trout from the Vojmån river, and hunt for the black vanilla orchid by the Ljusnan river.

10 Åre Fjällen p130

Mountains, rivers and some of Sweden's biggest and most impressive waterfalls feed a vast network of lakes, perfect for exploring by canoe. Slide down the river pools of Ullån with wild swimming galore. Forage for cloudberries, try the local birch sap wine and stay in a cosy mountain lodge.

11 Höga Kusten p140

Famous for its soaring granite coast, this breathtaking landscape has superb hiking, remote beaches and uninhabited islands. For the more intrepid, canoe out to find secret caves, sleep in a lighthouse or try the famously pungent Swedish delicacy of fermented herring.

12 Dala-Floda p148

This is a highly accessible yet fairytale landscape, rich in both wildlife and heritage, where girls dance around the Maypole wearing fresh flowers to sounds of traditional fiddle music, and wolves and lynx still roam. Be enchanted by the red timber houses, explore by horse and cart and stop to swim in the myriad lakes.

13 Stockholm Archipelago p158

A short boat ride from the Swedish capital takes you to the heart of over 30,000 islands, islets and rocks that make up this spectacular archipelago. There's snorkelling, swimming and canoeing galore, but you can also find gemstones, ruined castles and an ancient labyrinth – all linked by simple passenger ferries.

14 Tjörn p170

A spectacular granite island, with sheltered and shallow waters easily explored with a rented kayak. Wild camp on uninhabited islands, resupply at the small harbour villages, and enjoy an abundance of seafood. Inland you'll find wildflower meadows and remains from the Bronze Age and Viking periods.

15 Österlen p178

This is the setting for the popular *Wallander* books and films, a pastoral coastal landscape rich in ancient standing stones and rock carvings. Make a slow tour by bicycle, swim from white-sands beaches, camp in the dunes and taste produce from the many organic farms – including delicious local cider.

Iceland

16 South West & Reykjavík   p190

Convenient for Reykjavík, this is an area packed with huge waterfalls, black-sand beaches, volcanic thermals, glaciers, secret hot springs and much more. Geysers spout boiling water 40 metres up into the air and you can snorkel a fissure between two continental plates. Unusual delicacies include rotten shark!

17 North West Iceland   p204

Stretching from the glacier-covered volcano of the Snæfellsnes peninsula, where Jules Verne set off to find the centre of the earth, to the West Fjords with their remote fishing villages and fjords. There are numerous hot springs, often in amazing coastal settings, and in the north the indigenous horses outnumber the people.

18 North East Iceland   p214

A steamy volcanic region of remote plateaus and volcanic sands. There is Dettifoss, the most powerful waterfall in Europe, mighty glacial rivers that have carved deep canyons and glaciated mountain peaks. Spend a day inspecting boiling mud pots, subterranean springs and colossal lava features before relaxing in a restorative thermal bath.

19 South East Iceland   p222

Iceland's most remote region, where the lone main road hugs the coast, taking you past the blue glow of an iceberg-filled lagoon and the Vatnajökull glacier, home to the largest national park in Europe. Hunt for ice diamonds on black-sand beaches, and shower under a steaming waterfall. Discover why this is called the 'Land of Fire and Ice'.

Denmark

20 Sealand Coast & Copenhagen p232

Largest of the over four hundred islands that make up Denmark, Sealand is also where you'll find the capital, Copenhagen. From the city it's an easy bicycle trip out to one of the many long, sandy beaches. Spend a long weekend camping by the sea, visiting incredible Viking remains and eating delicious organic food at the Fuglebjerggaard café.

21 Funen   p240

Spend halcyon days exploring the idyllic and magical island of Funen in a horse-drawn caravan. Then take to the sea in a kayak and explore the archipelago of 96 islands that decorate the south coast – with a great network of unique architect-designed coastal shelters so you can camp overnight in style.

22 North Jutland   p246

Defined by its dune-backed white sandy beaches, the northern area of the Jutland peninsula is the perfect place for a laid-back summer adventure filled with fresh fish dinners, glorious sunsets and beach combing for amber. Rent a bicycle and visit one of the many ruins, museums and Viking remains.

23 Bornholm & South Sea Islands p258

Bornholm, as well as the South Sea Islands of Ærø, Langeland, Lollan, Falster and Møn, has its own unique flavour of Danish island life and all can be explored by a mixture of ferry (if no bridge) and bicycle. Bornholm alone has ruined castles, prehistoric burial sites, sandy beaches, towering cliffs and ancient woodland to be explored.

Introduction

The Scandinavian countries and Iceland have a shared linguistic and cultural heritage and, with the exception of Denmark, they are home to some of the largest remaining tracts of true wilderness in Europe. Sweden and Norway alone are so vast that it would be impossible to do the entire countries justice in a single guide. For these two countries, the book focuses on eight different areas or specific journeys in each. The selection has been made to give you, the reader and potential visitor, a meaningful and satisfying taste of the different landscapes that both Sweden and Norway have to offer.

For the considerably smaller countries of Denmark and Iceland, each has been divided up into four geographical areas. And for each of these areas – and this applies to all countries – you will see an obvious focus on a particular mode of transport or type of activity. These suggestions offer you the chance to experience the very best of that particular area and direct you to places where opportunities for even more adventures are likely to open up. The book is primarily a summer guide for all the areas of Scandinavia and Iceland, but many of these places offer wonders at all times of year.

Landscapes shaped by fire and ice

Mainland Scandinavia's landscape has been largely shaped by glaciation during the last ice age and its immediate aftermath. The most obvious evidence are the lakes and fjords, but you'll find examples of other glacial landforms all over the region. In the High Coast area of Sweden, for example, the land is still rising at a rate of about 8mm per year. This phenomenon is known as post-glacial rebound, which occurs because the land is no longer being forced down by the

weight of ice. It will continue to rise until it reaches an equilibrium level. In this area alone the land has already risen 800 metres since the end of the last ice age.

Iceland is altogether different and in geological terms a much younger country. It also lies on the divergent boundary between two tectonic plates – the Eurasian and the North American – directly above a hotspot known as the 'Iceland plume'. Seismic activity at this boundary around 16 to 18 million years ago is believed to have caused the creation of Iceland's land mass, which is characterized by numerous volcanoes and hot springs.

Language and culture

Danish, Swedish and Norwegian are all mutually intelligible, whereas modern Icelandic has changed very little from the Old Norse that the original settlers from mainland Scandinavia brought with them to Iceland in the ninth century.

These countries display many other cultural similarities such as shared customs and festivals, but at the same time there are also obvious differences. These are often the basis of stereotypical jokes and friendly rivalries between the different nations.

In the north of Sweden and Norway, where a spine of mountains forms their common border, you'll meet the indigenous Sami people. Their lands also span Finland and the Kola Peninsula of Russia. The Sami, who have kept their own language and customs, traditionally herded reindeer in the mountains and forests, or fished in the lakes, rivers and along the Norwegian coast. Families that are no longer nomadic and are settled at a particular farm are known as 'sedentary Sami'. Some of the areas of Norway and Sweden included in this book have significant Sami communities, and details of where you can find out more about their fascinating culture are included.

Friluftsliv

The concept of *friluftsliv*, which roughly translates as 'open-air life', is the Scandinavian philosophy of having a true connectedness with the natural environment. It means being outdoors, breathing the fresh air and living in harmony with nature and the landscape. The term itself, written down for the first time in 1859 by the Norwegian poet Henrik Ibsen, is relatively new but the concept itself is older. If you intend to explore the outdoors in Scandinavia, make some time to read a little more about the benefits of *friluftsliv* before you leave.

The Scandinavian good life

Also included in the book are my selection of special places to eat and stay. Generally speaking, the cafés and restaurants recommended specialise in local food prepared with organic or sustainable ingredients. In terms of places to stay, those listed are unusual, particularly convenient for outdoor adventures, or perhaps require a little local knowledge to discover. In some areas covered by the book, where spectacular wild camping is a very obvious and possible option, then you'll find fewer accommodation options.

If you want to forage, the rural and coastal landscapes in the book offer ample opportunities for gathering berries and mushrooms, as well as fishing. Indeed, this is how many of the rural restaurants included in the book obtain their super-fresh and delicious ingredients. Using local, traditional and seasonal produce but preparing it in new ways even has its own name – 'New Nordic' cuisine – and it's delicious!

My love of this region has led me to study the Scandinavian languages and spend many years exploring its spectacular landscapes. With its fascinating culture and history, I'm confident that like me, you will also enjoy discovering wild Scandinavia.

Ben Love

adventure@wildthingspublishing.com

Finding your way

Each wild place can be located using the overview maps and the directions, but to be sure of finding your way you'll need to use the latitude and longitude provided. This is given in decimal degrees (WGS84) and can be entered straight into any web-based mapping program, such as Google, Map.krak.dk (Denmark), Kartor.eniro.se (Sweden) or Ja.is/kort (Iceland). Print out the map before you go or save a 'screen grab' in case there's no mobile reception. You can also enter the co-ordinates into your GPS, car Sat Nav (enable decimal degrees) or your PDA/telephone, if it has GPS enabled. Approximate walk-in times are given for one way only, and abbreviations in the directions refer to left and right (L, R) and north, east, south, west (N, E, S, W).

Wild, safe & responsible

1. Remember that some areas included in the book are extremely remote. Always ensure you have suitable equipment and know how to use it, carry local maps and a compass, and, if necessary, leave a route plan and time of return with a third party. Destinations where experienced guides are needed, e.g. glacier walks, are indicated.

2. Make sure you're aware of the laws regarding access in each country (see the back of the book for more information).

3. Keep to paths and obey safety notices in geothermal/volcanic areas in Iceland.

4. Follow the safety advice given for driving on mountain and summer roads. Only ford rivers if you have an appropriate vehicle, and obey road closures.

5. Check local weather reports before heading into remote areas.

6. Be aware that apparently calm rivers and lakes can suddenly feed into huge waterfalls. Check before swimming.

7. In Norway and Sweden make sure you have plenty of mosquito repellent.

8. Leave nothing behind you but footprints.

Right to roam

The Scandinavian countries and Iceland have a centuries-old tradition called 'every man's right'. People are allowed to roam just about anywhere as long as they do not disturb or destroy the environment. In protected areas such as national parks there may be restrictions, for example cycling on marked trails only.

For fishing, local signs will indicate the need for a permit.

Norway (*Allemannsrett*)
All uncultivated land is accessible. Cultivated land may only be walked on when frozen and covered in snow. You can pitch a tent for up to two days on any uncultivated land, no closer than 150m from a dwelling. Canoeing and swimming in rivers, lakes (but not reservoirs for drinking water) and the sea is permitted. Foraging is allowed.

Sweden (*Allemansrätt*)
Everyone has the right to access and camp on land except in private gardens, the immediate vicinity of a dwelling and land under cultivation. You can also forage (don't pick protected species). Canoeing and swimming in rivers, lakes, and the sea is allowed – unless explicitly forbidden.

Iceland (*Almannarétt*)
You can cross uncultivated private property without special permission unless signs have been posted. Public land is open to everyone. Off-road driving is forbidden when the ground is not covered with snow. Canoeing and swimming in rivers, lakes and the sea is allowed – unless explicitly forbidden. You can pitch up to three tents on uncultivated ground for a single night, unless there's a notice to the contrary. Foraging for immediate consumption is allowed.

Denmark (*Offentlighedens adgang til naturen*)
Dunes, beaches and all publicly owned forests are accessible. Uncultivated, unfenced areas have daytime access irrespective of ownership. Privately owned forest can be accessed by road and track only and foraging is allowed on public land. You can wild camp but only at specified locations. Canoeing and swimming in rivers, lakes and the sea is allowed.

See the links at the back of the book for more information.

Scandinavian wildlife

Most travellers come to Scandinavia for its spectacular nature. Its fjords, its snow-capped mountains and its evergreen boreal forests. But too few have paid attention to Scandinavian fauna. While most serious wildlife travellers still tend to head to the African continent, early pioneers are now turning their binoculars and cameras towards the North.

Scandinavia has an abundance of wildlife, and although nature is suffering from exploitation of forestry and mining, many of the large mammals – and especially large carnivores – are actually increasing in numbers. For example, the wolf used to be extinct in Scandinavia, wiped out by hundreds of years of hunting. But since the 1980s when a few wandered back in from the Finnish/Russian population, more have followed and these have led to a population of about 500 wolves, most in central Sweden.

Perhaps most characteristic of all Nordic animals is the majestic moose (European elk), which can be found throughout most of Swedish and Norwegian mainland. Also iconic to these lands are reindeer, and still today semi-domestic reindeer are herded by the indigenous Sami people in most parts of northern Sweden and Norway. Wild reindeer can only found in mountainous southern Norway.

Scandinavia has its own 'big five', and these large carnivores are exciting, if hard to spot. They include wolves, wolverines, the elusive and rarely seen lynx, brown bears and the golden eagle. Brown bears can be found in large parts of Sweden and Norway, but are threatened by overhunting. Whereas golden eagles as well as white-tailed sea eagles have made a major comeback in recent years.

Other fascinating fauna include the Eurasian beaver in Sweden and eastern Norway; Arctic foxes in northern Norway, Sweden and Iceland; and huge colonies of the delightful Atlantic puffin on the coast of Iceland and northern Norway.

Largest of all the land mammals is the musk ox, which can be seen in Dovrefjell-Sunndalsfjella National Park, Norway. This population was reintroduced in 1932 and 1947 and now consists of around 200 animals. In the summer they typically live in groups of 10 to 15 individuals, and one of these groups has migrated into Härjedalen in Sweden where a small group has established.

Scandinavia also has an incredible wealth of sea mammals, and Iceland and northern Norway are among the best places in Europe for species like sperm whales, white-beaked dolphins and orcas, often called 'killer whales'.

Top tips for seeing Scandinavian wildlife

1. Season – behaviour patterns change during the year.

2. Habitat – type of landscape and plantlife – i.e. meadows and clearings are best for summer moose spotting.

3. Time of day – when does it feed? Rest? Drink? Dawn and dusk are usually best.

4. Be quiet – listen carefully.

5. Stay downwind – so your scent doesn't carry.

6. Be invisible and still – wear natural colours and keep your distance. Find a good spot and wait.

7. Equipment – bring binoculars and a camera.

8. Local knowledge – employ a local guide or seek advice.

By Marcus Eldh,
founder & head guide
Wild Sweden www.wildsweden.com

Best for
Wild camping

In Sweden, Norway and Iceland you're allowed to wild camp pretty much anywhere (with a few caveats – see Right to Roam p18) and there are some spectacular locations.

Camp by a river or lake and start the next day with a refreshing swim, or choose somewhere with a fantastic view for when you open the tent door next morning. With so much space, it's not hard to find a great spot all to yourself. When driving you don't, on the whole, need to stray very far from the main road to find a pleasant spot to break your journey.

If the weather is good and there are no mosquitoes, sleep in a tarp or bivvy bag for a real 'under the stars' experience. Remember to bring a decent sleeping mat and a sleeping bag appropriate for the temperature. When you break camp make sure you leave nothing behind to indicate that you were ever there.

Kvalvika Beach (Norway, Lofoten 1)

Bunes Beach (Norway, Lofoten 3)

Femundsmarka National Park (Norway, Røros 7)

Haugastøl (Norway, Mountain Railway, 14)

Besseggen Ridge (Norway, Jotunheimen 13)

Kungsleden (Sweden, Kiruna Lapland 19)

Vålådalen Nature Reserve (Sweden, Åre Fjällen 18)

Þingvellir National Park (Iceland, South West & Reyjkavik 31)

Archipelago Shelters (Denmark, Funen 18)

Thy National Park (Denmark, North Jutland 26)

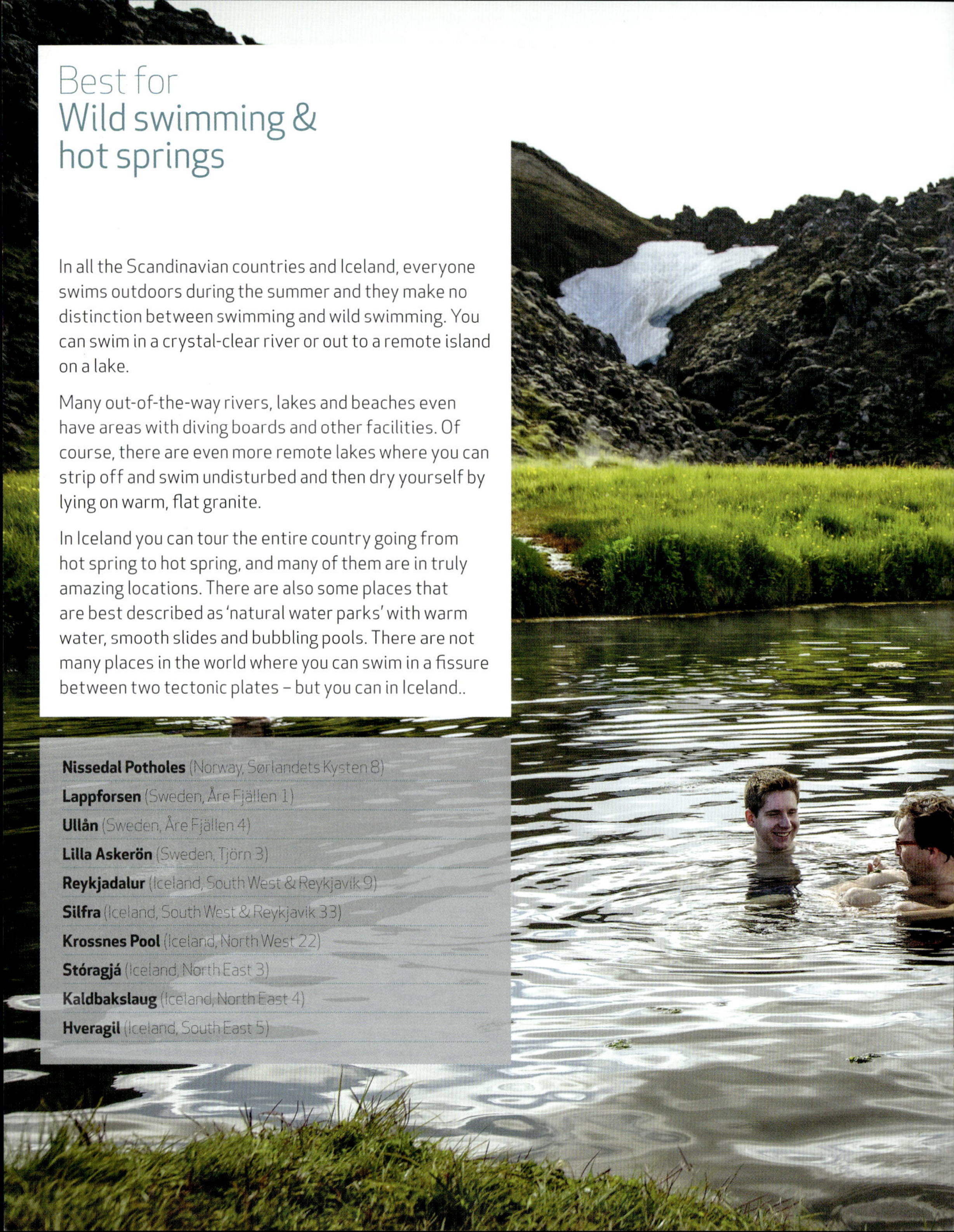

Best for
Wild swimming &
hot springs

In all the Scandinavian countries and Iceland, everyone swims outdoors during the summer and they make no distinction between swimming and wild swimming. You can swim in a crystal-clear river or out to a remote island on a lake.

Many out-of-the-way rivers, lakes and beaches even have areas with diving boards and other facilities. Of course, there are even more remote lakes where you can strip off and swim undisturbed and then dry yourself by lying on warm, flat granite.

In Iceland you can tour the entire country going from hot spring to hot spring, and many of them are in truly amazing locations. There are also some places that are best described as 'natural water parks' with warm water, smooth slides and bubbling pools. There are not many places in the world where you can swim in a fissure between two tectonic plates – but you can in Iceland..

Nissedal Potholes (Norway, Sørlandets Kysten 8)

Lappforsen (Sweden, Åre Fjällen 1)

Ullån (Sweden, Åre Fjällen 4)

Lilla Askerön (Sweden, Tjörn 3)

Reykjadalur (Iceland, South West & Reykjavik 9)

Silfra (Iceland, South West & Reykjavik 33)

Krossnes Pool (Iceland, North West 22)

Stóragjá (Iceland, North East 3)

Kaldbakslaug (Iceland, North East 4)

Hveragil (Iceland, South East 5)

Best for
Canoe & kayak adventures

The numerous sheltered archipelagos in Scandinavia offer amazing opportunities for exploring by canoe or kayak. Take your camping gear with you in the boat and camp out on a secret island or beach.

In all the areas where there's great paddling, there is also the possibility of hiring both boats and equipment. Paddlelapland in Kiruna will even take care of the logistics of more complex excursions, including arranging for you to be flown to a river or lake with your kayak or canoe dangling in a net below the helicopter. In Iceland there's some great sea and lake kayaking, but the rivers mainly require considerable experience in negotiating whitewater: nearly all of them involve a substantial and very spectacular rapid or waterfall.

Whatever your skill level or experience, there are wonderful adventures to be had in each of the countries, and nothing beats floating across the landscape.

Reine Kayaking (Norway, Lofoten 6)

Tømmerrennene (Norway, Røros 10)

Vistas Paddle (Sweden, Kiruna Lapland 6)

Laddjujokka Paddle (Sweden, Kiruna Lapland 7)

Ottsjön (Sweden, Åre Fjällen 9)

Harpikön (Sweden, Dala-Floda 6)

Norra Stavsudda (Sweden, Stockholm Archipelago 34)

Stora Dyrön (Sweden, Tjörn 9)

Stigfjorden (Sweden, Tjörn 12)

South Funen Archipelago (Denmark, Funen 6)

Best for
Beaches & coast

Think of white sandy beaches with turquoise waters and your first thought might not be of Sweden, Norway or Denmark, but know where to go and you will discover hundreds of miles of secluded beach and coastal paradises.

Denmark is made up of 400 islands, and wherever you travel, you're never far from a beautiful sandy beach – and the same goes for the south of Sweden.

On Iceland the beaches are of black, volcanic sand, whereas the white sand and azure-blue sea of Norway's Lofoten Islands' beaches lends a special quality to the light. The smooth granite coastlines of the Stockholm archipelago, the Swedish west coast and the south coast of Norway also have fantastic coves and beaches – in short, you're spoilt for choice.

Sandnessjøen (Norway, Hurtigruten 12)

Geiranger (Norway, Hurtigruten 6)

Sandvika beach (Norway, Sørlandets Kysten 4)

Knäbäckshusen Beach (Sweden, Österlen 1)

Hvítserkur (Iceland, North West 31)

Diamond Beach (Iceland, South East 7)

Røsnæs (Denmark, Sealand Coast & Copenhagen 13)

Kandestederne (Denmark, North Jutland 6)

Møns Klint (Denmark, Bornholm & South Sea Islands 13)

The Hammer (Denmark, Bornholm & South Sea Islands 14)

Best for
Sacred & ancient

Boasting huge riches in historic and cultural remains, these lands full of myth and traditions offer a wide variety of intriguing sites. From prehistoric stone ships and circles to tombs and fortresses, you will discover wonderful ancient rock art and learn how early settlers lived and worshipped.

The stave churches in Norway date back to Viking times and feature extraordinary carvings depicting a fascinating mixture of images from Norse mythology as well as Christian symbols. There's also a pilgrim route across Sweden and Norway that takes you through some very rugged yet beautiful landscapes. In Iceland, some sacred springs and pools are said to have healing properties where you can soothe aches and pains.

Many of these places have a very special atmosphere as well as being in wild and wonderful locations. Take time out to pause and reflect and let your imagination run free.

Urnes Stave Church (Norway, Jotunheimen 4)

Pilane Grävfält (Sweden, Tjörn 17)

Havängsdösen (Sweden, Österlen 6)

Järrestads Hällristningar (Sweden, Österlen 18)

Kungagraven (Sweden, Österlen 19)

Glavendrupstenen (Denmark, Funen 9)

Mårhøj Jættestue (Denmark, Funen 10)

Troldkirken (Denmark, North Jutland 14)

Krosslaug (Iceland, South West & Reykjavik 15)

Goðafoss (Iceland, North East 10)

Best for
Food & foraging

To travel is also to taste, and in these special places you will often be spoilt with incredible fresh and preserved food bound by local tradition and culture to the land.

With so much forest and uncultivated land, wild berries and woodland mushrooms are plentiful, and you're likely to see bilberries and cloudberries on every summer walk. Many restaurants source ingredients through foraging and their menus will give you a good idea of what's available locally and at that time of year.

Near the coast you can expect an abundance of amazing seafood, and there's nothing like catching your own fish from your kayak. But in the mountains you're likely to be eating reindeer and Arctic char.

If you're feeling adventurous, why not try one of the more unusual dishes? Sheep's head or rotten shark might be on offer in Iceland, or there's the more palatable fermented herring in Sweden.

Best for
Sunrise, sunset & the midnight sun

When you cross the Arctic Circle around midsummer, the sun never sets and the Arctic sun shines through the night, bathing everything in a very special warm light.

This extraordinary phenomenon can make for some amazing photographs, and there are great places to experience it. Immediately below the Arctic Circle, it's still light at night so you can make the most of the long days. As you head further south (and when the summer solstice has passed), you start to see fiery red sunrises and sunsets. Arrive early in the evening or morning, or alternatively set up camp in a location where you'll be guaranteed an amazing show before bed or when you wake up.

Horseid Beach (Norway, Lofoten 2)
Narvikfjellet (Norway, Narvik 6)
Midnattsolstigen Walk (Sweden, Kiruna Lapland 13)
Aurora Sky Station (Sweden, Kiruna Lapland 21)
Låktatjåkko Mountain Station (Sweden, Kiruna Lapland 31)
Högbonden Fyr (Sweden, Höga Kusten 21)
Hamneberget (Sweden, Tjörn 21)
Ales Stenar (Sweden, Österlen 15)
Grímsey (Iceland, North East 14)
Rubjerg Knude (Denmark, North Jutland 17)

NORWAY

LOFOTEN

Our perfect week

→ **Jump** across the horns of the goat on Svolværgeita.

→ **Scramble** to the summit of Higravstinden – the highest point in the Lofoten Islands.

→ **Surf** above the Arctic Circle then relax in a hot tub.

→ **Wild** camp on Kvalvik beach with a roaring driftwood fire.

→ **Watch** the white-tailed sea eagles hunting in Trollfjord.

→ **Kayak** round Henningsvær with seals for company.

→ **Learn** about the fishing community in the Lofoten Islands at a living museum.

→ **Spend** the night in a remote mountain cabin.

→ **Stroke** a puffin hound on Værøy.

→ **Swim** in the sea under the midnight sun.

The many islands that make up the Lofoten Islands Archipelago are characterised by their towering peaks, sheltered inlets and white-sand beaches, all set against a background of a turquoise sea. Although this is well above the Arctic Circle, summers here can be very warm and the midnight sun means you don't have to worry about darkness curtailing your adventures.

Getting there is easy: you can fly direct to the small airport in Svolvær or alternatively fly to Bodø on the mainland and take the ferry across. This stops en-route at the remote islands of Værøy and Røstlandet, so if you choose that route you could start your adventures there.

The E10 road links all the main islands of the archipelago via an impressive network of tunnels and bridges. This road is a national tourist route and an adventure in itself – you'll find yourself constantly stopping to take in the breathtaking views. A great way to explore is by bike, which gives you plenty of time to absorb the scenery.

Fishing has been the main industry in the islands for many hundreds of years. From mid-February to end of April the Arctic cod migrate in vast numbers from nutritious areas of the Barents Sea to their spawning grounds near Lofoten. Traditionally fish would be caught and then hung to dry on huge racks. This very important fishery is carefully managed, and you can learn more about it at the Norwegian Fishing Village Museum. Unsurprisingly, seafood also features significantly in the local cuisine.

The coastline is easily explored by kayak, and these can be rented from numerous places. Many of the beaches can only be reached by sea or require a substantial walk, so as a kayaker you can often have a breathtakingly beautiful beach all to yourself.

Wild camping is easy, but if you want a real bed then an old fisherman's cabin or *rorbu* is a classic Lofoten experience. One end is over the water, so you can easily start the day with a bracing swim. In the summer it's very easy to forget that you're above the Arctic Circle.

BEACHES

1 KVALVIKA BEACH

One of the most scenic beaches in the islands. The surfing documentary *North of the Sun* was filmed here, and the shelter built in the film still stands. Make a roaring driftwood fire and camp on the edge of the dunes by the turquoise sea. You won't want to leave.

→ From E10 S of Ramberg take FV808 onto Moskenesøya island and L for Fredvang after crossing bridge. Follow road about 3km to red boat shed on L and parking (68.0695, 13.1305) up on R just after. An obvious trail inland leads to the beach.
1 hour, 68.0776, 13.0982

2 HORSEID BEACH

Narrow wedge of white sand between high mountains with some grassy areas great for camping. There should be plenty of driftwood to make a fire but it's advisable to bring your own fresh water. Otherwise hike up one of the mountains until you find clean water flowing off the slopes. For the best camping spot, walk to the end of the beach and then climb up a little to the right. This is close to the sea and very sheltered. You'll want to spend at least one night here.

→ From harbour in Reine take the ferry to Kjerkfjorden (67.9924, 13.0137). At end of pier turn R. After 100m on L you'll see a path and sign. Follow about 3.5km to beach. Reinefjorden ferry,
+47 76 092090, www.reinefjorden.no
2 hours, 68.0220, 12.9923

3 BUNES BEACH

Isolated and beautiful beach, perfect for escaping from civilisation. Lying below the west face of Helvetestinden mountain, it's a great place for watching the sunset in late summer. There's usually plenty of driftwood for a roaring fire and water can be collected from a waterfall. There is nowhere to buy provisions in Vindstad, so ensure you bring everything you need with you – although you could fish for your dinner. Great camping.

→ Take the ferry from the harbour in Reine to the village of Vindstad (67.9578, 13.0037). From here follow the path 2km through the village and along the fjord. When the village ends take the path L signed 'Bunes'. Reinefjorden ferry,
+47 76 092090, www.reinefjorden.no
1 hour from village, 67.9778, 12.9665

4 RAMBERG BEACH

Beautiful white sand beach with contrasting turquoise water, easily accessible and perfect for a midnight-sun swim. Behind the village is a rock formation said to be a troll (68.0859, 13.2343). The legend is that he came to the village to propose to a beautiful girl who turned him down, so he sat down and stayed there until the sun rose, turning him to stone. He still watches all the pretty girls down in the village, and loose falling rocks are said to be his tears.

→ The beach is in the village of Ramberg on the E10.
68.0959, 13.2408

5 UNSTAD SURFING

Campsite and board rental by a world-class surf break above the Arctic Circle. Run by the daughter of one of the 1960s pioneers of surfing here. Stay in a cabin or camp with access to a sauna and hot tub when you come in after surfing under the midnight sun. Lessons available for beginners.

→ Unstadveien 105, 8363 Bøstad.,
+47 970 61201, www.unstadarcticsurf.com
68.2652, 13.5910

KAYAK

6 REINE KAYAKING

Hire kayaks in the beautiful village of Reine on Moskenes and explore the sheltered Reinefjord. Around midsummer you can paddle at night under the midnight sun. Fish as you go and stop on a remote beach to cook and camp. From here you can also paddle (with a little walking) to the beaches of Horseid (see 2) and Bunes (see 3).

→ ReineAdventure, Reine, 8390 Reine, +47 932 14596. www.reineadventure.com
67.9325, 13.0895

7 HENNINGSVÆR KAYAKING

The fishing village of Henningsvær is spread over several small islands. Hire kayaks and launch into the large harbour in the centre of Henningsvær, with open sea at one end and a causeway you can go through at the other. Paddle round the islands, perhaps stopping for lunch on one of the outlying skerries. By the time you return you may well find you're being followed by an inquisitive seal!

→ Book kayak hire from XXLofoten in Svolvær: Johan E. Paulsens gate 12, 8300 Svolvær, +47 916 55500. www.xxlofoten.no
Allow 3 hours+, 68.1543, 14.2054

BOAT TRIPS & FISHING

8 TROLLFJORD BOAT TRIP

Impressive fjord off Raftsund, a sound between the Lofoten islands and the Vesterålen Archipelago. Its entrance is only 100m wide, framed by sheer cliffs; further along its 2km length it widens to a maximum of 800m. Take a boat trip and look for white-tailed sea eagles spectacularly diving for fish. Your voyage will take you past several small islands such as Skrova (see p40).

→ Collective of companies offering trips to Trollfjord from Svolvær: Trollfjord Cruise, Torget 16, 8300 Svolvær, +47 451 57587. www.trollfjordcruise.com
2–3 hours, 68.3638, 14.9466

9 FISHING TRIP

The waters around the islands are rich fishing grounds, and for centuries fishing has been the main industry. Have a go at catching one of the legendary huge cod. Nigel Hearn, an English fisherman who's made these islands his home, can provide tackle and take you to some great spots in one of his small boats. Any fishing trip here is also a marine safari, so be prepared to be distracted by sea eagles, seals and dolphins.

→ Leave from various harbours, book at: vestpollen vei 61, 8316 Laupstad, +47 997 59342. www.noproblemsportfishing.com
68.3585, 14.7200 🛏️🍴🏖️🎣

10 RØST ISLANDS

Accessible only by boat, this stunning group comprises 365 islands, holms and skerries. A 65km ferry journey takes you from Moskenes to the main island of Røstlandet. While this is only 12m above sea level, the surrounding islands tower above the sea – Storfjellet is the highest at 259m. A quarter of Norway's seabird population is said to live here, and you're likely to see rarities such as the greater and lesser storm petrels and fulmars. There's accommodation and wild camping on the island.

→ Ferries run by Torghatten Nord, +47 906 20 700. www.torghatten-nord.no
105 mins one way, 67.5194, 12.1152
🛏️🍴🦌🏖️⛺🎣

HISTORY & CULTURE

11 VÆRØY

Craggy island of 18km² where the birds far outnumber the 775 permanent human residents. There are numerous hikes around the island and you'll have no trouble finding space to wild camp undisturbed, from beautiful white-sand beaches to vantage points up on the cliffs. The island also has an abandoned village (Mostad), numerous Viking Age burial sites and the oldest church in Lofoten, dating from 1714. The rare six-toed Norwegian Lundehund is from here and was used to hunt for puffins. The ferry runs from Moskenes to the main village of Sørland.

→ Ferries run by Torghatten Nord, +47 906 20 700. www.torghatten-nord.no
75 mins one way, 67.6769, 12.6675
🛏️🍴🏖️🚣🦌⛺🏖️✝️

12 SKOMVÆR LIGHTHOUSE & HELVETET CAVE PAINTINGS

Take a boat from Røstlandet to explore the birdlife and secrets of other islands in the group. The furthest, at 15km, is Skomvær (67.4108, 11.8751). Its lighthouse dates from 1887 and is now automated – there was a lighthouse keeper here until 1978. The island of Trenyken (67.4369, 11.8912) has a 100m-long cave with paintings and seal remains dated to 1500 BC. Landing here is not allowed from April 15th to August 15th due to nesting birds. Bring binoculars.

14

15

16

→ Lofottur sightseeing boats leave daily in summer from Røst Bryggehotell on Röstlandet. +47 934 97445. www.lofottur.com
2.5 hours, 67.5057, 12.0772

13 VIKING MUSEUM LOFOTR

The largest Viking longhouse ever found has been reconstructed as a fascinating museum of the history of the Vikings in the Lofoten Islands. Every year in August it hosts a festival with numerous fun and informative events. In a nearby inlet is a replica of the Gokstad Viking ship that you can try your hand at rowing.

→ Lofotr Vikingmuseum, Prestegårdsveien 59, 8360 Bøstad, +47 76 154000. www.lofotr.no
68.2439, 13.7565

14 BALLSTAD FISHING VILLAGE

Located on a small island off Vestvågøya, Ballstad is one of the largest and oldest fishing villages in the Lofoten Islands, and still very active. Walk round the harbour and see the traditional fishermen's cabins (rorbuer), built on land but with one end supported on poles over the water to allow easy access to the boats. Over the other side of the island, look at the racks used for drying cod.

→ Book a rorbu with Kræmmervika Rorbuer, 8373 Ballstad, +47 76 060920. www.kremmervika.no
68.0743, 13.5505

15 FLAKSTAD CHURCH

Second-oldest church in Lofoten, from the 18th century – a storm destroyed the 15th-century original. It's constructed of wood from Russia that was exchanged for fish, and has an onion dome more in keeping with a Russian church. One window is from the original building. The tower was blown down by a hurricane in 1874 and restored in 1938. Ramberg beach (see 4) is close by.

→ Flakstad Kirke, Kjerkveien, 8380 Ramberg.
68.1046, 13.3062

16 SUND BLACKSMITH

The blacksmith in Sund makes little wrought-iron cormorants. In north Norwegian folk legends an enchanted land called Utrøst sometimes emerges from the sea with fields full of corn and cattle, and the three farmers who inhabit it are able to transform into cormorants. Visit the smithy and see the blacksmith at work.

→ Smeden i Sund, 8384 Sund, +47 76 093629. www.smedenisund.no
68.0049, 13.2070

22

17 LOFOTEN FISHING VILLAGE MUSEUM
Fascinating living museum of life in a fishing village over the past 200 years. Learn about Lofotfiske (seasonal cod fishing) and see how cod liver oil was processed. During the summer there is also a working traditional bakery. Guided tours are available.

→ Å i Lofoten, 8392 Sørvågen, +47 76 09 14 88. www.museumnord.no 67.8799, 12.9829

HIKES

18 HIGRAVSTINDEN HIKE
You can scramble almost to the summit of the highest point in the Lofoten Islands – 1,146m above sea level. It's hard work, but on a good day the views will make it more than worthwhile.

→ Park at junction of E10 with Lilandveien in the village of Higravseidet (68.3555, 14.7473). The path starts here but is not always obvious, so use a local map.
3–4 hours, 68.3562, 14.7913

19 SVOLVÆRGEITA
Pinnacle of rock 150m above Svolvær that resembles two horns – its name in Norwegian means Svolvær Goat. It's possible to climb to

the top of the larger horn and then jump to the smaller one.

→ Northern Alpine Guides take fit people, including non-climbers: Kalleveien 21, 8310 Kabelvåg, +47 942 49 110. www.alpineguides.no 68.2461, 14.5883

LOCAL FOOD

20 AALAN GÅRD
Delicious organic goats' milk cheeses made using traditional local techniques. There's also a fascinating herb garden and in summer, a café serving home-cooked food.

→ Lauvdalen 186, 8360 Bøstad, +47 76 08 45 34. www.aalan.no 68.2448, 13.8981

21 LOFOTEN GÅRDSYSTERI
Small organic farm and dairy selling scrumptious cheeses, eggs, hand-made sausages and honey – ideal if you are putting together a beach picnic.

→ Unstadveien 235, 8360 Bøstad, +47 76 08 96 31. www.lofoten-gardsysteri.no 68.2672, 13.5873

CABINS & CAMPING

22 NØKKSÆTRA HYTTA
Easy hike in to a mountain cabin on the edge of Austre Nøkkvatnet lake. There are amazing panoramic views and you can take a swim to cool off after the walk. This cabin sleeps up to 16 and the key is collected from the tourist office in town. There are several mountain huts throughout the islands run by Lofoten Turlag, the local branch of the DNT (Norwegian Trekking Association). Visit www.vesteralen.turistforeningen.no for booking and details.

→ Park at the Red Cross building on Leirskoleveien in Svolvær (68.2473, 14.5492). Head N on the gravel road which becomes a marked trail. The climb is about 250m.
1.5 hours, 68.2630, 14.5035

18

23 KÅRØY RORBUCAMPING

Very cool bunkhouse-style accommodation on the tiny island of Kårøy just off the coast of Røstlandet. With no direct link to the main island you will need to use the (provided) boat and row for 5 minutes. Everything here is much the same as it would have been during the sixties. There are several shared kitchens and bathrooms. Cook your own food or row to Røstlandet for a selection of restaurants.

→ On Røst (see 10) follow the road past the Røst Bryggehotell and then turn R. Wait by the jetty and unless already given instructions call Kårøya: Kårøy Rorbucamping, 8064 Røst, +47 760 96 238. www.karoy.no
67.5049, 12.0777

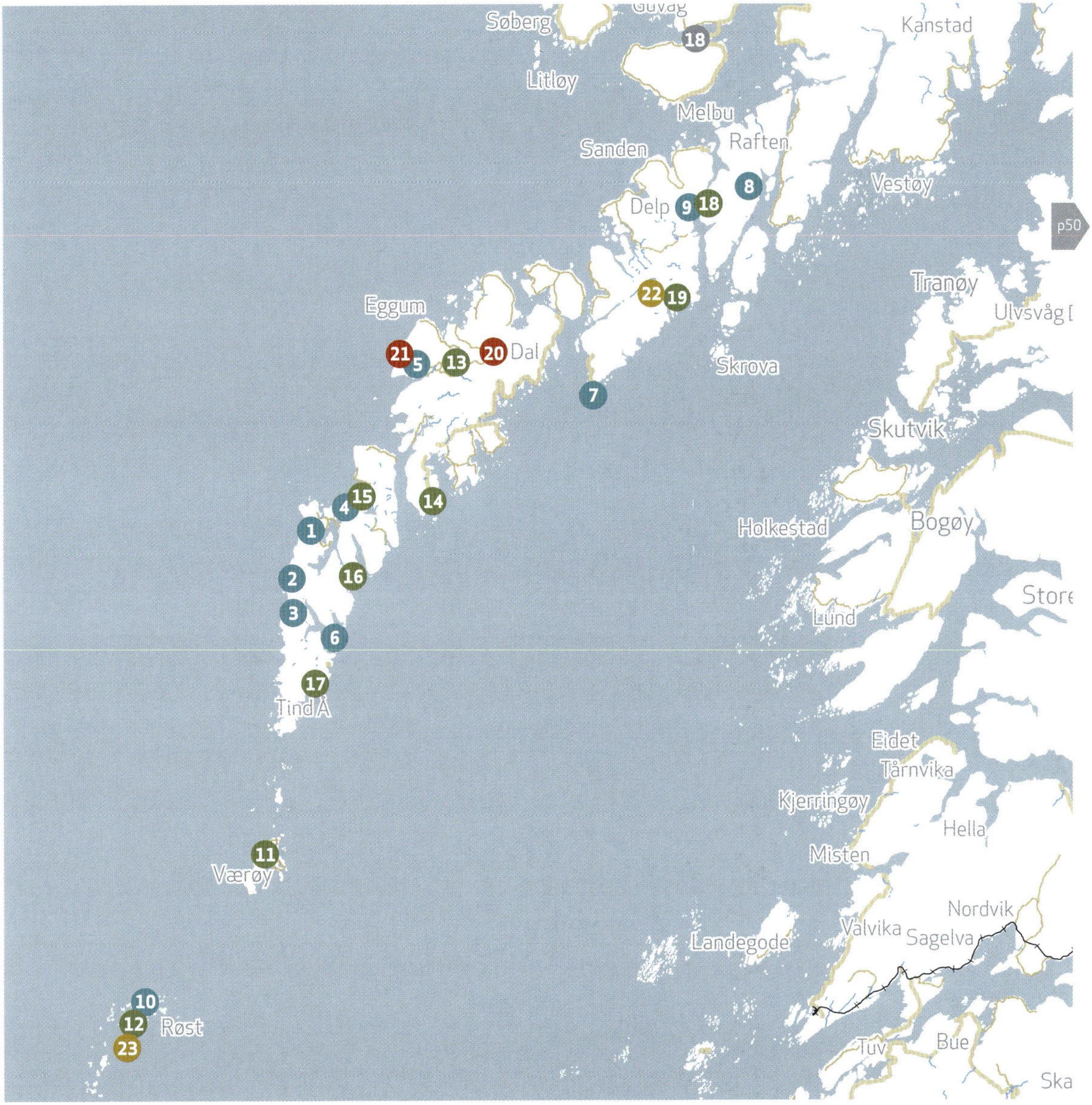

NARVIK

Our perfect week

→ **Crawl** into the mystical caves of the Trollkirka.

→ **Taste** a traditional Sami soup made with reindeer meat.

→ **Learn** how Nordland boats are constructed at the North Norwegian Boat Museum.

→ **Shower** under a geyser at Taraldsvikfossen.

→ **Meet** the wolves at the Polar Park.

→ **Walk** in the footsteps of British navvies along the Rallarvegen.

→ **Find** the rock carvings on the shore of Skjomen Fjord.

→ **Scavenge** for interesting finds on an old mountain battlefield.

→ **Toast** the midnight sun with an aquavit made from yarrow.

→ **Weave** a traditional Sami basket from birch bark at Pippira Siida.

Take the train from Narvik along the 43km-long Ofotbanen as it climbs up into the mountains and the border with Sweden. Just before the border, alight from the train and join the trail built by the railway construction workers. At every turn of the descent, until you reach the tree line, you'll be captivated by alternating views of the mountains and the dark water of the fjord. Heading back towards town on a boat, you might see an otter or maybe a sea eagle.

From the turn of the 20th century, the town of Narvik, located on the shore of the Ofotfjorden, has benefited from a symbiotic relationship with Kiruna, just across the border in Sweden. Iron ore from the mine in Kiruna is brought by rail to be loaded into ships in Narvik for export worldwide. Following a breathtaking route, the line connects the mine with a harbour that's ice-free all year round and, without it and the resulting infrastructure, Narvik would very likely still be a village.

Narvik's connection with Kiruna also gave the area significant strategic importance during the Second World War, when the fjords and mountains became the scene of a very hard-fought campaign. Owing to fierce naval battles, the bottom of the fjord is now littered with sunken ships, and on the rocky plateaus by the Swedish border you can still come across the remains of containers of German equipment that were dropped by parachute in 1940.

Long before the mines and railways, the nomadic Sami would spend the summer in settlements along the coast before heading back to spend the winter in Sweden. Some families still follow the reindeer across the border while other sedentary Sami tend their animals on mountain farms.

At 220km above the Arctic Circle, Narvik town enjoys the midnight sun at midsummer, while a combination of the Gulf Stream and the shelter offered by the surrounding mountains results in a relatively mild climate considering its northerly location.

Looking down on the town and harbour from 656m above sea level on Narvikfjellet puts the industry in perspective – you hardly notice it. What you do notice is the panorama. It takes your breath away.

2

FJORDS

1 ROMBAKSFJORD BOAT TRIP

From the end of the Rallarvegen at Rombaksbotn (see 9), catch a fast boat from the site of the old construction-workers' village to Sildvik (68.4101, 17.7953) further along the fjord. From here you transfer to a bus that takes you to Narvik. Look out for white-tailed fish-eagles and otters. During the Second World War the German destroyer Georg Thiele was scuttled here and the wreck is still visible.

→ The boat goes a couple of times a week during the summer. Contact Visit Narvik for times and to make a booking:
+47 7696 5600, www.visitnarvik.com
30 mins, 68.4182, 17.9001

2 SKJOMEN FJORD

Stunningly beautiful 25km side fjord off the Ofotfjorden. Framed by steep mountains including the spectacular Skjomtind, Reintind and Klubbviktind, the water is crystal-clear and perfect for a bracing swim. On the southern side of the fjord in the shadow of Reintind (68.2856, 17.3079) there are around 80 rock carvings, believed to date from around 5000 BC. Although there is no obvious path, the carvings are worth searching out and remarkably distinct.

→ Head south from Narvik on the E6 and after 10km turn left onto the 761 towards Elvegård. The road runs alongside the water and you can stop to explore at several points.
68.2958, 17.3193

SEALIFE

3 WRECK DIVING

At 78km long, Ofotfjorden is Norway's 12th longest fjord and during the Second World War several notable naval battles were fought here. Those with previous diving experience can visit spectacular submerged wrecks, but others can board the dive boat Jane R (originally from Scotland and with a Scottish skipper), which offers sightseeing trips to visible wrecks and other coastal fortifications. There's also a good chance of seeing plenty of wildlife, including killer whales, seals, otters and white-tailed fish-eagles, as well as lots of other marine birds.

→ Dive Norway, Roald Amundsens vei 14, 8516 Narvik, +47 994 74234.
www.divenorway.com
68.4305, 17.1332

MOUNTAINS & HIKES

4 SKJOMTINDEN

Mountain visible from Narvik, also known as the 'Sleeping Queen'. It was named in honour of Queen Victoria by British navvies who were constructing the Ofot railway. Hike to the top for impressive views over Skomenfjord.

→ The path is clearly marked with a red letter T and starts just south of the road bridge at the end of Nervatnet lake on Håkvikdalveien (68.3763, 17.3779).
4 hours (round trip), 68.3436 17.3527

5 TROLLKIRKA

The Troll Church, 5km north of the city of Tårstad, is one of Norway's longest and most spectacular limestone caves. It drains the Arnfinnvannet lake, but nobody knows where the water then exits. The total length of the cave system is about 4km with numerous chambers and you can only explore it with appropriate equipment. Guided trips are available.

→ For organised trips contact: Aktiv Events, Samasjøveien 26, 9404 Harstad,
+47 900 74666. www.aktivevents.no.
68.4893, 16.6410

6 NARVIKFJELLET

Take the cable car to the Mountain Lodge and summit of Narvikfjellet at 656m above sea level. From here you have a breathtaking panoramic view of the Ofotfjorden and many of the local mountains including Skjomtind (see 4). The 1,810-metre journey to the top takes around 8 minutes. Eat and stay at the lodge or bring a picnic.

→ Base station for cable car: Narvikfjellet AS, Skistuaveien 7, 8505 Narvik, +47 905 40088. www.narvikfjellet.no. Narvik Mountain Lodge: +47 995 38045. www.nmlodge.no
10 mins, 68.43319, 17.4595 🚶📷

7 OFOTBANEN

The Ofot line, a 43km-long section of railway between Narvik and the Swedish border, is considered one of the most spectacular railway lines in the world. Forming part of the Malmbanan (Ore Line), it crosses the mountains between Narvik and Luleå on the Swedish Baltic coast. It was constructed in two phases, from 1884–1888 and from 1898–1903, to transport iron ore from the LKAB mine in Kiruna (see Kiruna Lapland, Sweden) to the harbour in Narvik. If you take the train from Narvik to the Swedish border at Bjørnfjell (68.4322, 18.0711) you'll pass

through six stations and 18 tunnels, with breathtaking views of the Rombaksfjord and the mountains. Combine this with the Rallarvegen (see 9) and boat trip in Rombaksfjord (see 1) for a circular route back to Narvik.

→ Narvik Railway Station, Stasjonsveien 1, 8514 Narvik. Online timetable at www.sj.se
68.4416, 17.4415 🚆📷

8 STETIND

Striking peak of 1,400m voted Norway's national mountain in a poll hosted by NRK (the Norwegian Broadcasting Corporation). A very distinct profile with steep and smooth granite faces makes it an obvious landmark for seafarers. Reaching the summit requires specialist equipment and a guide, but it can be viewed from a distance or you can hike as far as the approach.

→ Visit the website run by the local council (Tysfjord kommune) for details of hiking routes and mountain guides: www.visitstetind.com
68.1652, 16.5927 🥾📷

9 RALLARVEGEN

Trail built by navvies working on the Ofotbanen. Starting from their village base at Rombaksbotn, it leads up to the railway

11

line at Katterat, then goes through Bjørnfjell and crosses into Sweden. (See Kiruna Lapland, Sweden for details of the Swedish trail section). From the station at Katterat the trail zigzags 15.5km down to the head of the Rombaksfjord. On your way you'll pass numerous marked sites of historical importance concerning the construction of the railway and the Second World War. Arrange your walk to coincide with a boat back to Narvik along the fjord (see 1).

→ The path is clearly signposted from the stations at Bjørnfjell or Katterat and ends at Rombaksbotn (68.4182, 17.9001).
2.5 hours, 68.3976, 17.9660 ❤🔭📷🏔

10 NARVIK GEYSIR

For great views overlooking Ofotfjord head up to Taraldsvikfossen mini-hydro overlooking Narvik. Here an enormous geyser (geysir in Norwegian) erupts twice a day during the summer. The huge spout of water, which is visible from town, is created by the opening of a large valve. Kids love running under the falling water. Several hikes start from here.

→ Taraldsvikfossen kraftverk, Reinveien, 8516 Narvik.
68.4404, 17.4703 🏞🏔

WILDLIFE

11 POLAR PARK

The world's northernmost wildlife park, featuring Arctic animals in over 114 acres of natural habitat. Here you'll find creatures that, even in this region, are scarce in the wild, including wolves, brown bear, lynx, wolverine, moose, reindeer and mountain foxes. Guided tours are available.

→ 9360 Bardu + 47 77 186630.
www.polarpark.no
68.6913, 18.1100 🐾🏔

CULTURE & HISTORY

12 RED CROSS WAR MUSEUM

The strategically important iron-ore exporting port of Narvik was invaded by Germany in 1940 at the start of Operation Weserübung – Hitler's assault on Denmark and Norway. A bitter two-month campaign followed with the invading Germans pitted against the allied French, Polish, British and Norwegian forces. Although victorious in the Battles of Narvik, the Allied forces later withdrew from Norway, leaving Narvik under Nazi occupation until 1945. The museum documents the period from 1940–1945

9

8

and interesting exhibits include an original Victoria Cross and an Enigma Machine.

→ Torgsvingen 15, 8509 Narvik, +47 76 944426. www.warmuseum.no
68.4383, 17.4287 📷

13 OFOTEN MUSEUM

Museum that complements Narvik's war museum by focusing on the town's railway, the local Sami, fishing and iron ore. Lots of interactive displays for children. A good place to visit before walking the Rallarvegen as it also documents the work of the navvies, many of them British, who built the Ofotbanen.

→ Administrasjonsveien 3, 8514 Narvik, +47 76 969650 www.museumnord.no
68.4317, 17.4261 ✈📷

14 ROCK CARVING

Very well-preserved rock carving of a moose or reindeer located in a small park in the middle of Narvik. Discovered in the 1960s, it's believed to date from around 3000–4000 BC.

→ Follow the signed path at the end of Einerveien.
10 mins, 68.4454, 17.4293 ✝📷

15 REINDEER ACTIVITIES

Spend some time with the Njala Sami family, who have for generations herded reindeer in the mountains around Narvik. Learn about Sami culture while participating in seasonal activities such as herding, labelling calves or maybe even the autumn slaughter. Traditional meals can also be arranged. Learn how to lasso a reindeer!

→ Njalasouka Adventures, Hesjemoen 6, 8522 Beisfjord, +47 427 63992
www.njalasoukaadventures.no
68.3693, 17.5959 ✈🍴🚴

16 ST HANS FEIRING

Midsummer's Eve, the Feast of St John, is celebrated throughout Norway with huge bonfires and festivities on June 23rd. In Narvik there's an impressive fire with food and amazing views at the upper cable-car station (Øvre Fjellheisstasjon) on Narvikfjellet overlooking the town.

→ Narvikfjellet, 8517 Narvik, +47 76 942799. www.narvikfjellet.no
68.4331, 17.4602 ✈📷⛰

17 BJØRNFJELL WAR WALK

During the Second World War, fighting in the mountains around Narvik was particularly

21

fierce, and during battles the Germans were resupplied by parachute drops. Look carefully and you might spot the remains of various equipment. Do not remove anything you discover but photograph any finds and pass on the location to the war museum in Narvik (see 12). Keep children well away from anything that looks like old munitions.

→ Head E out of Narvik on the E6 turning off onto the E10 towards Bjørnfjell and Sweden. Stop in the lay-by on the R just after the bridge over the Øvre Jernvatnet. You will see a 'krigsminne' sign and the area to explore is between here and the shore of the lake.
68.5087, 17.9454 ▾⬛◲

18 GÁLLOGIEDDI

Fascinating open-air museum of Sami history and culture housed in a collection of traditional buildings in a coastal area with many summer settlements. These were populated by nomadic reindeer herders who travelled from their winter habitat around Jukkasjärvi in Sweden (see Kiruna Lapland, Sweden). A 2km self-guided culture trail starts at the museum, where on certain days there are also handicraft and cooking demonstrations.

→ Bedringens vei 9, 8536 Evenes, +47 76 985020. www.vardobaiki.no
68.4968, 16.7019 ▾⬛◲

19 BALLANGEN MUSEUM

From the 17th century up until 1964, the beautiful Ballangen area about 40km south of Narvik was the centre of mining in northern Norway, for mainly copper and pyrite. The Ballangen Museum documents the history of mining in the area as well as everyday life and culture over the centuries. Learn about what the region was like before the Ofotbanen and iron ore put Narvik on the map.

→ Syllaveien 36, 8540 Ballangen, +47 76 929120. www.museumnord.no
68.3287, 16.7928 ⬛◲

20 FREDSKAPELLET

Chapel built in the name of peace on the foundations of one destroyed in 1940 during the Battles of Narvik. The building is surrounded by a substantial war cemetery with graves for the fallen from several different countries.

→ Rombaksveien 44, 8517 Narvik
68.4431, 17.4528 ✝◲

15

21 NORTH NORWEGIAN BOAT MUSEUM

Fascinating maritime museum with the world's largest collection of Nordland boats. Built to a design used by the region's fishermen for centuries, they're closely related to the old Viking longships. The boat was a lifeline for coastal communities and considered to be the most important possession a man could own. Learn about its uses from fishing to summoning the midwife.

→ Hellarbogen, 9470, Gratangen, +47 77 020370. www.nnfa.no
68.6695, 17.6789 ⬛▾⬛◲

22 TINJA MOUNTAIN LODGE

Sedentary Sami farm located in a rugged mountain landscape offering food and accommodation. The kitchen uses only locally farmed or foraged produce, such as grouse, trout, mushrooms, cloudberries and other berries. They also brew their own beer and produce a home-made yarrow aquavit.

➜ Kong Olavs vei, 8517 Narvik,
+47 40 60600. www.tinja.no
68.4788, 17.7567

23 PIPPIRA SIIDA

Sami settlement where you can learn about sedentary Sami who renounced their nomadic lifestyles in favour of farming in a fixed location. Traditional Sami food is served in the café, including the bidos - a soup with plenty of reindeer meat, onions, potatoes and carrots. Try your hand at lassoing reindeer or traditional handicrafts such as birch bark weaving. Accommodation is available in cabins.

➜ Kalvås, 8540 Ballangen, +47 91 150282.
www.pippirasiida.blogspot.no
68.3212, 16.6816

24 FJELLKYSTEN GUEST HOUSE

Coastal hotel in an unusual eco-building inspired by traditional construction techniques. Built into a hillside and partially underground, it features Norway's largest turf roof. The kitchen specialises in local seafood, but you can also camp and cater for yourself. Stunning sea views.

➜ Fjellkysten, Åbrekka, 9357 Tennevoll,
+47 47 924792. www.fjellkysten.com
68.7817, 17.7954

25 TROLLVIKEN LODGE

Idyllically located lodge on the edge of the Ofotfjord close to the village of Bjerkvik. Originally a fish farm, the barn has been converted to provide various accommodation options. Run by Narvik Mountain Guides, you can also book on numerous guide-led outdoor activities – see www.narvikguides.no.

➜ Located just S of Route E10 about 6km SE of Bjerkvik: Herjangen 290, 8530 Bjerkvik,
+47 45 295395. www.trollvikenlodge.no
68.5253, 17.4383

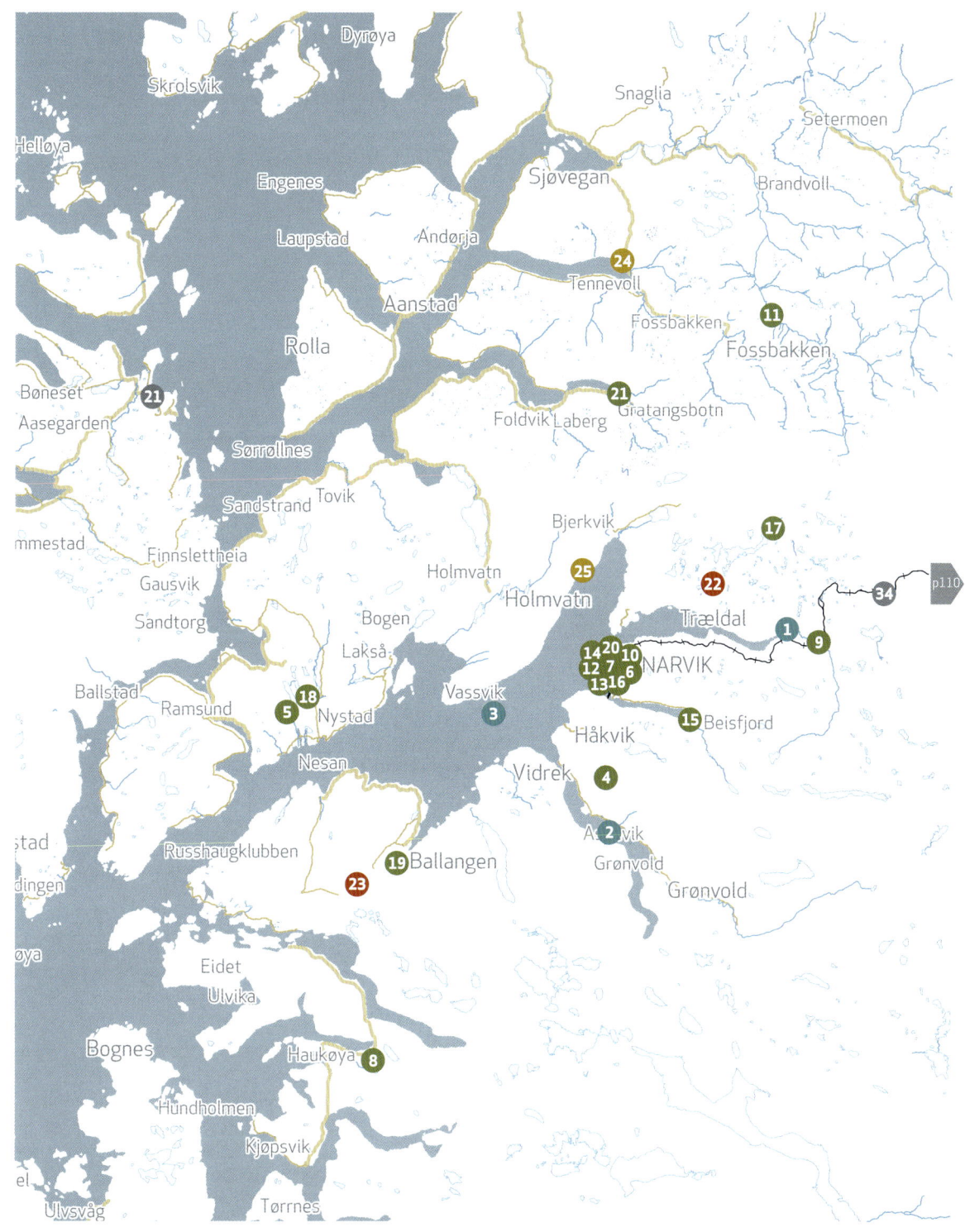

HURTIGRUTEN

Our voyage highlights

→ **Marvel** at the waterfalls cascading down the sides of the Geirangerfjord to the deep water below.

→ **Navigate** the crazy inland hairpin bends of the Trollstigen mountain road.

→ **Taste** klippfisk that has been naturally dried in the sun and wind.

→ **Celebrate** and make merry as you cross the Arctic Circle.

→ **Spot** a large sperm whale and log the number of seabird species.

→ **Discover** legends and folklore associated with many of the islands.

→ **Feel** the midnight sun on your face as you stand on Nordkapp.

→ **Notice** climate and habitat changes as you get closer to the Russian border.

→ **Learn** how several distinct cultures co-existed in harsh environments.

Sailing north along the Norwegian coast as far as the Russian border, you sit on deck, mesmerised by some of the most spectacular coastal landscapes in the world. Stopping at remote villages on a route that threads its way along fjords and through breathtakingly beautiful archipelagos, hop ashore to explore the communities or perhaps venture even further inland. As the boat crosses the Arctic Circle on a midsummer night, everything is bathed in the warm light of the midnight sun and you'll want to stay up on deck to take it all in.

At the end of the 19th century, reaching the many remote fishing villages along the wild 1,255km coastline from the main trading port of Bergen up to Kirkenes on the Russian border was only practical by boat. All manner of steamers and sailing boats plied this treacherous route, but with only 28 lighthouses north of Trondheim, sailing at night was too dangerous, making the journey long and unreliable. To improve coastal communications with these isolated communities, in 1893 the Norwegian government offered the Hurtigruten company a contract to provide a regular service. Although the Hurtigruten ships still carry freight as they cruise along one of the world's most beautiful and dramatic coastlines, passenger comfort is now a priority.

A round trip from Bergen to Kirkenes takes 12 days and is a popular choice – on the return leg you get to see the parts you sailed past at night on the journey north. With daily sailings in each direction from every port of call, it's also possible to hop on and off, camping overnight onshore rather than booking a cabin. Fellow passengers will be a mixture of locals using the route as a ferry and tourists taking the 'cruise'. For the latter, each ship has someone on board to help with booking the various organised excursions available at the different ports.

The name Hurtigrute – literally 'the Express Route' – describes the service offered by the company when it was first contracted to provide a coastal freight and passenger service. But rest assured, although journey times and facilities have improved, you will never feel rushed.

THE HURTIGRUTEN ROUTE

1 BERGEN

An old Hanseatic city, Bergen is the most southerly port on the Hurtigruten route. The harbour area of Bryggen, with its medieval wooden buildings, is now a fascinating UNESCO World Heritage Site. Take the Fløibanen funicular railway from close to the harbour up to the summit of Mount Fløyen. From here there's a spectacular panoramic view over the city and the islands, sea and mountains beyond. Until the 19th century Bergen was the trading centre of Norway and larger than the capital Oslo. Known as the 'Gateway to the Fjords', many trips to the nearby fjords not visited by the Hurtigruten ships start from here. Two – to Hardangerfjord and Sognefjord – are highly recommended. Leaving Bergen, the Hurtigruten takes you along Hjeltefjord, thought to be the same route the Vikings followed when they invaded Shetland around AD 800.

60.3922, 5.3107 🖼

2 FLORØ

Norway's most westerly town was for centuries a centre for shipbuilding, then fish-farming, and more recently a supply base for the offshore oil industry. After leaving Florø the ship passes to the west of Vingen and one of the largest rock carving sites in Northern Europe, featuring over 2,000 images of mainly deer, but also human figures and other animals. To the west is the towering peak of Hornelen where, according to legend, witches gather to dance with the Devil at midsummer and Christmas. Just before arriving in Måløy the ship crosses the mouth of Nordfjord – a long fjord stretching inland to Jostedalsbreen, the largest glacier in mainland Europe.

61.6017, 5.0258 ✝

3 MÅLØY

Fishing port on the south side of the island of Vågsøy and linked to the mainland by a long bridge. The coastline has four spectacularly positioned lighthouses, one of Norway's most beautiful beaches, and the Kannesteinen – a unique mushroom-shaped rock formed over the centuries by the power of the sea.

61.9391, 5.1222 🌊🗺🏖

4 TORVIK

Small village on the island of Leinøya in one of Norway's most important areas for fishing and fish-farming. Set in a beautiful, rugged landscape with numerous glaciers, waterfalls and national parks a short distance inland from the coast. The neighbouring island of Runde is home to over 240 different species of seabird, with more than 500,000 nesting there every year. After leaving Torvik you'll glimpse the spectacular Sunnmørsalpene (Sunnmøre Alps), widely considered to be the most spectacular mountain range in Norway. Its classic Alpine profile was shaped by ice over thousands of years, and the snow-capped peaks are popular with hikers in summer and skiers in winter.

62.3368, 5.7283 🧗🥾🏔

5 ÅLESUND

Town with a fairy-tale feel that was rebuilt in the art-nouveau style following a catastrophic fire in 1904 when 850 houses burned to the ground and 10,000 people were left homeless. Mount Aksla overlooks the town, and from the path up to the summit there are magnificent panoramic views of the islands and of the Sunnmøre Alps. A short drive inland will take you to the Trollstigen (Troll's Road) – a dramatic mountain road that zigzags its way up the

mountainside. Each spectacular hairpin bend is named, often after the foreman of the construction gang responsible for that section. Cascading beside and then under the road is the equally impressive Stigfossen waterfall. Not recommended for nervous drivers!

62.4756, 6.1529 ▨ 🚲 🏔

6 GEIRANGER

Often referred to as the most beautiful of all the Norwegian fjords, the Geirangerfjord area is a UNESCO World Heritage Site. During the summer Hurtigruten ships stop at the small village of Geiranger at the head of the fjord and you can go ashore to explore. Geirangerfjord's blue water is about 300m deep and thundering down into it from the surrounding mountains are numerous spectacular waterfalls. Brudesløret (the Bride's Veil) and De Syv Søstrene (the Seven Sisters – with seven separate falls) are the most famous and you can see both clearly from the ship.

62.1035, 7.2028 🏔 ▨

7 MOLDE

Small coastal town and port surrounded by wonderful landscapes and home to one of Norway's largest folk museums. Much of the city was rebuilt after the Second World War when it was largely destroyed by German air raids. An 8.3km dramatic section of road between Molde and Kristiansund, known as the Atlanterhavsveien (Atlantic Road), is considered one of the world's best road trips and many car manufacturers have filmed advertisements here. The series of causeways, viaducts and bridges links together several small islands and skerries, to connect the island of Averøy with the mainland and the Romsdalshalvøya peninsula.

62.7363, 7.1669 ▨

8 KRISTIANSUND

Fishing port located on four islands whose fortunes were founded on dried salted cod, known locally as *klippfisk* – literally 'cliff fish' because the fish was sun- and wind-dried on cliffs and bare rock. Small passenger ferries take visitors between the islands. The old part of town, which has many narrow streets and well-preserved wooden houses, is particularly interesting.

63.1147, 7.7367 ▨ 👥 🍽

9 TRONDHEIM

Before entering Trondheimsfjord the ship will pass the Kjeungskjær lighthouse. Perched atop a very small skerry, it's no longer manned but you can rent the lighthouse-keeper's flat. Trondheim has many interesting old wooden houses, some along narrow medieval streets and others on wide, 17th-century boulevards designed to stop fires from spreading. The cathedral, which dates from 1070, is at the final destination of the St Olav pilgrims' route (see Åre, Sweden).

63.4426, 10.4068 🖼️🍴

10 RØRVIK

Perfectly situated for exploring the thousands of islands and skerries that make up the beautiful Vikna Archipelago, this town has a mild, maritime climate and in summer plum and apple trees flourish in many gardens. The ship will pass Torghatten Island, an unusual granite mountain with a large hole at its centre, which has a legend attached. Spurned by Lekamøya, the troll Hestmannen fired an arrow at the young girl but the king threw his hat between them and the arrow pierced it. As the sun rose they were all turned to stone, including the hat.

64.8604, 11.2390 🚶🖼️🗺️✝️

11 BRØNNØYSUND

Located on a narrow peninsula surrounded by islands at the geographical mid-point of Nordkapp and Lindesnes, the landscape around Brønnøysund has all the classic Norwegian ingredients – sea, islands, fjords, mountains, lakes, wild rivers and waterfalls. One of the local industries, the production of eiderdown, has been pursued sustainably for more than 1,500 years. Breast feathers are harvested from the nests of female eider ducks and replaced with hay. The down is then processed by hand.

65.4756, 12.2106 🚣🚲🗺️

12 SANDNESSJØEN

Between Brønnøysund and the island port of Sandnessjøen is a section of coast said to be among the most beautiful in the world. The boat travels the length of the island of Alsta and the De Syv Søstre (the Seven Sisters) – a range of seven peaks set so close together they can be hiked in one long day. Their beauty gave rise to the legend that they must be female trolls turned to stone.

66.0237, 12.6372 ✝️🚶🖼️

13 NESNA

Stopping briefly at this village for passengers and to deliver and collect goods and mail, you then catch sight of the white tongue of the mighty Svartisen glacier. Centuries ago the glaciers in the region stretched all the way to the sea, but climate change is hastening their retreat. At 66° 33' latitude, when the ship crosses the Arctic Circle, the sun shines for 24 hours a day throughout the summer. A large globe on the island of Vikingen marks the point and you can expect celebrations on board.

66.2003, 13.0085

14 ØRNES

Coastal village just above the Arctic Circle set against a mountainous backdrop with an archipelago of over 700 islands and skerries offshore. This marks the end of the section of coast known as Helgelandskysten. By the harbour is the kjærlighetsbenken (love bench) – a romantic spot where you can simply sit with your beloved, or maybe fasten a padlock to the bench and throw the key into the sea.

66.8689, 13.7034

15 BODØ

Largest town in the Nordland region, founded as a trading centre in 1816 and often described as the gateway to the true north. South-east of the town, the impressive tidal overfalls of Saltstraumen generate a current of 22 knots – the strongest in the world. Leaving Bodø the ship sails into Vestfjorden, not a true fjord and best described as a firth between the Lofoten archipelago and mainland Norway. It's also a famous cod fishery (see Lofoten p42). Approaching the archipelago, the silhouettes of the Lofotveggen mountain range appear to rise from the sea in a single, unbroken line.

67.2892, 14.3959

16 STAMSUND

Fishing village on the south side of the island of Vestvågøy in the Lofoten archipelago. During the Second World War, British and Norwegian commandos carried out one of the first successful raids on Nazi-held territory here. They returned with prisoners and Norwegian volunteers, as well as a codebook for an Enigma machine and some of its wheels. From here the ship heads east along the spectacular southern edge of the Lofoten archipelago.

68.1214, 13.8411

17 SVOLVÆR

The main town on the Lofoten Islands is a centre for both the fishing industry and tourism. The ship also visits the nearby Trollfjord (see Lofoten p42).

68.2307, 14.5666 🧍➡️

18 STOKMARKNES

This small settlement on the north side of the island of Hadseløya is the headquarters of the Hurtigruten line. The museum tells the fascinating story of the coastal route from its establishment in 1893 up to the present day, including thrilling stories of sinkings and shipwrecks. Next to the museum, the old coastal steamer MS Finnmarken, which was commissioned in 1956, sits on dry land. A modern vessel of the same name was launched in 2001 and currently sails the route.

68.5702, 14.9080 🖼️

19 SORTLAND

Risøyrenna (the Risøy channel), a shallow sound that could be crossed on horseback at low tide, was dredged and widened in 1922 to become a major shipping lane. The deep channel allows the Hurtigruten ships to call at the regional town of Sortland. At the turn of the millennium the town decided to turn itself blue and has continued to develop this colour scheme with help from both local artists and the community. Very quirky!

68.6987, 15.4207 🍴

20 RISØYHAMN

Tiny village on the island of Andøya and a stop on the Hurtigruten route, despite its size. Numerous seabird colonies nearby including one with more than 160,000 puffins. Complete skeletons of ichthyosaurs have been found in the mine at Ramså, and close to Risøyhamn are several burial mounds and the remains of a settlement from the Iron Age. Keep an eye out for huge sperm whales.

68.9676, 15.6414 🧍🖼️✝️🔭

21 HARSTAD

Port and town on the island of Hinnøya, the largest island in Norway, that each June hosts the Festival of North Norway – an eclectic mix of both local and international live music. Recent archaeological excavations indicate a well-developed culture in the area during the Bronze Age, with finds including a bronze axe and collar close to the town centre. Harstad was an important centre of Viking power and the

current name is probably from the Old Norse word Harðarstaðir – a combination of the male name Hörðr and staðir, meaning homestead or farm.

68.7988, 16.5481

22 FINNSNES

Small town on the mainland beside the bridge to the island of Senja, the location of the Ånderdalen National Park. Established in 1970, this protected section of coast retains diverse wild habitats, including pine and birch forest. You'll see seals, otters, moose and reindeer as well as many colourful species of alpine flowers.

69.2290, 17.9733

23 TROMSØ

The Arctic city of Tromsø was once the starting point for many polar expeditions, and you can learn about them in the Polar Museum by the harbour. Now described as 'Paris of the north', the town is rich in both culture and history, all with a majestic mountainous landscape as a backdrop. For breathtaking views take the Fjellheisen cable car to the summit of Fløyfjellet. You can also visit the University of Tromsø museum, where displays explain the culture

and nature of the area, with a focus on the indigenous Sami. After leaving Tromsø there are dramatic views of the Lyngsalpene (the Lyngen Alps) – a mountain range that plunges down into the sea. During the winter it's possible to do an unusual backcountry ski trip here. You arrive by sea and climb to a summit before skiing back to your boat.

69.6484, 18.9629

24 SKJERVØY

Island village on a wild and remote section of Arctic coast, where the main industries are fishing and fish-farming. In 1896 it was the first port of call for the ship MS Fram returning from Fridtjof Nansen's attempt to reach the geographical North Pole. Nansen and his 'musher' Hjalmar Johansen returned separately to Vardø a week earlier after being dropped off in the Arctic Sea, and the whole of Norway anxiously awaited the safe return of the ship and its crew.

70.0352, 20.9826

25 ØKSFJORD

Fishing village and the first port of call in the Finnmark region, where colourfully painted houses cling dramatically to the mountainside. On a clear day you get a glimpse of Øksfjordjøkulen, one of Norway's largest glaciers and the only one on mainland Norway to 'calve' directly into the sea. According to a local story, a Tromsø solicitor (who spoke poor English) mistakenly sold the hunting rights here to a wealthy Englishman for just $2,000.

70.2379, 22.3492

26 HAMMERFEST

At 70°7' north, Hammerfest claims to be the most northern town in the world, and although at roughly the same latitude as northern Alaska and Siberia, it's free from permafrost. A fishing port, it has traditionally also traded along the coast with Russia. Many burial sites dating from the Stone Age show that the site has been settled for a long time. The name Hammerfest comes from the Old Norse *hamarr* meaning 'steep mountainside' and *fest*, a 'fastening' (for boats) – in other words a sheltered anchorage.

70.6642, 23.6837

27 HAVØYSUND

Remote island fishing community in the Barents Sea with colourfully painted, mainly post-war, houses characteristic of the small fishing villages in the area. Most of the older houses were burned to the ground at the end of the Second World War when the Germans adopted a 'scorched earth' policy while retreating southwards from the Red Army. The rocky island of Hjelmsøystauren, just off the coast, has the most densely populated bird colony in Europe: kittiwakes, common guillemots and razorbills are among the species nesting here. Between 1740 and 1917 this was also an important bartering area for Russian Pomors – settlers from the White Sea area and the Kola Peninsula.

70.9948, 24.6863

28 HONNINGSVÅG

Close to the town of Honningsvåg but not directly on the Hurtigruten route, Nordkapp (North Cape), at 71°10'21", is the northernmost point of the European mainland. It was discovered in 1553 by three English ships searching for the Northeast Passage: two failed to return and the crew of the third named it North Cape. It's a high rocky plateau overlooking the sea and boasts an iconic globe monument. In the spring you may witness the Norwegian Army transport around 3,800 reindeer in landing craft from the mainland to Magerøya Island,

but the most exciting time is autumn when the animals and their calves swim back across the 1.8km strait to reach their winter grazing area.

70.9816, 25.9682

29 KJØLLEFJORD

On the west coast of the Nordkinn Peninsula, this big fishing village is at the head of the Kjøllefjord, which empties into the much larger Laksefjorden. Every year, several Sami families move their reindeer to summer pastures in the area. Leaving Kjøllefjord, the ship sails past the magnificent Finnkirka –

a dramatic cathedral-shaped rock that was once a Sami sacrificial site. Fishermen would stop here as they left the fjord to pray for good weather, and on their return they would give thanks for a safe passage. When the Hurtigruten ships sail past at night, Finnkirka is illuminated. ▲✚⬛
70.9489, 27.3364

30 MEHAMN

This northernmost port on the route lies on the north coast of the Nordkinn Peninsula. In 1903 there was a civil disturbance at the large whaling station here that became known as the Mehamn Rebellion. Local fisherman blamed whaling for their poor catch, believing that whales encouraged the fish to come near the shore. When the manager of the whaling station refused to help a fishing boat in trouble, the fishermen reacted angrily and by the time military forces arrived, the whaling station was completely destroyed. Some of the perpetrators received light sentences and the following year the Labour party, which wanted whales protected, won seats in the Norwegian parliament. These first four MPs were from the north of Norway and 'rode to victory on the back of a whale'. A law was subsequently passed to protect whales in the waters off the regions of Finnmark, Nordland and Troms. ▲⬛➡
71.0414, 27.8438

31 BERLEVÅG

At the mouth of Tanafjord the ship passes the sacred Sami mountain of Tanahorn, towering 270m above the water. Soon it arrives in Berlevåg, a large fishing village with several fish-processing plants around the harbour. Here, a museum documents the fascinating history of the community, focusing on the building of the breakwater over a period of 70 years. On an upland plateau, the nearby Varangerhalvøya National Park is a complete alpine eco-system with reindeer, wolverine and Arctic fox. After leaving the harbour, you pass one of the most striking lighthouses along the Hurtigruten route, built on a small strip of land stretching out into the Barents Sea. The Kjølnes lighthouse was once home to four families but is now fully automated. ▲⬛➡⬛✚
70.8574, 29.1148

32 BÅTSFJORD

An important centre for the Norwegian fishing industry, this port is at the head of the fjord on the remote coast of the Varanger Peninsula. The unusual stripes you can see in the local cliffs are sedimentary rock, originally formed underwater and known as the Båtsfjord formation. The rock is made up of violet and green mudstones, grey and pink sandstones, yellow-grey dolomite, and grey limestone. ⬛
70.6294, 29.7245

33 VARDØ

On the island of Vardøya, this is the oldest town in Northern Norway. At a longitude of 31°E, it's the most easterly in Scandinavia and even further east than St Petersburg and Istanbul. An underwater tunnel connects the island to the mainland. Just offshore, the island of Hornøya has a lighthouse at its highest point and a population of thousands of seabirds. Vardø has a museum about the Pomor trade and a fascinating local history museum with displays that emphasise the town's proximity to Russia and Finland. The 14th-century fortress didn't see action until the Second World War. 🏰⬛➡
70.3746, 31.1045

34 VADSØ

With a mixed Norwegian, Finnish and Sami population, this is a very multi-cultural town. It lies at the mouth of the Varangerfjord and like the other coastal towns and villages in the Finnmark region it was traditionally a centre for fishing. The town was almost destroyed during the Second World War, but two buildings survived and these are now part of the town museum, which also records the story of Finnish immigration. By the sea, you'll come upon the mooring mast of the Norge – the airship used by Roald Amundsen and then Umberto Nobile for their Arctic expeditions in 1926 and 1928. ⬛
70.0708, 29.7961

35 KIRKENES

At this final stop on the Hurtigruten route, the ship turns round and heads back. Lying on the Bøkfjord, very close to the Russian and Finnish borders, the inhabitants of the town are a mixture of Sami, Norwegian, Finnish, and some recent immigrants from Russia. At the end of the Second World War, the Red Army liberated Kirkenes and grateful local people continue to enjoy strong bonds with Russia. The climate here is more similar to that of Siberia and there are brown bears, wolverine, lynx, as well as occasional wolves crossing over from Russia. Fishermen catch the enormous and delicious king crab, which is exported to restaurants all over the world. ➡⬛🍴⬛
69.7288, 30.0722

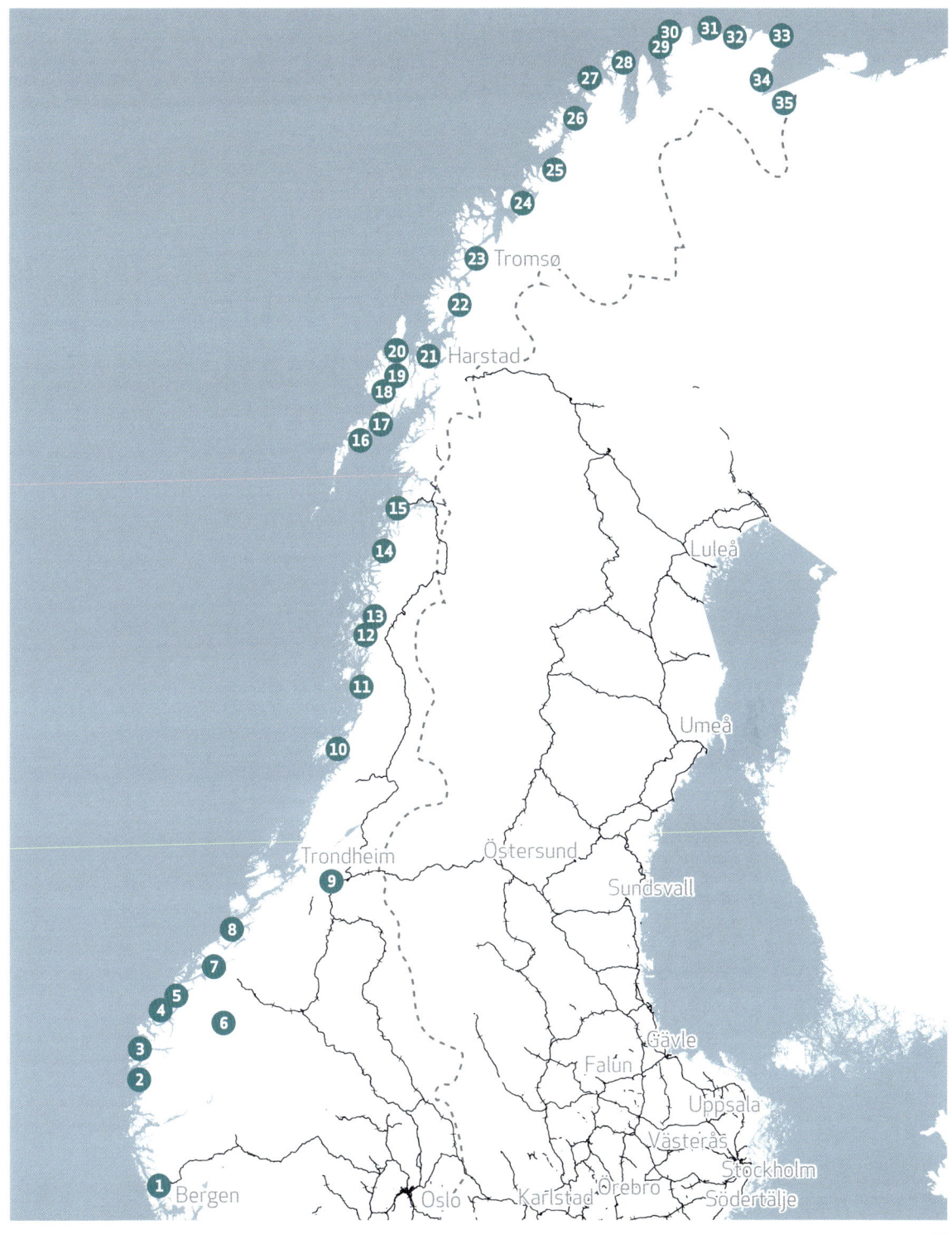

JOTUNHEIMEN

Our perfect adventure

→ **Discover** Norse mythical creatures in the intricate carvings of a stave church.

→ **Go** off-grid in a traditional Norwegian mountain farm and soak in a wooden bath.

→ **Dance** in the mountains at the Vinjerock Festival.

→ **Cycle** the Søgnefjellet pass, climbing high over the roof of Jotunheimen.

→ **Explore** beneath a glacier and find signs that point to climate change.

→ **Walk** the precipitous Besseggen Ridge and be captivated by panoramic views.

→ **Find** some precious thulite in the mountains around Lom.

→ **Feel** the power of the water thundering over Europe's highest free-fall waterfall.

→ **Climb** to the summit of Northern Europe's highest mountain.

This high alpine landscape was given the name Jotunheim by the poet Aasmund Olavsson Vinje in the 1860s. In Norse mythology Jötunheimr is the Land of the Giants and this is where you'll find 29 of the highest mountains in Norway. Now the Jotunheimen National Park, the area covers 3,500 square kilometres and it's the most popular area in the country for year-round outdoor activities.

The mountain slopes attract skiers in winter and hikers in summer, while the wild, fast-flowing rivers are a magnet for white-water kayakers from all over the world. It's a paradise for climbers, mountaineers, flat-water canoeists, cyclists and even cavers, who can choose to explore traditional limestone caverns or ice caves under glaciers.

Evidence of people living in the area since 1800 BC has been discovered in a glacier, including a shoe, several arrows and a wooden spade. It's worth a trip to the fascinating Norwegian Mountain Museum, not only to see these finds but also to learn about how people have lived, worked and travelled in the mountains over centuries.

Some of the surrounding mountain villages seem to be stuck in time. There are timber farm buildings (now guest houses) dating back to Viking times, and majestic wooden stave churches where if you look closely you'll see symbols from Norse mythology.

The village of Lom, home to a fine stave church, makes an ideal base for exploring the area. One of the roads out of town, the Sognefjellet National Tourist Route, takes you over the highest mountain pass in Northern Europe and the scenery is truly breathtaking.

The name Jotunheim is apt, not just because of the vastness but also the power of this landscape. Visit and be enchanted, energized and filled with the urge to explore.

RAPIDS & WATERFALLS

1 VETTISFOSSEN

Extraordinary waterfall with a single vertical drop of 275m, making it the highest free-falling waterfall in Europe. It's also one of Norway's tallest – those ranked higher will have multiple drops. Walking up past an interesting old farm, you reach the falls and will be amazed by the volume of water.

→ Reach the waterfall (61.3791, 7.9476) by walking from Øvre Årdal (61.3089, 7.8028) up the Utladalen valley. Local map and compass are essential.
1 hour, 61.3791, 7.9476

2 RIDDERSPRANGET

The Knight's Leap – a very narrow gorge across the Sjoa river – features a section of white water that's very popular with rafters and kayakers. According to local legend, a knight and a beautiful girl who were in love and running away from the girl's fiancé leapt over the water here. Not a good jumping spot but the views are impressive.

→ Signed from route Rv51. Parking, information and toilets close to the gorge. Local map and compass are essential.
61.6825, 9.0752

ANCIENT & SACRED

3 LOM STAVE CHURCH

One of the largest stave churches still standing, it was built in the second half of the 12th century. The inside has many intricate carvings and the roof is adorned with dragons' heads – symbols from Viking tradition. During the Middle Ages the church was at a busy intersection for pilgrims and other travellers passing through the area. It's still used for services by the community.

→ Bergomsvegen 21, 2686 Lom, +47 61 217300, www.lom.kommune.no
61.8398, 8.5661

4 URNES STAVE CHURCH

12th-century stave church on the edge of Lustrafjorden directly across the fjord from the village of Solvorn. A UNESCO World Heritage Site since 1979. It may well be the one of the oldest of its type and features medieval Christian imagery but also art from the Viking Age. Some amazing wooden carvings appear to show a four-legged animal biting a snake. This may be the Christ lion fighting Satan in the form of a serpent, or it could be a portrayal of Níðhöggr gnawing at the roots of Yggdrasil from Norse mythology.

→ 6870 Ornes, Luster, +47 57 678840. 61.2982, 7.3226

CULTURE & HISTORY

5 NORSK FJELLMUSEUM

The theme of the Norwegian Mountain Museum is the interaction between people and mountains and how this relationship has developed from the Ice Age up until the present day. Learn how prehistoric man travelled in the mountains and what archaeological evidence melting snow and glaciers are now revealing – almost 1,600 artefacts from the Upland region, including many from Jotunheimen, are on display. The museum also functions as a visitor centre for the Jotunheimen National Park.

→ 2688 Lom, +47 61 211600. www.fjell.museum.no
61.8376, 8.5677

6 VALDRES FOLK MUSEUM

Outdoor museum that the whole family will enjoy, offering fascinating insights into Norwegian culture. Look through Norway's biggest collection of regional costumes, enjoy traditional folk music and learn the local dances. You can enjoy local food,

regular concerts, and children will welcome the opportunity to befriend the museum's farm animals. There are numerous events and festivals taking place here throughout the year. Check the website for up-to-date information.

→ Tyinvegen 27, 2900 Fagernes, +47 61 359900. www.valdresmusea.no
60.9812, 9.2306 🔲🔳🏛

7 FOSSHEIM STONE CENTRE

Geological specimen collection with Norway's largest selection of minerals and semi-precious stones and a particularly interesting fossil section. There's also a workshop where you can buy jewellery and other handicrafts. Find out about the striking reddish mineral thulite, Norway's national gemstone, which is often made into earrings, necklaces and pendants. The stone is quarried locally in Lom.

→ Bergomsvegen 30, 2686 Lom, +47 61 211460. www.fossheimsteinsenter.no
61.8388, 8.5740 🔲♻

8 MÍMISBRUNNR KLIMAPARK

A very unusual and special museum where you can learn about climate change by descending 70m into an ice tunnel below a glacier. Your guide will explain what secrets it reveals – in particular what these tell us about the global climate over the last 6,000 years. In Norse mythology, Mímisbrunnr is the well below Yggdrasil in Asgard and the source of all knowledge and wisdom. The original finds from the ice are displayed at the Norwegian Mountain Museum (see 5).

→ 2688 Lom, +47 61 211600.
www.mimisbrunnr.no
61.6750, 8.3531 🔲🔳♻

9 VINJEROCK

Visitors are encouraged to hike to this music festival at 1,060m above sea level in Eidsbugarden. Great music and other outdoor activities in a spectacular mountain location. The festival is named after the famous Norwegian poet Aasmund Vinje – the first person to build a cabin in this area and the person who coined the name Jotunheimen – (Land of the Giants). The festival takes place in July every year.

→ Eidsbugarden, 2985 Vang i Valdres, +47 971 09903. www.vinjerock.no
61.3729, 8.2988 🔲🏛

MOUNTAINS & CLIMBS

10 SOGNEFJELLET TOURIST ROUTE

Spectacular mountain pass that has been described as both one of the world's best road trips and one of its best bike rides. Open to traffic only in the summer, this celebrated national route climbs to 1,434m above sea level at its highest point, offering a succession of breathtaking panoramic views from start to finish. Make the trip in spring when the road has just been opened and you'll be amazed by the 10m-plus walls of snow beside the road and understand why it's closed during the winter. There are several rest areas, each located at a point with really exceptional views. Drive or cycle.

➜ The road is designated the FV55 and runs for 108km between Gaupne (61.4026, 7.2934) by the Sognefjord and Lom (61.8366, 8.5666) in the Gudbrandsdalen Valley.
61.5536, 8.4842 🏕🏖🏔📷

11 GALDHØPIGGEN

Highest mountain in Norway and also in the whole of Northern Europe at 2,469m above sea level. The summit can be reached without climbing equipment, but it is a demanding hike and for one of the routes you'll need a guide to cross the glacier. If you're keen, you need to be fully prepared and use a local map. In 1850 three local men, including the church warden and teacher, were the first to reach the summit. Several thousand people now make the ascent every summer. There's a small cabin on the summit where you can buy drinks and chocolate.

➜ For guiding on the mountain contact: Aktiv i Lom SA, 2687 Bøverdalen, +47 61 212799.
61.6370, 8.3092 🏕🏖🏔📷

12 GLITTERTIND

The Jotunheimen National Park is not known as the Land of the Giants for nothing. Glittertind, the second highest mountain in Norway at 2,465m above sea level, was once a contender for the top spot, but the glacier at its summit reduced in size. The first ascent was made in 1841 and it's a popular summer hiking destination. The best access is from the west via the Spiterstulen lodge, but you will need to be well prepared and have a local map and compass. Alternatively, use a local guide. The view from the summit is magnificent.

➜ For guiding on the mountain see Galdhøpiggen (see 11).
61.6512, 8.5575 🏕🏖🏔📷

13

14

17

17

13 BESSEGGEN RIDGE

One of the most famous day hikes in Norway. The Besseggen trail starts at the edge of Gjende lake, climbs up onto the ridge and then drops back down to the lake again. The path is clearly marked with red letter T's painted on rocks. Either walk from Gjendesheim to Memurubu and take the regular ferry back, or do it the other way round. The walk is hard work and requires a good level of fitness. Save it for a very clear day as the views will take your breath away. There's a DNT (Norwegian Trekking Association) hut at Memurubu (see 19), but it's also possible to wild camp.

→ The route starts at Gjendesheim (61.4941, 8.8134), the highest point is at Veslfjellet (61.5073, 8.7637) and it finishes at Memurubu (61.4910, 8.6311). For ferry route back to Gjendesheim see below. Local map and compass are essential.

7–8 hours, 61.5010, 8.7174

14 GJENDE BOAT TRIP

A regular ferry service runs on this high mountain lake that is 20km long and, at 150m, the deepest in the area. Take a sightseeing trip and enjoy a cruise on the beautiful blue-green water; the colour comes from glacier particles. You can also use the ferry to access a hike such as the Besseggen Ridge (see 13).

→ The regular ferry runs from Gjendesheim (61.4941, 8.8134), to Memurubu (61.49099, 8.63107) and on to the end of the fjord at Gjendebu (61.4511, 8.4882). Check timetables at www.gjende.no

61.4941, 8.8134

GLACIERS & CAVES

15 DUMMDALSGROTTENE

Limestone cave system created over thousands of years by the Dumma river (which runs through it), comprising several different caves with numerous chambers and interesting rock formations. Organise a guide and specialist equipment for a great family adventure.

→ For guided trips with equipment provided, contact: Aktiv i Lom SA, 2687 Bøverdalen, +47 61 212799.

61.5564, 8.0521

16 SMØRSTABBREEN GLACIER

Spectacular glacier and a remnant of the ice that shaped this landscape. Take a guided tour to learn how glaciers work, explore all the different parts and then go right underneath the glacier and into several amazing caves.

→ Jotunheimen Glacier Guides, 2688 Lom, +47 91 301906. www.jotunheimenglacierguides.com

61.5414, 8.1064

FOOD

17 BRIMI SÆTER

A lovely traditional dairy farm hosting a timber-built café and restaurant with several accommodation options. Enjoy local food, such as farm cheeses and home-made waffles in an idyllic mountain ambience. Children will love the animals and getting involved with the milking, and you are bound to stay longer than you intended.

→ Smørlivegen, 2685 Garmo, +47 91 137558. www.brimi-seter.no

61.8070, 8.9144

EAT & SLEEP

18 KROSSBU TURISTSTASJON

This privately owned lodge located off the Sognefjellet mountain pass makes a great base for exploring the numerous marked trails in the area. During the summer there are guided tours across the Smørstabbreen and Fannaråkbreen glaciers. Excellent views and meals available in the restaurant.

→ 2687 Bøverdalen, +47 61 212922. www.krossbu.no

61.5742, 8.0324

19 GJENDEBU MOUNTAIN HUT

DNT (Norwegian Trekking Association) hut with 119 beds at the western end of Gjende lake in the heart of the Jotunheimen National Park. At an elevation of 995m above sea level, there are commanding views over the lake and mountains beyond. To get here you'll need to hike or take a boat over Gjende (see 14). The DNT has numerous other cabins in the Jotunheimen area. For details go to www.turistforeningen.no/cabin.php?lo_id=NO_jotun

→ 2684 Vågå, +47 91 574 965. www.gjendebu.com

61.4511, 8.4882

20 VALBJØR GARD

High above Vågå, and over 2,100 feet above sea level is Valbjør Farm, which dates back to Viking times. With amazing views of Vågå lake and with Jotunheimen in the background this is truly a stunning location. The farm is organic, rears sheep and goats

and also grows some vegetables and herbs. There are 12 wooden cabins that you can rent, as well as beds in the old hayloft. All the food served is local, home-cooked and really delicious. A number of marked hiking trails pass the farm.

➜ Øvre Nordheradsveg 472, 2680 Vågå, +47 61 237301. www.valbjoer.no

61.8745, 9.0858

21 RØISHEIM

Small hotel in an 18th-century coaching inn. This is an ideal location if you're climbing mountains in the national park. The kitchen serves delicious local food and hearty, traditional Norwegian breakfasts. Some bedrooms have distinctive wooden baths.

➜ 2687 Bøverdalen, +47 61 21 20 31. www.roisheim.no

61.7493, 8.3851

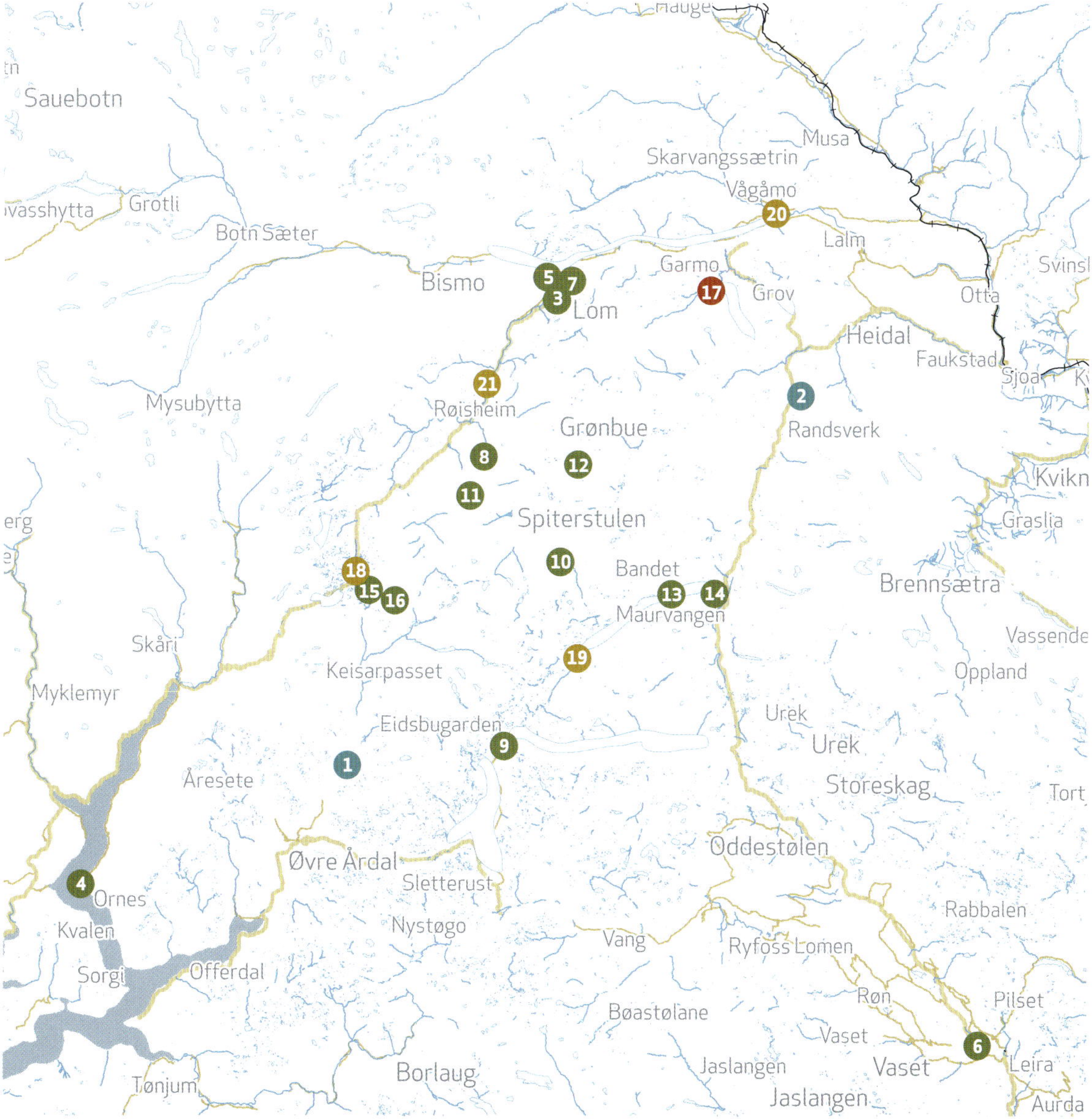

RØROS

Our perfect week

→ **Explore** Northern Europe's largest canyon at Jutulhogget.

→ **Be** captivated by the lights of the Hessdalen Phenomenon.

→ **Sleep** in a 17th-century timber-built hotel in central Røros.

→ **Drink** beer and learn to dance the polka at the Røros Folk Festival.

→ **Observe** a huge reindeer stag in the Forollhogna National Park (and try to find a set of antlers).

→ **Sing** to test the acoustics in the new stave church in Haltdalen.

→ **Descend** 50 metres underground at Olav's Mine and walk the tunnels.

→ **Listen** to the superstitions of the mountain farmers at the Husantunet Museum.

→ **Watch** copper ingots being produced at the Røros smelting works.

→ **Fish** for Arctic char from a canoe on the Doctor's Lake.

The mountain town of Røros is 600 metres above sea level and lies close to the border with Sweden. Now an idyllic and peaceful place, for 330 years it was a busy centre of copper mining. Once known as Bergstaden (the Mountain City), the town is almost unchanged since the 18th century and is a UNESCO World Heritage Site. To visit the old wooden miners' houses with their dark-pitch log facades that are often set around small medieval courtyards, is to go back in time.

The surrounding landscape was largely shaped by glaciation at the end of the last Ice age, and you'll discover numerous landforms such as kettle holes and eskers that are characteristic of those formed by glacial melt water. Røros even has its own drifting mini-desert.

The town grew up around the prosperous Røros Copper Works, which had several ore fields and numerous mines that were worked at different periods over three centuries. Life for the miners would have been very harsh here – a place where some of Norway's coldest winter temperatures are often recorded. You can visit one of the mines, descend into the shafts and walk along the adits that connect to neighbouring mines. The museum is on the site of the old smelting works and there are many other historical sites in and around the vicinity. A guided tour is the best way to learn more about this fascinating town.

The area around Røros features vast tracts of mountain wilderness along the border with Sweden, including two national parks. There are endless opportunities for hiking, canoeing and even living off the land if you want to.

Long before the advent of copper mining, Sami reindeer herders were working in the mountains and the area still has a very strong Sami culture. Look at the landscape through their eyes and you'll see that, far from being barren, it's a veritable larder of berries and plants to pick and lakes full of fish to catch.

Why not continue the medieval, fairytale theme of Røros by spending a night in Hessdalen and watching the mysterious and unexplained lights of the Hessdalen Phenomena (see 6). The experience is bound to fire your imagination.

LANDSCAPE & NATURE

1 MØLMANNSDALEN

Glacial valley created during the last Ice age. Follow the 8.5km marked trail, with information boards that help you appreciate the considerable history and point out interesting flora and fauna at the various points along the path. There are also several lakes to cool off in on a hot day. For very basic off-grid accommodation, you can rent the historic Mølmannsdalsgården farm building, which is owned by the Røros community.

➔ The signed path starts at the old farm: Mølmannsdalen, Prubergjellan, 7374 Røros. Booking contact: +47 72 410000. www.roros.no

62.5327, 11.4746 🅿️🅶🅻🌲

2 DOKTORTJØNNA

At the end of the last ice age a large block of ice melted to form this kettle hole (or kettle lake) and it is now a nature area run by the local community. During the 19th century it was owned by the local physician, and in Norwegian the name means 'Doctor's Lake'. Fed solely by nutrient-rich ground water, it's home to both trout and char if you want to fish. Numerous signposted trails start

here and you can rent a canoe or dinghy to explore the lake, then stop off at the café for refreshments. During the summer there are regular activities for children.

➔ Johan Falkbergets vei 16, 7374 Røros. +47 72 410880

62.5825, 11.3670 🅿️🚣🅻🌲

3 SAKRISODDEN

Protected area on the northern shore of Lake Aursund where you can find Norway's rarest plant – the Siberian aster (Aster sibiricus), which also grows on the Kola Peninsula in Arctic Russia. From four specimens in 1975, numbers have increased to over 800. If you would like to visit, contact Jorunn Sakrisvoll at the plant sanctuary.

➔ Jorunn Sakrisvoll, Sakrisodden, 7482 Glåmos, +47 72 414725.

62.6808, 11.5234 ✚

4 JUTULHOGGET CANYON

Largest canyon in Northern Europe at 2.4km long and between 150 and 500m wide, with 240m-high cliffs. Enjoy the dramatic view from the edge or make the steep descent on one of the precipitous paths. The canyon was formed by the draining of the Nedre Glåmsjø lake during the last ice age, some

10,000 years ago, but water no longer flows through it.

➔ From the village of Alvdal (62.1093, 10.6290) follow Route 3 for 20km to the hamlet of Urstrømmen. Turn L at the sign for Jutulhogget.

61.9976, 10.8882 🅿️🅻

5 KVITSANDA

A rare opportunity to explore a Norwegian desert! This conservation area of less than 1sq km, formed by sand and gravel deposited during the last ice age, looks like a mini-Sahara but is not a true desert. That would require a rainfall of less than 250mm per year, which is very unlikely in the Norwegian mountains. Pine trees and shrubs have been planted here to try to stop the sand drifting.

➔ Park at Doktortjønna (see 2) and follow the signed path for 1km.

62.5824, 11.3592 🅿️🅻

6 HESSDALEN LIGHTS

Since the 1940s, unusual white, yellow or red lights have been observed at night hovering over the Hessdalen Valley. Sometimes the lights move very fast and at other times they are stationary for hours. Explanations for the phenomenon range from UFO activity

to scientific theories. Why not see them for yourself and draw your own conclusions?

→ The best place to observe the lights is the Hessdalen Valley. The address for the research station is: Hessdalen AMS, 7380 Holtålen. www.hessdalen.org

62.8214, 11.2019

7 FEMUNDSMARKA NATIONAL PARK

Offering 573 sq km of pristine wilderness on the border with Sweden, this landscape has barely changed since it emerged from beneath the ice. Femundsmarka National Park is the perfect place to hike, canoe, forage for berries or fish for trout, char and grayling as you paddle between the interconnected lakes. Start your adventure at the visitor centre, where you can obtain local maps and details of the numerous mountain huts in the area. This is also the southernmost Sami reindeer herding area in Norway and has a strong tradition of Sami culture.

→ National Park Visitor Centre: 2446 Elgå, +47 62 458787, www.femunden.no

62.1653, 11.9440

8 FOROLLHOGNA NATIONAL PARK

In this national park renowned for its large wild reindeer herd, you can spend time observing the stags, which are particularly large and crowned with magnificent antlers. With gentle slopes rising from the valleys to meet higher alpine areas, this is 1,061 square kilometres of fantastic prime hiking territory. On the lower slopes are mountain farms where, for centuries, animals have been put out to pasture during the summer months. Start at the visitor centre in the mountain village of Vingelen (see 12) where you'll find all the information you need to plan your trip.

→ Vingelen Visitor Centre, 2542 Vingelen, +47 479 21187, www.midtnorsknatur.no

62.4173, 10.8663

BIKE & CANOE

9 BIKE RENTAL

→ There are numerous bike trails along old mining tracks in the Røros area and the tourist information office has a wide selection of route maps. Hire a hybrid, mountain or electric bike to explore the immediate area.

→ Bergmannsgata 13, 7374 Røros, +47 72 411218, www.gsport.no

62.5750, 11.3863

12

10 TØMMERRENNENE

With mining operations around Røros needing timber for pit props or turned into charcoal for the smelter, the immediate area quickly became deforested. Wood had to be brought in from further afield, so this series of lakes, canals and chutes were built in the 18th century to float timber from Femund Lake to the Feragen (62.5617, 11.8597) closer to Røros. You can walk, cycle or canoe the route.

→ Follow the 532 (Femundsveien) from Røros for 34km until the road ends at Femund Lake, then either head NE (use a local map) for 2km or follow the path (or paddle) along the edge of the lake until after approx 8km you reach the first section of waterway at the end of the lake. For a guided summer canoe trip contact: Rå Røros AS, Ol Kanelsaveien 2, 7374 Røros, +47 95 475690. www.raaroros.no
62.4345, 11.9177 ⛺📷🏔

HISTORY & CULTURE

11 HUSANTUNET OPEN-AIR MUSEUM

Fascinating village museum with one of Norway's best collections of old buildings, where you can get inspiration for your own modern eco-home by looking at how the 17 turf-roofed houses from the 18th century were constructed. Learn about traditional mountain farming in the area, discover how farmers coped with the often harsh winter climate, and hear about their strong superstitions.

→ Husantunet, 2560 Alvdal, +47 62 4878/7. www.alvdal.kommune.no
62.1201, 10.6293 📷🚲🐾

12 VINGELEN MOUNTAIN VILLAGE

Unspoilt village surrounded by summer pastures and meadows that are still traditionally worked. Set on the edge of the Forollhogna National Park and widely considered one of the most beautiful villages in the country, its 800-plus wooden houses are more than 100 years old, and many offer accommodation during the summer. Leave the present behind and take a tour of the village environs on a horse-drawn cart, then browse the quirky bric-a-brac and handicraft shop. There are several open farms to choose from, all serving home-cooked, home-grown food.

→ Vingelen, 2542 Vingelen, +47 47 921187. www.vingelen.no
62.4172, 10.8663 🍴🛏📷🚲♻

10

11

13 RØROS SMELTHYTTA

Fascinating museum on the site of the old smelting works, which burned down in 1975. In the smelter, an essential part of the mining operation, copper was produced from the ore extracted from the local mines and working models show how horsepower was used in the process. On summer weekdays there are smelting demonstrations when copper ingots are cast using traditional techniques. The museum also includes a collection of 19th-century clothing.

→ Malmplassen, 7374 Røros, +47 72 406170. www.rorosmuseet.no
62.5769, 11.3918

14 STORWARTZFELTET

At the Storwartz Field, one of Røros' principal sites, nine separate copper mines were worked at different times from 1645 until 1972. Located 10km N of Røros, the path is well signed or you can cycle along the old mining road from the centre of town. Explore this fascinating landscape and discover clues to its heavily industrialised past – including piles of stones carried out of the mines by hand during the 17th century.

→ Storwartz, 7374 Røros, +47 72 406170. www.rorosmuseet.no
62.6224, 11.5327

15 OLAVSGRUVA

Olav's Mine, one of the richest and most important mines in the Røros area and which operated from 1936–1972, can be found in the Storwartz Field (see 14 above). It is connected to the older Nyberget mine (worked from 1650–1717 and 1861–1890) and both are maintained by the Røros Museum and open to visitors. Descend 50m underground to walk in the footsteps of the miners from the town.

→ Rørosmuseet (Røros Museum), 7374 Røros, +47 72 406170. www.rorosmuseet.no
62.6320,11.5600

16 BERGVERKDIREKTØR HIORTS BAROKKPARK

Unusual Baroque park created by former mine director Peder Hiort between 1759 and 1780. Here you'll find an interesting mixture of Norwegian trees, plants and 18th-century wooden buildings. The park is laid out in grand European style with paths, walled gardens and sculptures.

→ Barokkparken i Hiort-Engan, Engan, 7374 Røros.
62.5640, 11.3072

17 RØROS CHURCH

Built on the highest point in the town, this is one of Norway's biggest churches with seating for 1,600. It was consecrated in 1784 during the heyday of mining and construction was paid for by the Røros Copper Works – you can see their symbol on all four walls of the tower. The sign over the entrance reads 'Til Guds Ære og Bergstadens Ziir' (to God's Glory and Bergstaden's beauty) and for this reason the church is also known as 'Bergstadens Ziir'.

→ Kjerkgata 7374, Røros, +47 72 410000. www.roroskirke.no
62.5773, 11.3883

18 HALTDALEN NEW STAVE CHURCH

The original stave church in Haltdalen was built around 1170, but in 1882 it was taken down and moved further north to Trondheim. At the turn of the 21st century, the local history association decided to replace it with a new stave church with exactly the same dimensions and in the same style as the original building. In the new church, built from wood using traditional methods, the acoustics are amazing. Why not try them out with a song?

→ Aunvegen 14, 7383 Haltdalen, +47 90 658772. www.stavkirka.no
62.9265, 11.1406

19 SLEGGVEIEN

Street of restored wooden houses once lived in by those who did not have a farm or keep livestock: mainly craftsmen, gypsies, casual workers and single people. Five of the houses at the top of the street are managed by Røros Museum and open for visits during the summer. Contact the museum for details of special events.

→ Malmplassen, 7374 Røros, +47 72 406170. www.rorosmuseet.no
62.5770, 11.3917

LOCAL FOOD

20 RØROS FOLK FESTIVAL

Annual folk festival where you can spend the day sampling local produce and the evening working it off by learning to dance a traditional polka. The events take place at various venues around Røros.

→ Contact the tourist office for tickets and info: Røros Tourist Information Office, Peder Hiorts gate 2, 7374 Røros, +47 72 410000. www.rorosfolkfestival.com
62.5753, 11.3865

ACCOMMODATION

21 LAVVO CAMP

Stay in a traditional Sami lavvo (essentially a wooden 'tent') with a wood-burning stove and reindeer skins to sleep on. Choose the one with the glass roof if you plan to watch out for the strange Hessdalen Lights (see 6).

→ Hessdalen UFO Camp, 753, Hessdalen, 7380, +47 95 075601.
www.visithessdalen.no/en/ufo-camp
62.7894, 11.1807

22 ERZSCHEIDERGÅRDEN

Small and cosy hotel situated right next to the church in Røros in a 17th-century wooden building. In German *erzscheider* is someone responsible for ore processing – a reference to the town's industrial past. The hotel, which dates from 1945, has 24 unique rooms and the kitchen specialises in dishes prepared from local produce.

→ Erzscheidergården Hotell, Spell-Olaveien 6, 7374 Røros, +47 72 411194.
www.erzscheidergaarden.no
62.5783, 11.3889

23 VERTSHUSET

Central Røros hotel with 32 bedrooms in a traditional timber house dating back to the 17th century. The kitchen specialises in dishes that fuse traditional and innovative ingredients. In the basement there's a micro-brewery producing several different types of beer. Just ask if you'd like to be shown round and do some tasting!

→ Vertshuset Røros, Kjerkgata 34, 7374 Røros, +47 72 419350.
www.vertshusetroros.no
62.5763, 11.3868

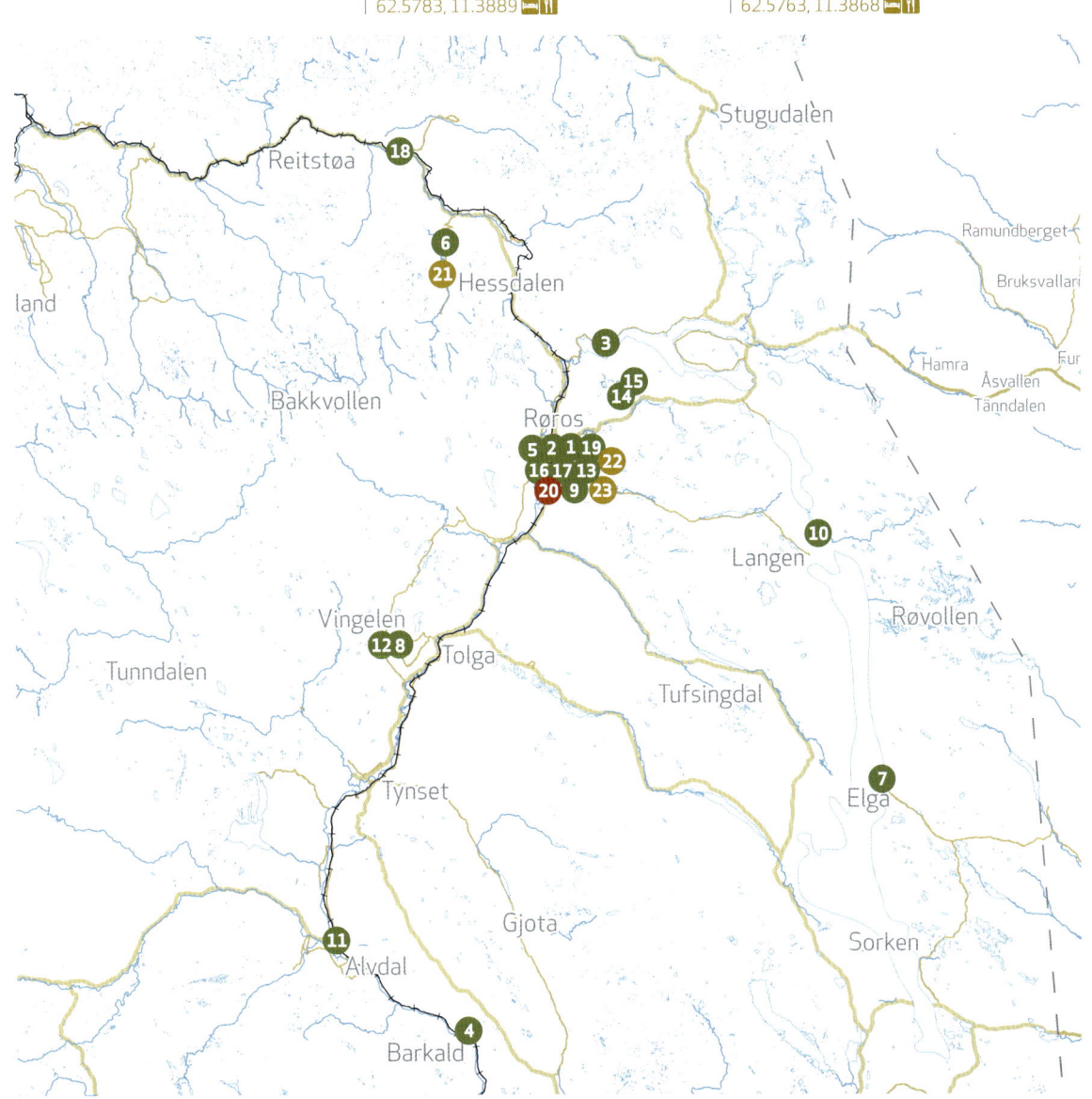

MOUNTAIN RAILWAY

Our perfect week

→ **Explore** the area around Finse station where Captain Scott's team trained for their ill-fated South Pole expedition.

→ **Disappear** into 182 dramatic tunnels along the route between Oslo and Bergen.

→ **Descend** 861.6m in 55 minutes on the train from Myrdal to Flåm.

→ **Imagine** the navvies excavating the tunnel at Gravhals, near Myrdal by hand over six years.

→ **Cross** 300 spectacular bridges on your journey between Oslo and Bergen.

→ **Follow** the Rallarvegen track on a breathtaking descent by bike from the Hardangervidda plateau down to the Aurlandsfjord.

→ **Watch** the *huldre* dance in the spray from the waterfall at Kjosfossen.

→ **Hike** in the footsteps of the *Heroes of Telemark* on the Hardangervidda plateau.

→ **Spend** the night in a remote mountain cabin by Hallingskeid station.

A famous railway that takes you through some of the most remote, beautiful and dramatic scenery that it's possible to experience on a train. Starting from either Oslo or Bergen (the other terminus), the 493-kilometre route works its way up mountain valleys and over Europe's largest mountain plateau, the Hardangervidda.

The construction of the line was a monumental achievement by the navvies and engineers. There are more than 20 km of tunnels, often hewn through solid gneiss and in very remote locations. The line is also so steep in places that the trains are fitted with multiple braking systems. In 1908, the first train completed the journey from Oslo to Bergen.

The whole route takes about seven hours, and for at least one of those you're above the tree line and well away from any sign of civilisation. During the winter months the train is often packed with skiers, but even in summer – the ideal time to travel on it to reach hiking trails that have no other means of access – you're likely to see substantial snow at the higher altitudes.

When constructing the railway, the navvies carved an access road into the mountains for transporting materials, which is now known as the Rallarvegen (the Navvy Road). Cycling along it from Haugastøl all the way down to Voss is great fun, especially if you choose the downhill route when very little pedalling is required. You can hire bikes at the start of the Rallarvegen and also at Finse station.

At Myrdal there's a junction with the Flåmsbanen branch line – one of the steepest railways in the world with eight stops for just 20km of line. The descent to Flåm station on the edge of the fjord below is so unhurried that the train even stops for passengers to look at a waterfall!

Whether you stay on the train and just admire the breathtaking views or alight at all of the mountain stops and explore, this is not only a voyage you'll never forget but also one of the most spectacular train journeys in the world.

3

BERGENSBANEN STATIONS

1 OSLO

Founded in 1000 and for many centuries an important trading centre, Oslo became the capital city of Norway in 1814. Lying at the head of Oslofjord the city covers 454 sq km, of which 245 are forest and green spaces. More of an inlet on the Skaggerak Straight than a true fjord, Oslofjord has over 60 islands and these can be reached by ferry. All the attractions you'd expect of a capital city are here including a royal palace and numerous fascinating museums. The Viking Museum and the Resistance Museum are two you should definitely make time for. The Bergensbanen's point of departure is Oslo's Sentralstasjon (Central Station) – the largest in the Norwegian railway system. The first section as far as Drammen was opened in 1872 and is known as the Drammenbanen (the Drammen Line).

2m above sea level, 493km from Bergen. 59.9111, 10.7525

2 LYSAKER

Once a farming community, Lysaker is now a residential area and part of Stor-Oslo (Greater Oslo). Just a short walk from the station, you'll see several beautiful waterfalls on the Lysakerelven and indeed Oslo is one of the few places in the world where white-water kayakers can run significant urban rapids. During the Second World War the Norwegian resistance sabotaged trains at this station on numerous occasions. You can find out more about this in the Resistance Museum at the Akershus Fortress. The train now leaves Oslo's city limits.

7.5m above sea level, 485km from Bergen. 59.9136, 10.6372

3 ASKER

Extending out to the Oslofjord, Asker has many forest areas and beaches that are great for swimming. It's a suburb of Oslo and many people commute into the city for work.

10m above sea level, 469km from Bergen 59.8336, 10.4346

4 DRAMMEN

The town grew up by the river of the same name (Drammenselva), where it widens to become the Drammensfjord. The river was once used for logging, and timber, paper and cellulose production were all important industries in the area. Nowadays you mainly see small boats and canoes on its waters.

Since 2011, the city (Norway's eighth-largest) has been heated by water-source heat pumps that draw water from the Drammensfjord.

2m above sea level, 452km from Bergen. 59.7400, 10.2040

5 HOKKSUND

Slightly further upstream from the town, there's good salmon fishing on the Drammenselva. Records show that 800 years ago the local people used nets and traps to fish below the Hellfossen falls.

8m above sea level, 435 km from Bergen. 59.7671, 9.9111

6 VIKERSUND

The section of line between here and Drammen is known as the Randsfjordbanen, (Randsfjord was the town's old name). Historically, the main industry was paper and pulp, but the area is now better known as a centre for ski-jumping. Although the line doesn't start to climb yet, the scenery becomes progressively more rugged and mountainous. During the summer a steam railway operates on a branch line from here.

67m above sea level, 409km from Bergen. 59.9693, 9.9982

7 HØNEFOSS

This town in Buskerud county is named after the large falls on the Begna river that flows through it. Much of the water is diverted for hydropower but during the spring melt the falls become very spectacular. The Ringerikes Museum, which has various local history displays and an interesting collection of runestones, is well worth a visit.

96m above sea level, 381km from Bergen. 60.1690, 10.2492 📷🚶🚻

8 FLÅ

By the time you reach the valley station of Flå, you are in the midst of a mountain landscape. The symbol of the town is a bear, and in the centre you'll find a very large wooden one. Go to the town's park to see the real thing – as well as other Norwegian animals – in large outdoor enclosures.

155m above sea level, 319km from Bergen. 60.4322, 9.4733 🚶🐾

9 NESBYEN

The train is now travelling through the Hallingdal Valley, which features large areas of mountain wilderness and numerous hiking trails. The Hallingdal Museum is one of the oldest in Norway and has a fascinating collection of buildings and artefacts. During the last week of August a ladies' market is held in the Kjerringtorge – all the stallholders are women and everything on sale is produced by local women. Although chilly in the winter, the town holds the record for the highest temperature ever recorded in Norway: 35.6°C on June 20th 1970.

168m above sea level, 285km from Bergen. 60.5766, 9.1134 🚴🚶

10 GOL

Lying in the middle of the Hallingdal Valley, the village of Gol is on an historical route between East and West Norway. Not far from the village the spectacular Hydnefossen waterfall on the Hydna river drops 155m over sheer cliffs to the valley below. There was once a stave church here but it was moved to the Royal Museum, now the Norwegian Folk Museum, in Oslo in 1885. The surrounding mountain landscape is a great area for hiking, cycling, canoeing and climbing.

207m above sea level, 268km from Bergen. 60.6990, 8.9712 🚶🏕️🚣🚴

11 ÅL

At the halfway point of the journey, this mountain village is popular with cross-

country skiers in winter while in summer it is the ideal base for a whole range of alpine activities. At the end of May it hosts Norway's oldest annual folk music festival – a week of singing, dancing and feasting on local food. In nearby Torpo the fairytale stave church, built in 1192 displays beautiful carvings and runic inscriptions. From here the train continues along the Hallingdal Valley.

436m above sea level, 243km from Bergen. 60.6265, 8.5619 ⚇✉✝🛶

12 GEILO

Norway's first ski resort, this mountain town is still one of the country's largest and during summer the many activities on offer include rafting and canyoning. From here, you can follow numerous marked trails of varying lengths and explore the vast wilderness of Hardangervidda National Park. During one of the most daring raids of the Second World War, Norwegian SOE agents parachuted onto the high plateau here. After spending a winter in hiding, they successfully destroyed the Vemork heavy water plant near Rjukan. After Geilo the train finally leaves the Hallingdal Valley.

794m above sea level, 218km from Bergen. 60.5346, 8.2068 🛶✉

13 USTAOSET

High mountain ski resort and the finishing point of the Skarverennet cross-country skiing race. For summer visitors, there are several marked hiking trails as well as great opportunities for canoeing on the Ustevatnet lake. The area features around 800 old mountain huts and strict Norwegian planning regulations make it almost impossible for new ones to be built. As the train leaves the station it follows the shore of first Ustevatnet and then Sløddfjorden until it reaches the next station.

990m above sea level, 207km from Bergen. 60.4963, 8.0454 🚴🛶🛶

14 HAUGASTØL

Small high-altitude station on the edge of the Hardangervidda mountain plateau. During the winter the village is a centre for the relatively new sport of snow-kiting, but during the summer it's the starting point of the Rallarvegen cycle trail (see p96). Many people bring their bikes on the train and alight here to start their ride.

998m above sea level, 196km from Bergen. 60.5117, 7.8690 🏔🚴🛶🛶

17

15 FINSE

Mountain village on the shore of lake Finsevatnet that is just on the edge of the Hardangervidda. At 1,222m above sea level it is the highest railway station in Norway and the line is the only means of access as there is no road. On the opposite side to the station building you'll see a museum about the construction of the railway line and two old snow-clearing engines. The members of Captain Scott's ill-fated expedition to the South Pole trained here and there's a monument outside the hotel. About 5km from the station you'll be amazed by the beautiful blue ice of the Hardangerjøkulen glacier, but don't venture onto it without a local guide. Based in the village, an alpine research centre run by the universities of Oslo and Bergen carries out valuable research into the ecology of high mountain areas.

1,222m above sea level, 169km from Bergen. 60.6017, 7.5041 ▲🏔️🏠🌄🏕️

16 HALLINGSKEID

Remote mountain station with no village or road connection where the train stops only for hikers and mountaineers. The station itself is inside a long wooden snow tunnel

15

16

and on four occasions (in 1948, 1953, 1960 and 2011) the tunnel has caught fire. The fire in 1960 also burned down the station building, while in 2011 a train also caught fire and was damaged beyond repair. The Norwegian Trekking Association (DNT) has a cabin nearby.

1,110m above sea level, 148km from Bergen. 60.6679, 7.2539 ▲🏔️🏠🚶🌄

17 MYRDAL

Located on a mountain pass between two tunnels, Myrdal station is the junction for the spectacular Flåmsbana (Flåm Line), often described as one of the world's most spectacular train journeys. This branch line descends 861.6m over 20.2km and takes you through some of Norway's most dramatic scenery to Flåm Station on the Aurlandsfjord. The line has eight stops, 20 tunnels and one bridge. Its maximum gradient is 5.5 per cent and at least 16km of the line has a 2.8 per cent gradient, which makes it one of the steepest railway lines in the world. The train is not permitted to go faster than 30km per hour downhill and 40km when climbing back up.

867m above sea level, 135km from Bergen. 60.7352, 7.1225 🚶🏠🌄🏕️▲

18 VOSS

The first town station you arrive at as you descend from the mountains. Voss, a centre for adventure sports, holds the Ekstremsportveko (Extreme Sports Week, or 'Veko' as the locals call it), every year at the end of July and people come here from all over the world. The town has numerous cafés and bars and is a great place to relax after spending time in the mountains. The Rallarvegen, which started in Finse, finishes here (unless of course you're doing it the hard way round). From Voss the line runs alongside Vossevangen lake and then follows the Vosso river as it flows through two lakes before heading south to Dale.

57m above sea level, 86km from Bergen.
60.6289, 6.4104

19 DALE

Village at the western end of the Bergsdalen valley and not far from Veafjorden where the knitwear manufacturer Dale of Norway – famous for its lusekofte sweaters – is based. This traditional Norwegian sweater, which dates from the 19th century, generally features a black and white design with colourful woven braid around the neck. At the visitor centre you can see how they prepare and spin the yarn before knitting the wonderfully warm sweaters. From Dale the line follows the Daleelven river and then the Veafjorden.

43m above sea level, 46km from Bergen.
60.5854, 5.8148

20 ARNA

Arna is on the east side of the Ulriken mountain, which at 643m above sea level is the highest of the seven that surround Bergen. From the station here the line goes into a tunnel and on into downtown Bergen.

8m above sea level, 10km from Bergen.
60.4201, 5.4661

21 BERGEN

The terminus of the Bergensbanen is Bergen stasjon, the main railway station in Bergen on the east side of the city centre. The station building, by the architect Jens Kielland, is listed and considered one of the best examples of the Norwegian national romantic style popular during the late 19th and early 20th centuries. Bergen is also referred to as the gateway to fjord Norway (see Hurtigruten chapter p63).

2m above sea level, 493km from Oslo.
60.3898, 5.3345

Rallarvegen

Cycle (mainly) downhill along the old construction road for the Bergensbanen along the edge of the high Hardangervidda plateau and down to the Aurlandsfjord in Flåm. The track is car-free and takes you through some breathtaking high-alpine scenery. On your descent, you'll come across the remains of the old navvies' dwellings and you'll also notice distinct changes in the landscape and vegetation. To cycle the entire route you normally need to wait until early or mid-July when the snow along the road has all melted. The road is then generally clear until the end of September, but this varies from year to year. It's also possible to do the entire journey in one long day, but it is more fun to break it up into three days and wild camp en-route.

Haugastøl–Flåm: 80km

Finse–Flåm: 57km

Haugastøl–Myrdal: 63km

Myrdal–Flåm: 18.5km

Cycle Hire: Haugastøl Turistsenter AS, 3595 Haugastøl. +47 32 087564. www.haugastol.no

23

FLÅMSBANA STATIONS

22 VATNAHALSEN

Originally built to give people living in the district of Sogn access to Bergen and Oslo via the Bergensbanen, the station is now primarily a tourist destination. Indeed, it's the third most visited tourist attraction in Norway. From Myrdal the Flåmbana heads in the Oslo direction before descending into the Flåmsdalen Valley. On this first section, the line passes through several short tunnels and snow shelters.

811.3m above sea level, 19.07km from Flåm.
60.7439, 7.1298 🖼️🎦🏔️⛰️

23 REINUNGA

After a horseshoe curve and a long tunnel followed by a precipitous artificial ledge, the train arrives at the next station at Reinunga.

767m above sea level, 18km from Flåm.
60.7439, 7.1391 🖼️🎦🏔️⛰️

24 KJOSFOSSEN

The next stop, with spectacular views, is at the Kjosfossen waterfall where the Flåmselvi (also known locally as the Moldåni) river makes a total drop of 225m over several spectacular falls and slides. In summer you might see strange female figures (*huldre*) in traditional dress (*bunad*) dancing in the spray. These huldrefolk, mythical Scandinavian female forest spirits, are students from the Norwegian National Ballet School who dance to entertain tourists – or are they…? There's also a small hydro-power station here that produces the electricity for the Flåmsbana.

670m above sea level, 15.8km from Flåm.
60.74698, 7.1356 🖼️🎦🏔️⛰️=

25 KÅRDAL

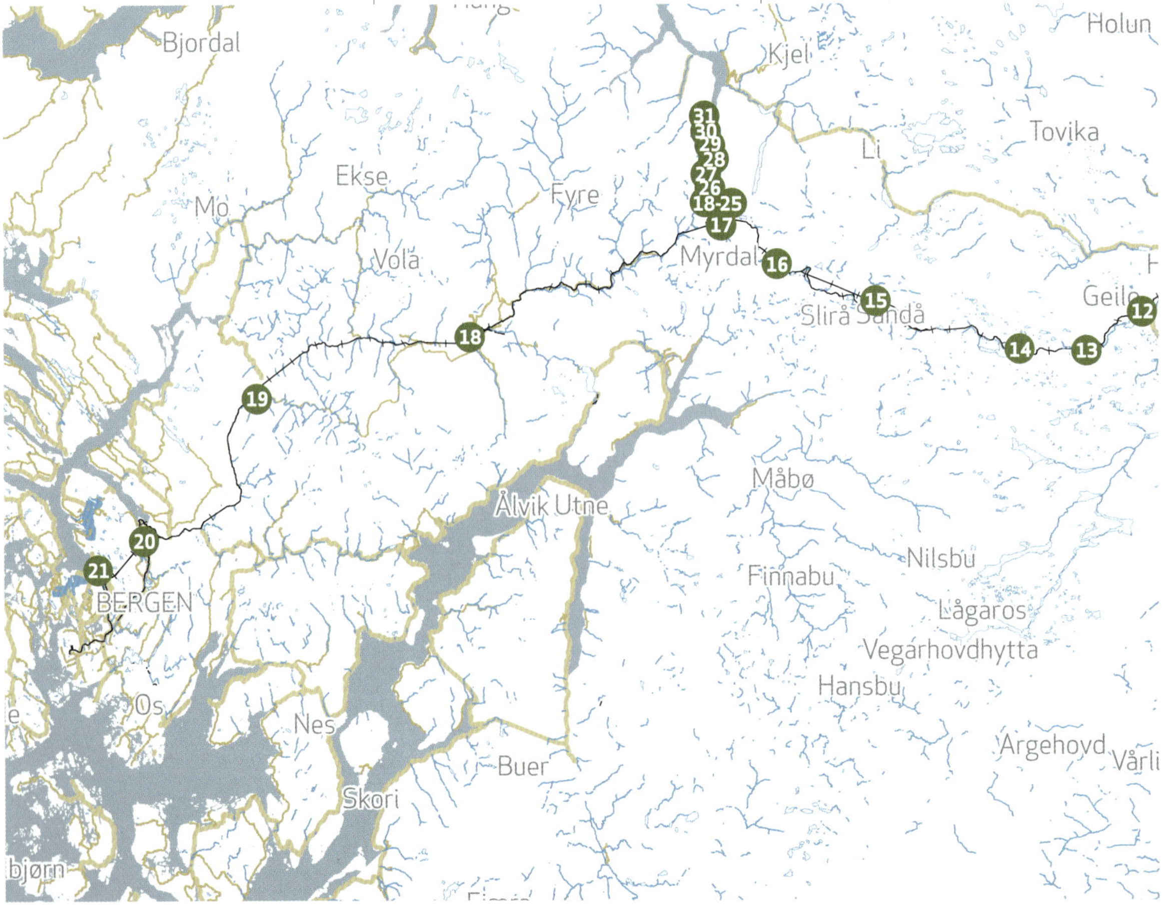

After running through the 1,341.5-metre Nåli tunnel (the longest on the line), the train arrives at Kårdal. Built to service the farms furthest up the Flåmsdalen valley, the station is on a very steep gradient and only trains that are descending stop here.

557m above sea level, 13.86km from Flåm.
60.7561, 7.1055 🖼️🚻🗺️🏔️

26 BLOMHELLER

The mountain beside the line here is called Trodlatoppen and every year this section is subject to numerous avalanches. The train stops at this station, just before crossing the Flåmselvi river again.

458m above sea level, 11.8km from Flåm.
60.7722, 7.1026 🖼️🚻🗺️🏔️

27 BEREKVAM

The valley starts to widen out as the train arrives at Berekvam station. This is the only loop on the line, so if two trains need to pass each other it has to happen here.

344m above sea level, 13.67km from Flåm.
60.7882, 7.0963 🖼️🚻🗺️

28 DALSBOTN

Dalsbotn station is situated just before the 424m-long Furuberget tunnel and the Rjoandefossen waterfall. You'll see the small river plunge 14m over a vertical cliff from the train, which runs alongside the valley.

199m above sea level, 11.56km from Flåm.
60.8135, 7.1243 🖼️📘

29 HÅREINA

Now the scenery changes: the gradient is much less steep here and there's lots of lush green vegetation beside the line.

48m above sea level, 2.99km from Flåm.
60.8395, 7.1229 🖼️♻️🗺️

30 LUNDEN

At the penultimate station of the descent, the valley opens up alongside the river and you'll see numerous small farms.

16m above sea level, 1.6km from Flåm.
60.8508, 7.1139 🖼️♻️🗺️

31 FLÅM

The terminus is the town of Flåm on Aurlandsfjord – a branch of the larger Sognefjord. Cruise ships sail into the fjord so their passengers can take the railway up the mountain. There's also a fast ferry service that connects to Bergen if you want to make a round trip. The old station building is now an interesting museum documenting the remarkable construction of the Flåmsbana.

2m above sea level, 20.2km from Myrdal.
60.8630, 7.1140 🚂🚶🗺️🖼️

31

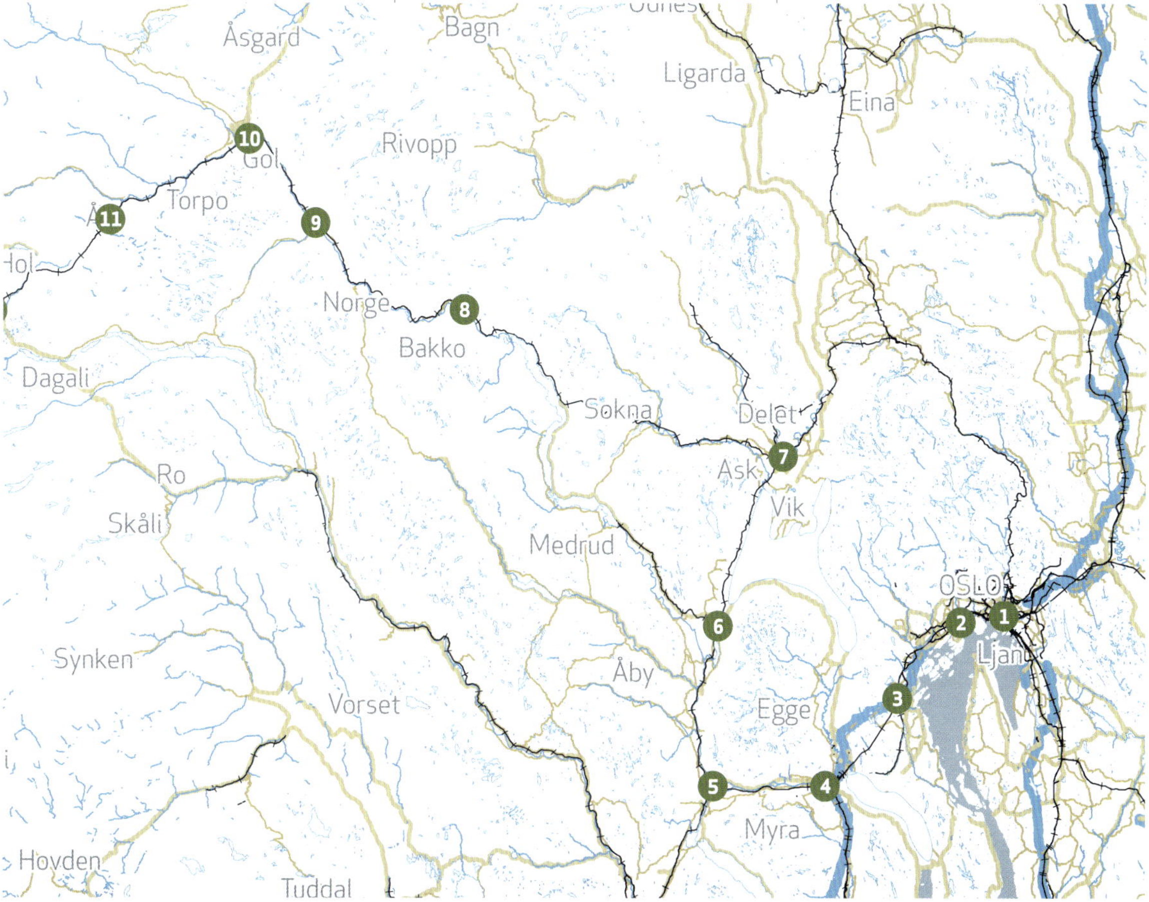

99

SØRLANDETS KYSTEN

Our perfect adventure

→ **Step** back in time during a visit to the coastal settlement at Romsviga.

→ **Marvel** at the power unleashed by the area's huge and spectacular waterfalls.

→ **Become** a lighthouse keeper for the night when you stay at the Lista lighthouse.

→ **Explore** the spectacular Brufjell potholes on the hike to Sandvika beach.

→ **Swim** from the beach outside the old captain's house on Merdø island.

→ **Descend** into the tunnels beneath the bunker at Nordberg Fort.

→ **Walk** along an old log flume, up over a bridge and through a dark tunnel.

→ **Cross** Gjeveden lake by raft, light a fire and enjoy a picnic at Svårthylkyrkja.

→ **Learn** about iron production at the Næs Ironworks Museum.

→ **Watch** the kite surfers fly along the Havikstrand beach.

Following the signs and waymarked stones, the route to Sandvika Beach is spectacular and there are iron handholds to help you navigate particularly steep sections of path. The smooth rock is riddled with large and dramatic hollows that were sculpted over 20,000 years ago during the last ice age by fierce waves, when the sea level was much higher. When you get to the white-pebbled beach you'll be more than ready to cool off with a refreshing swim in the clear water.

Sørlandet (the 'south country') is the name given to this sheltered region in the south of Norway. Along the coast are agricultural lowlands, but only a short distance inland you'll discover mountains, high plateaus and steep valleys where powerful rivers rush down to the sea. This chapter covers a 240-kilometre stretch of the Skagerrak coast from Sandvika beach in the west to Åsmundhavn in the east.

With the highest average summer temperatures in the country, Sørlandet is also known as the Norwegian Riviera. Here the Skagerrak coastline is rocky and characterised by an idyllic archipelago comprising hundreds of picturesque islands and skerries.

Working your way along the coast, your route will take you past remote lighthouses, hidden beaches, historic harbours and even elaborate bunker systems dating from the Second World War. If you travel slowly by bicycle and kayak, or even follow the coastal path on foot, you'll see much more and make the most of your adventure.

Stop off to eat and sample delicious and amazingly fresh seafood, as well as the many variations of traditional smoked, salted or pickled delicacies peculiar to each small coastal community.

After your explorations you may want to spend a day swimming and sunbathing. Head to the Nissedal valley, where you'll discover a series of natural bubbling pools and slides . On a hot day the water warms up very quickly and you can create your very own water-park adventure.

BEACHES

1 HAVIKSTRAND BEACH, LISTA

The Lista area has some of the best beaches in southern Norway. Haviksanden is probably the best known of these and the expanse of white sand and dunes make it especially beautiful. Very popular with kite-surfers, who can be fun to watch.

→ Park in Hanangermona (58.0734, 6.7175) on the Rv651. A short path through the dunes will bring you to the beach.

15 mins, 58.0698, 6.7137

2 KVILJOSANDEN BEACH, LISTA

Another of the beautiful Lista beaches. It shelves very gradually and the shallow water is great for families with small children. Picnic on the beach or in the dunes.

→ Park in the village of Kviljo at the end of Rv 662 (58.0752, 6.6844), then follow the footpath to the sea.

15 mins, 58.0698, 6.6792

3 HAUESTRANDA BEACH, LISTA

Yet another sandy Lista beach on a small peninsula south of Farsund. There are trees, dunes and plenty of places to set up your base camp for a perfect day by the beach.

→ Head SW out of Farsund on the Rv651, then turn R onto the Rv 664 and after a few minutes park in the area opposite the Lista Aluminium Smelter. Take the footpath to the beach from here (58.0694, 6.7812).

15 mins, 58.0715, 6.7717

4 SANDVIKA BEACH

A three-hour hike through a breathtaking coastal landscape south-west of Stornes brings you to Sandvika beach – a secret white pebble cove. On the way you'll pass the spectacular geology of the Brufjell potholes and rock formations. The path can be tricky at times – take utmost care with small children.

→ The area is part of the Magma Geopark. For info and maps see website. Guided walks with a geologist are also available. Magma Geopark, Elvegaten 23, 4370 Egersund, +47 91 782594, www.magmageopark.com

3 hours, 58.2757, 6.3857

WATERFALLS & POTHOLES

5 BJORLOFOSS

Start of a section of the Åkrogjen river, with several beautiful waterfalls. When the river is very low and the sun's shining there are some great potholes for swimming.

→ Drive W from Knaben (58.6657, 7.0638) on the FV839 (which follows the river) for 5 km. Park on the gravel verge beside the road and you'll see the falls on your R.

5 mins, 58.6673, 7.0216

6 DIGELVA WATERFALL WALK

Footpath alongside the spectacular waterfalls on the Digelva river. Walk downstream beside the dramatic slides and drops. Avoid the path during flooding or if you're not confident about rough walking and heights. Not suitable for small children.

→ Cross the bridge over the Tøvdalselva immediately N of Birkeland and head W on route FV258. After 1km you'll see the main falls on your L and a lay-by on your R. Park in the lay-by and follow the path downstream. Walk to the lake (2km) or enjoy the main falls.

1 hour, 58.3363, 8.2046

7 RAFOSSEN WATERFALLS

Series of spectacular waterfalls on the Kvina river. On a fine day you can sit on the flat granite slabs beside the falls and enjoy a picnic, or just contemplate the mighty power of the water. Not suitable for small children owing to the steep and unprotected drops.

→ From Kvinesdal, drive N on the Fv465 for

8.5km until you see a little wooden sign for Rafossen. Follow this road for approximately 2km until the road stops. From here the waterfall is a 5-minute signposted walk.

30 mins, 58.3650, 6.9571

8 NISSEDAL POTHOLES

Spectacular potholes formed in the last ice age and now filled with water, make this an ideal, secret swimming spot. The river that once flowed here is now dammed and on hot days the site becomes a spectacular natural waterpark. Deep pools and slides in very smooth granite that warms up and transfers its heat to the water. A fantastic family day out when the sun's shining.

→ From Haugsjåsund village head W on Route FV352 for 17km. Find a parking area on the L at 58.9521, 8.3657. Leave your car here, cross the road and follow the marked path for 50m.

5 mins, 58.9498, 8.3713

9 KVÅSFOSSEN

Kvåsfossen is one of the largest waterfalls in southern Norway with an impressive drop of 36m. When the Lynga river is low, numerous potholes become visible, and at very low water and on sunny days these make fantastic natural hot tubs.

→ The Lynga river runs alongside the Rv43. Park by the road 3.5km N of the village of Moi and you'll see the waterfall on your L.

5 mins, 58.2644, 7.1899

10 SILD ÅSMUNDHAMN POTHOLES

Very large potholes formed in smooth coastal granite. On a warm day you can swim and bathe in brackish water with amazing sea views. At almost 5m wide and 6m deep, they're the largest in Northern Europe. Bring a picnic.

→ From Risør head W on the Rv416, turn L onto the Rv411 then R onto the Rv1 and follow it until you reach the village of Krabbesund. Approx 500m further on turn L (58.6756, 9.2021). Drive to the end of the track and park. Follow the obvious path to the small harbour (Åsmundhamn) then walk NE along the shore for about 1 km to arrive at the potholes.

25 mins, 58.6736, 9.2105

11 SVÅRTHYLKYRKJA

Huge half-pothole hidden away at the northern end of the Gjevden lake. A great place for swimming and a picnic. Pull yourself across the lake on a raft attached to a cable. There's a fire pit, but you'll need to bring your own wood.

→ Heading E from Vindilhytta on the Rv271 (58.9649, 8.13759), park just off the road at the end of the lake and walk 25m to the jetty for the raft (58.9640, 8.1360).
20 mins, 58.9634, 8.1332

HISTORY & CULTURE

12 VENNESLA LOG FLUME

Wooden log flume (narrow, often raised, waterway) built to transport timber, and one of a few surviving examples in Norway. Enjoy an adventurous walk along the restored wooden canal, which is now dry, as it bypasses the picturesque rapids of the Otra river. The 4km route takes you over a couple of suspension bridges and through a low and rather creepy tunnel. Children will love it.

→ From Vennesla (58.2687, 7.9711) head W out of town on the R454 for 3km, following the shore of the lake. Turn R onto the Steinsfossvegen, for a further 2km. The flume is on your L.
1 hour, 58.3013, 7.9693

13 LINDESNES FYRSTASJON

Oldest lighthouse in Norway, built in 1656 (and lit by candles) on the very beautiful southernmost tip of the Norwegian mainland. It's now a holiday apartment, offering accommodation (for six). A visitor centre, with a cinema and café, documents the building's history. Entrance includes a visit to the top of the tower. Several scenic coastal footpaths pass the lighthouse.

→ Turn off the E39 at Vigeland, W of Mandal. Turn R on to the R460 via Spangereid and the Spangereid canal for 27km. 4521 Lindesnes, +47 38 255420. www.lindesnesfyr.no
57.9825, 7.0467

14 NORDBERG FORT

Fully restored German bunker with tunnels built from 1940–45, that was once part of Hitler's Atlantic Wall. This extensive system of coastal defences stretched for 2,690 km from the Norwegian border with Russia to the French border with Spain, and the location was obviously selected for its commanding views. At the fascinating museum here (part of the Lista Museum complex) you can learn more about a very dark period in Norwegian history.

→ From Vanse (58.0980, 6.6922), head NW on the Rv463 for 3.5km, turning R onto FV652, then very soon after L on to the Fv654. After 2.5km see the fort on the R, 500m off the road. +47 38 396900. www.vestagdermuseet.no
58.1304, 6.6212

15 ROMSVIGA

Traditional coastal settlement that dates back to the 17th century and there was a working farm here until the late 20th century. It is now a protected, historical area and owned by the local community. As well as farming, Romsviga was a busy fishing quay, small ships stopped here to stock up on food supplies, and it was also a pilot station for vessels heading into Kristiansand. Now open to visitors (contact them for seasonal opening times), it's also a great spot for swimming.

→ Head E out of Langenes on Route 456. After approx 2.5 km you will reach a turning on your R (58.0758, 7.9123) with a barrier and a white sentry box. This will take you to the parking area. Langenesveien 600, Søgne, +47 47 922301. www.facebook.no/romsviga

58.0756, 7.9145 📱🐾🏊

16 MERDØGAARD MUSEUM

Learn about the history of the tiny island of Merdø in this charming and informative little museum. Housed in an old 18th-century farm once owned by a ship's captain, and decorated as it would have been 200 years ago when he lived there. Find out about the extensive nautical history of the island and its connections with Denmark, the Netherlands and England. The grounds of the museum include a café and a great beach for swimming.

→ The car-free island of Merdø can be reached in 25 minutes by ferry from Pollen harbour, Arendal (58.45913, 8.76554). Ferries run during the summer season from June to August.

58.4942, 8.8669 📱✈️🍴

17 NÆS IRONWORKS MUSEUM

Iron works with historic buildings and industrial machinery that covers the 300-year period from 1665 onwards, when these works – the second-largest in Norway – were in operation. After suffering a catastrophic flood when a dam failed, the works closed in 1959. A visit offers fascinating insights into Norway's industrial past, with archive footage showing the manufacturing process from charcoal-burning in the forests and iron-ore mining to producing steel.

→ Head N out of the village of Nesgrenda on Route 415. The museum is signposted to the L with a brown tourist sign. Nesverkveien 240, 4934 Nesgrenda, +47 37 160500. www.jernverksmuseet.no

58.6303, 8.8542 📱

FORAGE

18 FISHING BOAT RENTAL

Hire a small boat to explore the myriad of beautiful islands that form the archipelago off Lindesnes. With the provided rods you can fish and then find a secluded spot to land and grill your catch. The sea is very protected here and novice sailors will be given appropriate instruction and directions.

→ The harbour is on the small peninsula just off Route 460 immediately SE of Spangereid. Båly Havn, 4521 Lindesnes, +47 93 036500. www.lindesneshytteservice.no
58.0403, 7.1459 🛏️🍴

SLEEP WILD

19 LISTA LIGHTHOUSE

Spectacular 34m-high lighthouse built in 1836 and now a popular birdwatching spot. During the Second World War it was incorporated into a coastal defence system. Two holiday apartments, each sleeping seven, come with a key to the tower. It's a rare opportunity to become a lighthouse keeper for a night.

→ Fyrveien, 4563 Borhaug, +47 38 397776. www.lista-fyr.com
58.1094, 6.5670 🛏️🖼️

20 SONGVAAR LIGHTHOUSE

Lighthouse on a small, remote island in the Søgne archipelago with accommodation for overnight stays or longer. The perfect retreat if you want to escape from civilisation and enjoy fantastic coastal views. Accessible by small boat.

→ 4640 Søgne, +47 48 240815. www.songvaarfyr.com
58.0153, 7.8096 🛏️🍴🖼️

21 CANVAS HOTEL

Unique camp situated far from any road with ten luxurious sleeping yurts a sauna, shower and a larger yurt for meals. On the edge of a lake and in an area full of biking and walking trails; you can either hire a bike to explore on two wheels or relax in the idyllic surroundings of smooth granite outcrops, wetland and birch forest. None of the structures are permanent and the food is delicious.

→ The camp is approx 3km SE of Tveitsund and 3km from the nearest road. When making your booking you will be advised on the best approach depending on whether you're cycling or walking – you cannot drive here. A local map will be required.
www.canvashotel.no
58.9849, 8.6785 🚶🚴

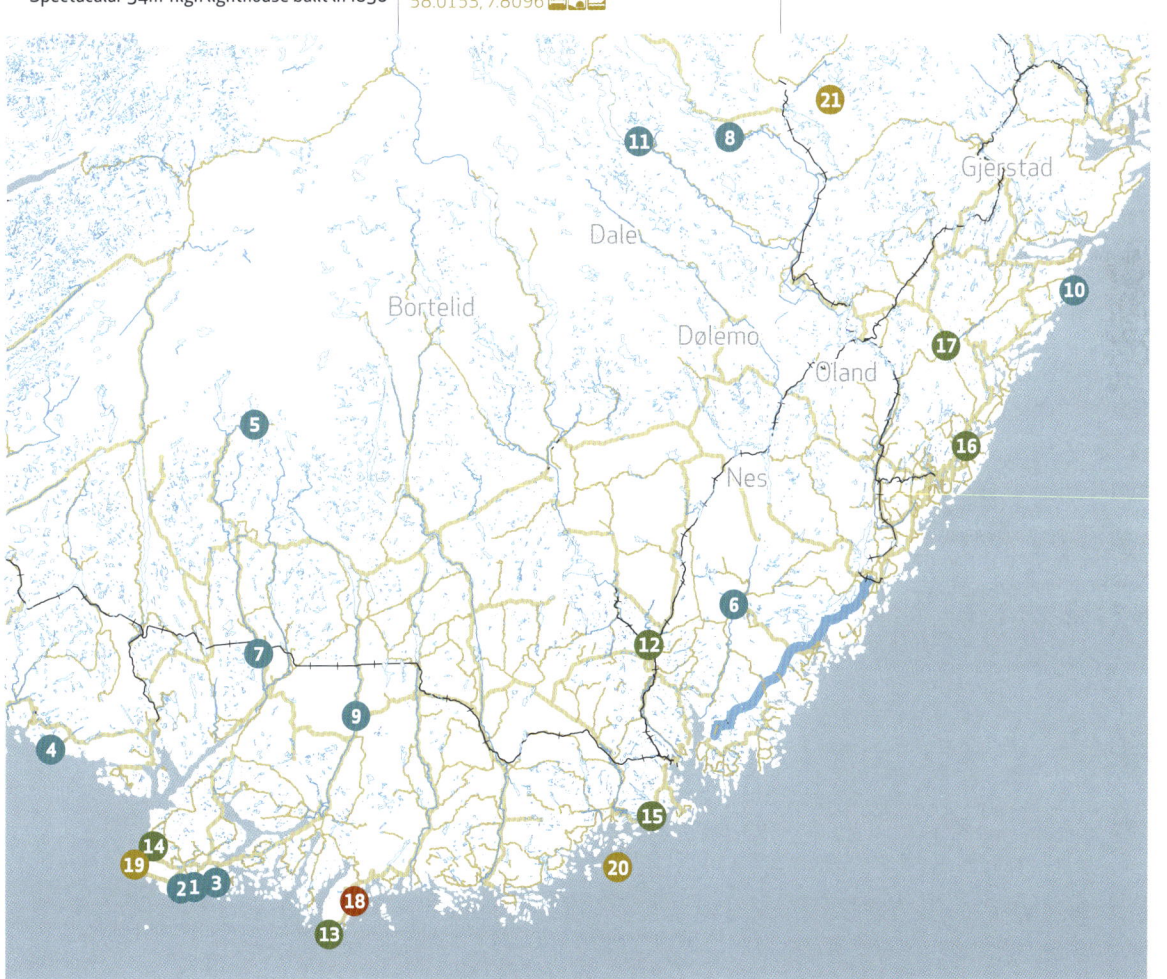

SWEDEN

KIRUNA LAPLAND

Our perfect week

→ **Watch** the midnight sun from the top of a mountain.

→ **Skinny** dip in an ice-cold and crystal-clear glacial lake.

→ **Stand** in three countries at the same time at Treriksröset.

→ **Climb** to the summit of Kebnekaise – Sweden's highest mountain.

→ **Wild** camp by the Rautas river in early autumn and gaze at the aurora borealis overhead.

→ **Hike** a section of the Kungsleden national trail.

→ **Shower** under the Silverfallet waterfall.

→ **Canoe** up into the mountains on the Vistas river and drift back downstream.

→ **Paddle** in the azure water of the Abiskojokk river above Torneträsk lake.

→ **Fly** in by helicopter to spend a few nights wild camping in true wilderness.

Aptly described as Europe's last true wilderness, Swedish Lapland is a vast and incredibly beautiful landscape. The indigenous Sami describe the area as having eight seasons, with each one reflecting distinct changes in nature. From the white cotton-grass of early summer to the golden yellow birch leaves of late autumn, there is plenty of colour in their calendar. The very special light can also make these colours almost glow, and the sunsets of late summer will take your breath away.

During midsummer you never run out of daylight, as the never-setting midnight sun will allow you to hike, paddle and explore late into the night. In the short nights of early autumn, when the sun starts to drop below the horizon again, it is likely to still be warm. On clear nights you may be able to watch the magical aurora borealis as it lights up the sky.

The focus in this chapter is on the rivers, lakes and mountains around the mining town of Kiruna. The town, which owes its very existence to the mine, will have to move 3km to the east over the coming years due to necessary mining expansion. Make some time to visit the mine and see for yourself the huge subterranean industry that makes this area so strategically and economically important. To see a completely different side of Lapland, visit a Sami camp and learn how they spend the summer following their herds of reindeer through the mountains. Taste traditional delicacies and be amazed by the detailing on their handicrafts.

The road network in Lapland is very limited, so you need to expect to have to do some walking in order to explore properly, but the destinations are all incredibly beautiful and more than worth the effort. Many also include the opportunity for a swim in a limpid glacial lake. Kayaks and canoes are also very practical for accessing remote camping spots and can be rented locally along with any other specialist equipment required.

To properly appreciate the vastness of the landscape, you can even arrange to get dropped off by helicopter for a few days. Drink straight from a mountain stream and fish or forage for berries to supplement whatever provisions you bring with you.

Conclude your explorations with a night in one of the mountain lodges, where a traditional wood-fired sauna does wonders for tired legs. Not just a wilderness, Swedish Lapland is a landscape of almost limitless opportunities for any aficionado of outdoor life.

SWIM & CANOE

1 SILVERFALLET

Spectacular waterfall where the Rakkasjokk drops into the valley to meet Lake Torneträsk. Swim in the deep pool of breathtakingly cold green water below the falls. In the winter this is a popular spot for ice climbing.

→ Park by bridge over the Rakkasjokk on E10 about 1km S of Björkliden and walk downstream.

10 mins, 68.4022, 18.6955 ⬚⬚⬚

2 TROLLSJÖN

Trollsjön (also called Rissajaure) is known as the clearest and purest lake in Sweden. You can see down through 34m of glacial meltwater all the way to the bottom. The lake is only ice-free for three months of the year. A great spot for a bracing wild swim after the spectacular (5km return) walk up the Kärkevagge valley.

→ About 10km E of Riksgränsen on E10, park in lay-by either side of the bridge over Kärkejåkka (68.4262, 18.3519, sign on bridge says Låktejåkka). The signposted trail to Trollsjön heads off to the S.

4 hours, 68.3857, 18.3417 ⬚⬚⬚

3 PADDLELAPLAND KAYAK & CANOE HIRE

Kayak and canoe hire run by a local family. Guiding and logistics are also available. They can help you plan a trip, provide all specialist equipment and get you to and from your chosen lake or river. Contact them for friendly and up-to-date advice on paddling in the area or even employ them as guides.

→ Uttervägen 5A, 98137 Kiruna, +46 70 5677744, www.paddlelapland.com
67.8510, 20.2591 ⬚

4 PUOLTSA PADDLE

The Kalix river is 461km long, flowing from Kebnekaise to the Gulf of Bothnia. It is one of very few big rivers in Sweden that are not dammed for hydropower. Explore the forks and bays of this upper lake section, which has no rapids, all with a fantastic backdrop of Sweden's highest mountains.

→ Put in on Kaalasjärvi lake on road to Nikkaluokta (signed from E10 just S of Kiruna) and head upstream dir Nikkaluokta. Return to the same point.

Up to 6 hours, 67.7968, 19.8528 ⬚⬚⬚⬚

5 SAUTOSBÄCKEN

A shallow stream with several wide and deep pools for swimming that warm up quickly on hot days. Swim upstream or downstream from the road bridge. Great for small children.

→ About 10km E of Kiruna turn off the E10 onto route 875 to Jukkasjärvi. In the village turn L signed Paksuniem. Stop in the lay-by after about 1.5km, just before bridge over the Sautosbäcken.

67.8536, 20.6385 ⬚⬚

6 VISTAS PADDLE

Paddle upstream on the glacial Vistas river as far as you are able, taking time to explore the numerous oxbow lakes. As the river meanders along the valley you'll have plenty of opportunities for spotting wildlife on the banks, and there are numerous sandy beaches and several promontories where you can set up camp. When you want to head home, just let yourself drift slowly and silently back downstream.

→ Enter and leave at the road bridge on route 870 at Nikkaluokta (signed from the E10 just S of Kiruna).

1–2 days, 67.8604, 19.0282
⬚⬚⬚⬚⬚⬚

7 LADDJUJOKKA PADDLE

Hike in with an inflatable kayak or a pack raft. Alternatively, get dropped off by helicopter

113

with your kayak. Follow the slow-flowing and low-volume glacial river downstream from the mountains to the dense, moose-filled birch woodland near Nikkaluokta. The whole trip is 25km, or 7km if you start at the lake.

→ Put in S of Kebnekaise Fjällstation (67.8601, 18.6058), or at the end of Ladtjojaure lake (67.8452, 18.8882), and leave at route 870 (67.8554, 19.0218).

1.5 hours to 1 day, 67.8601, 18.6058

CANYONS, CAVES & GLACIERS

8 TORNETRÄSK

The sixth-largest lake in Sweden, with a total area of 330km² and a length of 70km. The mighty Torne river flows out of the south-east end. Swim from the pebble beach by the old boat jetty in Abisko or pick up a timetable for boat trips on the lake from the Mountain Station. Arrange to get dropped off and picked up later so you can explore the remote north shore where there are remains of old Sami settlements. Maybe wild camp for a night on one of the few islands?

→ Park at Abisko Mountain Station and follow the signposted footpath to the boat jetty. Abiskovägen 7, 981 07 Abisko.

30 mins, 68.3615, 18.8024

9 ABISKOJOKK CANYON

The Abiskojokk river flows down from the mountains in the Abisko National Park into Torneträsk lake. Its final 3km starts with a spectacular tunnel that once formed part of a hydroelectric scheme used for railway construction. A waterfall at the end of the tunnel signals the start of an incredible canyon with sheer rock walls and rapids with azure water. The canyon then slowly recedes until it eventually meets the lake, and the very last bit is great for paddling and swimming. There are paths on both sides as well as a bridge partway down. A scientifically important, and also breathtakingly beautiful, environment.

→ Park at the Abisko Mountain Station and follow the signposted footpath to the canyon. Abisko Mountain Station, Abiskovägen 7, 981 07 Abisko.

15 mins, 68.3598, 18.7763

10 KÅPPASJÅKKA CAVES

Cave system with three different caverns formed by the Kåppasjokken stream. The caves were first discovered in the 1980s and exploration since has shown they are among the largest in Sweden. The rock is an interesting mix of slate and limestone with

13

both vast chambers and narrow passages. Specialist equipment and guiding is essential if you want to enter the caves.

➔ Just S of Björkliden. For guiding contact Anders Bergwall, Arctic Guides AB, Syster Syrenas väg 1, 981 07 Abisko, +46 980 40120. www.arcticguides.com
68.3949, 18.6890

11 TRERIKSRÖSET

The Treriksröset is the cairn that marks the point where the borders of Sweden, Finland and Norway meet. There has been a cairn here since 1897 and the current structure dates from 1926. There is no road access near it, but in summer a small ferry comes to the boat jetty at Koltaluokta on Kilpisjärvi lake (69.0467, 20.6093), from just over the border in Finland. The journey takes 30 mins and the boat waits for 2 hours before returning. This is a very remote and beautiful spot and a visit here helps you to fully comprehend the vastness of Lapland.

➔ The ferry M/S Malla is operated by Kilpisjärvi Cruise, +358 40 0669392. www.mallalaiva.com
3 hours, 69.0599, 20.5486

12 KÅRSA GLACIER

Learn how the landscape of Lapland was formed by visiting an active glacier. As it's in a very remote location you can either hike in or your guide will arrange a helicopter. If you fly in, the trip can be done in a day, otherwise add a day each way for approaching on foot. On the glacier itself a local guide is essential. As well as hiking, you will also be able to go into caves formed under the glacier. See for yourself the power of glacial ice and the effect of climate change on this very special region.

➔ For guiding contact Dick Johansson, Abisko Mountain Lodge, Lapportsvägen 30, 981 07 Abisko, +46 980 40100. www.abiskomountainlodge.se or Anders Bergwall, Arctic Guides AB, Syster Syrenas väg 1, 981 07 Abisko, +46 980 40120. www.arcticguides.com
1 day, 68.3577, 18.3237

HIKES

13 MIDNATTSOLSTIGEN WALK

From around the 30th of May until the 14th of July the top of Luossavaara mountain is a great place for viewing the phenomenon of the midnight sun. There are also fantastic views of Kiruna town, the LKAB mine, and on the horizon, the mountains of the Kebnekaise massif. It's possible to drive to the summit, but the best way is to walk up the Midnattsolstigen trail. Bring a picnic. Distance 7km, ascent 225m.

➔ The path is well signposted. Start and finish at the crossroads in front of Camp Ripan, Campingvägen 5, 981 35 Kiruna.
2–3 hours, 67.8603, 20.2405

14 RALLARVÄGEN HIKE

This is an old construction road through

the mountains, used for building the Narvik to Kiruna iron-ore railway. Known as the Rallarvägen (Navvies Road), it is now a great hiking path that will take you through some fantastic scenery with plenty of opportunities for wild camping along the way. Follow the section from Abisko to the Norwegian border at Riksgränsen. At the start of the trail is a small museum recording the construction of the railroad and its strategic importance during the Second World War.

→ Start at Abisko Mountain Station. The signposted path runs 45km to Riksgränsen (68.4256, 18.1271). See the chapter on Narvik (Norway) for details of the final section.
3 days, 68.3583, 18.7806 ▣▣

15 LADTJOVAGGE VALLEY HIKE

Walk as far as you want up an ancient glacial valley for fantastic views of some of Sweden's highest mountains. Follow the signposted path from Nikkaluokta. It's possible to head high up into the valley by taking a boat along Ladtjojaure lake (67.8451, 18.8879). Why not split the walk over two days and wild camp for a night before heading back the next day? To the lake and back is 10km; a timetable for the boat is available at Nikkaluokta.

→ Start at Nikkaluokta Sarri AB, Nikkaluokta (signed from E10 S of Kiruna), 981 99 Kiruna
2–3 hours, 67.8507, 19.0135 ▣▲▲▣▣

16 NAKERIJÄRVI WALK

Follow the marked path up the mountain to Nakerijärvi lake (68.1981, 19.6908) where you can skinny dip in the crystal-clear and ice-cold water. The walk up takes you through glacial moraine and you gives stunning views over Torneträsk. By the lake you'll see an eclectic collection of small huts, which are dragged out onto the ice in winter for fishing.

→ Park at Torneträsk railway station and follow the obvious path in a south-westerly direction up the mountain.
3–4 hours, 68.2174, 19.7114 ▣▲▣▣▣

17 HELICOPTER – GO ANYWHERE

Due to the vast expanses of wilderness without any roads in this region, helicopters are often used for access. The Sami also use them to assist with herding their reindeer. For the ultimate remote adventure, arrange to be dropped off by helicopter at a location of your choice and either head back to civilisation on foot or arrange for a later

20

collection. Helicopters can even take kayaks. There are several bases servicing the Kiruna region.

➔ Bases at Nikkaluokta (67.8511, 19.0063), Kurravaara (67.9424, 20.3689) and Abisko (68.3458, 18.8307). For flights contact Kallax Flyg AB, Vargbackenvägen 1, 942 94 Sikfors, +46 911 251030. www.kallaxflyg.se

18 RAUTAS WALK

A level path that takes you on duckboards over a bog before it meets the Rautas river. Follow the grassy bank upstream for about 4km. There are some great places to stop and make a fire or wild camp, and you can also fish for Arctic char and gather berries.

➔ From Kiruna take route 874 N dir Kurravaara. Follow for 12km, passing the sign for S Kurravaara. Turn L onto Norra Vägen signed N Kurravaara. Take second L onto Rautasälvsvägen, then next R after 1.5km. Park on L by next junction. Follow path to L.

2 hours, 67.9443, 20.2981

19 KUNGSLEDEN

The Kungsleden (King's Trail) stretches from Abisko 450km S to Hemavan (65.8148, 15.0875). There are numerous

hiking shelters and huts along the way. Walk a short (return) section from Abisko or the entire 103km first leg past Kebnekaise to the Sami camp at Nikkaluokta (67.8508, 19.0160). The trail is signposted, and there are numerous maps available with all the shelters marked.

➔ The start of the trail is clearly marked with a wooden archway near the entrance to the parking across the E10 from the Abisko mountain station. The trail can also be followed in the opposite direction from Nikkaluokta.

68.3578, 18.7780

VIEWS

20 LAPPORTEN

This perfect U-shaped valley was carved by ice in the last glacial period. Known as Lapporten (the Lapponian Gate), it is one of Sweden's most photographed natural landforms. There is no defined trail in the valley and it's most spectacular when viewed from a distance.

➔ Best viewed from anywhere along the E10 between Abisko and Björkliden.

68.2678, 18.9832

18

21 AURORA SKY STATION

Viewing point and café on the summit of Nuolja Mountain (68.3616, 18.7234). Travel the 900m to the top by ski lift in only 20 minutes. With almost no light or sound pollution, this is a very special place to view the midnight sun or the aurora borealis. The café sells local specialities and dinner can be booked.

➔ Aurora Sky Station, STF Abisko Mountain Station, 981 07 Abisko, +46 980 40200. www.auroraskystation.com

30 mins, 68.3583, 18.7806

CULTURE & HISTORY

22 RALLARKYRKOGÅRDEN

The iron-ore railway through the mountains between Kiruna and Narvik was built between 1884 and 1903. The construction was a dangerous occupation and the 'navvies' lived in very harsh conditions. The Rallarkyrkogården (Navvies' Graveyard) is where those who died were buried. Look for the grave of Anna Hofstad, known as Black Bear, one of the few women there, who was a popular and now legendary Norwegian canteen cook.

→ Park in layby N of Paktajåkka on E10 and walk back. About 150m S of bridge, look for unmarked paths from scree area (68.4337, 18.6543). One leads S towards the railway and you will see the cemetery ahead after 100m; the other reaches it via Tornehamn church.
10 mins, 68.4312, 18.6470 🅿

23 NIKKALUOKTA

Small Sami village at the point where the three valleys of Vistasvagge, Ladtjovagge and källsjöars (the source of the mighty Kalix river) meet. Also the starting point for several hiking trails to some of Sweden's highest mountains and a stop on the Kungsleden (King's Trail). A variety of accommodation options are available, including camping, and the village restaurant specialises in preparing traditional Sami dishes from local produce.

→ Signed from the E10 just S of Kiruna. Nikkaluokta Sarri AB, Nikkaluokta 1104, 981 99 Kiruna, +46 980 55015. www.nikkaluokta.com
67.8508, 19.0160 🍴🚻🚌♿⛺

24 JUKKASJÄRVI CHURCH

The oldest building in the village, dating from around 1607, this red wooden church has a fairytale feel to it. A brightly coloured altarpiece depicts the coming together of traditional Sami and Christian traditions. More images from Sami mythology can be seen on the organ, which is made from birch and reindeer horn.

→ Jukkasjärvi Kyrka, Marknadsvägen, 981 91 Jukkasjärvi.
67.8466, 20.6208 ⛪🚐

25 SAMI SIIDA VISITOR CENTRE

Sami camp located on the old Sami marketplace in the village of Jukkasjärvi. Learn about their nomadic way of life and try to lasso a reindeer! Traditional food and handicrafts can be purchased.

Accommodation in wooden cabins on the bank of the Torne river is also available.

→ Marknadsvägen 84, 98191 Jukkasjärvi, +46 980 21329. www.nutti.se
67.8468, 20.6199 🚐♿🛌🍴

26 ICE HOTEL

The actual Ice Hotel is built new every year on the frozen Torne river, but once the hotel has melted in the spring there is still a spectacular exhibition of ice sculptures located in a solar-powered and turf-covered cold room on the riverbank. You can warm up afterwards with a hot drink served in a glass made of ice. Accommodation is also available in wooden cabins by the river.

→ Marknadsvägen 63, 981 91 Jukkasjärvi, +46 980 66800. www.icehotel.com
67.8508, 20.5952 ♿🛌

27 LKAB

Kiruna is home to the world's largest underground iron-ore mine (67.8518, 20.1922). Without the mine it's doubtful if the town and railway would even exist. Visit the visitor centre 540m underground; learn about the history of the mine, modern mining and why the town needs to move.

→ Make bookings and catch the bus at Kiruna Tourist Office: Lars Janssonsgatan 17, 981 31 Kiruna, +46 980 18880.
67.8553, 20.2251 🚐🚌🚐

28 MALMBANAN

Use the 130km section of the iron-ore railway between Kiruna and Riksgränsen (68.4257, 18.1275) to access the mountains and enjoy fantastic views. The line was originally built as part of a network to move ore from the mines.

→ Kiruna currently has a temporary railway station due to the mine expansion, and a new permanent position has yet to be decided. For timetables see www.sj.se
67.8673, 20.2005 🚉🚐

LOCAL FOOD

29 LAP DÅNALDS

Probably the world's most remote burger bar, located in the shadow of the Kebnekaise massif and serving very local food. Fill up on nutritious reindeer burgers, followed by waffles with delicious berries and cream. Definitely worth the walk!

→ Follow the signs for the first 5.5km of the Ladtjovagge valley hike (see 15).
67.8457, 18.8901 🍴⛺

30 CAMP RIPAN

Campsite in the heart of Kiruna that also has a well-regarded Sami-inspired restaurant specialising in dishes made from local produce. There are cabins for rent and a spa with a unique Lapland feel.

➔ Campingvägen 5, 981 35 Kiruna, +46 980 63000. www.ripan.se

67.8607, 20.2405 ⧉⧉

31 LÅKTATJÅKKO MOUNTAIN STATION

A mountain station spectacularly located between two mountain peaks, on a pass 1,228m above sea level (68.3985, 18.4611). Only accessible on foot. It has a small number of beds as well as a great restaurant, bar and sauna. The classic Låkta waffles with fresh cloudberries are highly recommended.

➔ Follow the marked trail from Björkliden Fjällby for 12km. Låktatjåkko Fjällstation, Björkliden, 98 193 Björkliden, +46 980 64100. www.bjorkliden.com

3 hours, 68.4069, 18.6750 ⧉⧉

ACCOMMODATION

32 KEBNEKAISE MOUNTAIN STATION

Kebnekaise is the highest mountain in Sweden, at about 2,100m depending on the ice thickness. The mountain station is run by the STF and is situated at the foot of the mountain (67.8681, 18.6203), providing basic accommodation facilities and food. It's a 19km walk on a marked trail to here from Nikkaluokta, or approx 5km less if you take the boat along Ladtjojaure lake. This is a remote alpine environment, and you need to be equipped accordingly. If you would like to attempt the summit you're recommended to use a local guide.

➔ For bookings contact +46 980 55000. www.svenskaturistforeningen.se and for a summer ascent of Kebnekaise contact UIAGM guide Mikael Amlert, +46 705 680091. www.amlert.se

4–7 hours from Nikkaluokta, 67.8508, 19.0160 ⧉⧉

33 ABISKO MOUNTAIN STATION

Lodge located in northern Abisko National Park with views over Torneträsk lake and Noulja mountain. Run by the STF, it has a restaurant specialising in local dishes. There is a small shop and outdoor equipment for hire. A great base for exploring the area, especially if you like a sauna after walking.

➔ Abiskovägen 7, 981 07 Abisko, +46 980 40200. www.svenskaturistforeningen.se

68.3586, 18.7828 ⧉⧉⧉

34 KATTERJÅKK TOURIST STATION

Lodge on the border with Norway at Riksgränsen, run by the Friluftsframjändet (Swedish Outdoor Association). Easily accessible by train or car it is an ideal base for explorations up into the mountains or along the Rallarvägen (see 14). Simple self-catering accommodation with a sauna and communal area with an open fire.

➔ Katterjokk Turiststation, 981 94 Riksgränsen, +46 730 360595. www.katterjokk.se

10 mins, 68.4198, 18.1622 ⧉⧉

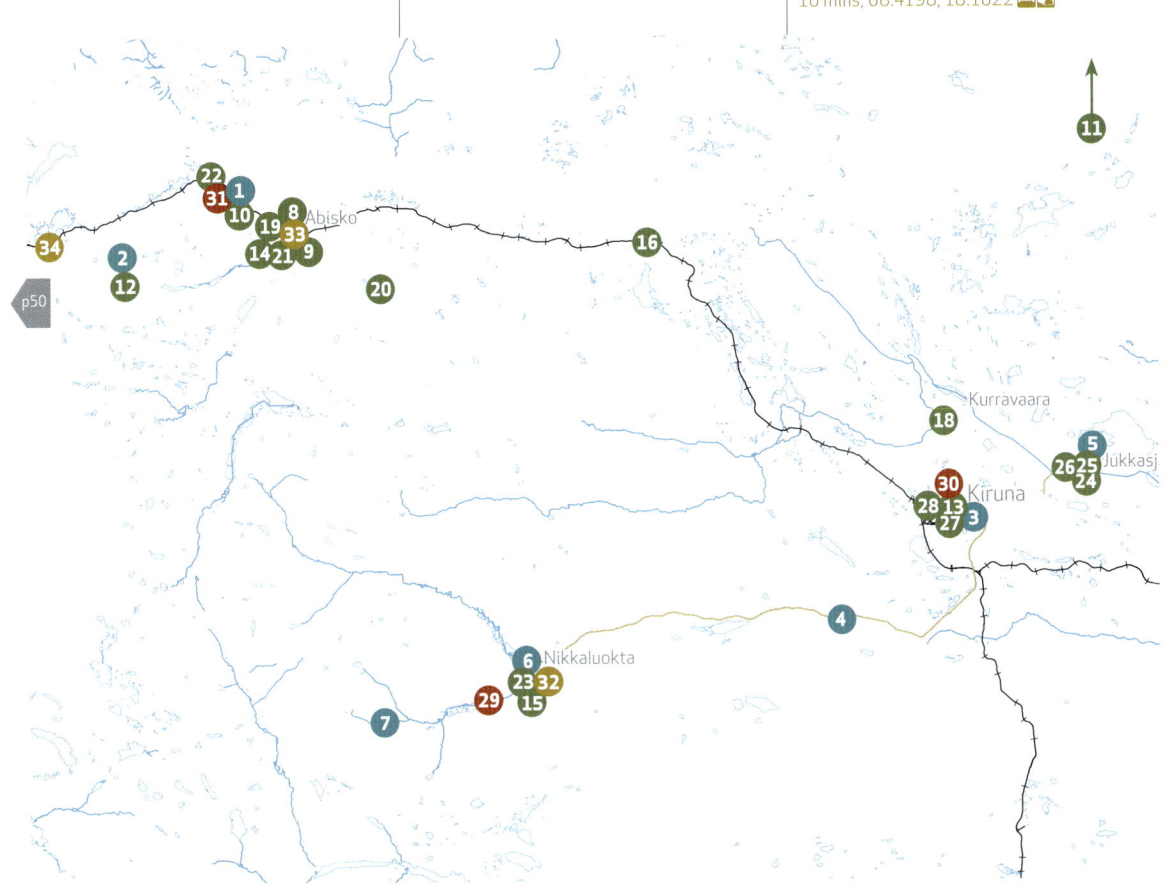

INLANDSBANAN

Our perfect adventure

→ **Look** for bears in the forest north of Orsa.

→ **Search** for a black vanilla orchid on the banks of the Ljusnan river.

→ **Watch** the surface of Storsjön lake for Storsjöodjuret – the legendary lake monster!

→ **Taste** smoked trout or grayling from the Vojmån river.

→ **Forage** for traditional Sami medicinal plants at the Båtsuoj Sami Centre.

→ **Stand** astride the Arctic Circle.

→ **Go** back in time at the Jamtli living museum.

→ **Find** and stand at the geographical centre of Sweden.

→ **Climb** the Brunflo clock tower for a view of the mountains.

→ **Discover** Europe's oldest tapestry in Överhogdal.

The Inlandsbanan (Inland Line) is a railway that travels up the centre of Sweden. Its original purpose was to be a line of communication running through the resource-rich interior that was not strategically vulnerable, as the routes up the Baltic coast were. Used mainly to transport timber to the south, the trains were slowly replaced by road transport, and in 1992 the entire line was mothballed.

Since then the line north from Mora has been sold to the municipalities along the route, and they jointly own and operate the company Inlandsbanan AB, which runs a passenger service along the route from mid-June to the end of August. There's also some new freight traffic on the line, which helps ensure its upkeep. The line south of Mora operates a less frequent service, but this chapter does not include that section.

The Inlandsbanan is a unique rail travel experience. The line from Mora to Gällivare is divided into two sections – north and south of Östersund – and just one train travels in each direction along each section each day. Either section takes the best part of a day, so to do the entire route non-stop would require spending a night in Östersund between the two sections.

The timetable varies each year, and the train stops frequently for food at a restaurant or from a stall on a platform, or where interesting wildlife is spotted. Some of the stops are big, old wooden station buildings and others are simply a sign and some steps in the middle of the forest.

The best way to travel is to purchase an Inlandsbanan Card, which gives you unlimited travel for 14 days. You just hop on and off, but you can still reserve a seat. This means you can use the train to wild camp and explore all the interesting stops along the line. This chapter lists the stations from Mora northwards, with their distance from Mora, but you can start wherever you want. For tickets and booking details see www.inlandsbanan.se

43

MORA TO ÖSTERSUND

1 MORA STATION

A town on Siljan lake with numerous food and accommodation options. In winter the Vasaloppet cross-country ski race finishes here. It follows the route taken in 1521 by Gustav Eriksson when fleeing the Danes. He then returned to Mora to lead an uprising against the Danes, eventually united the realm and became Gustav Vasa, Sweden's first dynastic king.

61.0088, 14.5586 ▯🚆▯

2 VATTNÄS

Small rural halt on the shore of Orsasjön lake. Start your trip here with a wild camp and swim, if you want to avoid Mora town.

5km, 61.0492, 14.5979 🏊△🚆

3 ORSA

A small town dating back to the Iron Age, with a history of producing grindstones. The area has a Finnish heritage, as many settled here in the 17th century to work in the forest. Variety of food and accommodation.

13km, 61.1189, 14.6211 🚆▯🚆

4 TALLHED

Halt in the middle of the forest. Shortly after leaving the train stops on a bridge high above a gorge with views of the impressive Storstupet waterfall (61.226, 14.790).

25km, 61.2101, 14.7089 🚆▯🚆◻△

5 BJÖRNIDET

The train stops in a swamp area at the Inlandsbanan's highest point (524m above sea level) where you can walk to take a look at an old bear den.

42km, 61.3797, 14.7467 🚆🐾

6 ÄLVHO

Small rural halt. This is brown bear territory, so watch the forest closely.

64km, 61.4972, 14.7482 🚆🐾

7 VASSJÖN

Remote forest halt on the edge of a lake. Opportunities for wild camping, swimming and foraging for bilberries.

79km, 61.5668, 14.7883 🚆△🏊🚆

8 LILLHAMRA

Halt in dense forest once cultivated by Finnish settlers. Wild camp by the Sundsjöån

river where you can also fish and swim.

82km, 61.6414, 14.7960 🚆△🎣🚆

9 TANDSJÖBORG

Small village and Sweden's smallest national park (Hamra, 27ha) renowned for its insect habitat. From here the track follows Tandsjön lake for a while.

89km, 61.6953, 14.7455 ◻🚆🎣🐾△

10 FÅGELSJÖ

The northbound trains stop for cinnamon buns and drinks on the platform. Southbound trains have a choice of sandwiches and drinks. Gammelgård, by the station, is a farm exactly as it was when abandoned in 1910 by Finnish foresters. Stay at STF Hostel or wild camp and swim on the beach at Myrsjön lake.

→ STF Fågelsjö, Fågelsjövägen 239, 820 50 Los, +46 657 30030
www.svenskaturistforeningen.se

102km, 61.8013, 14.6822 🚆🚆▯🚆🚆

11 BÄCKEDAL

Halt on the outskirts of Sveg. An opportunity to wild camp by the Ljusnan river.

133km, 62.0264, 14.3757 🚆🏊△

13

12 SVEG
Small town with a selection of accommodation and eateries. The Nordic Noir author Henning Mankell lived in the flat above the courthouse until he was 13.
136km, 62.0364, 14.3521

13 ÄLVROS
Station in the forest, a few kilometres from Älvros village, by the confluence of the Ljusnan and Norrälven rivers. Wild camp by the river and fish for trout, perch and char.
149km, 62.0600, 14.5747

14 YTTERHOGDAL
Minor rural halt close to Sweden's geographical centre, calculated as half the distance from the country's northernmost point to the southernmost point and half the west-east distance from the Norwegian border to the coast.
176km, 62.1972, 14.8556

15 ÖVERHOGDAL
Small village stop by the Ljusnan river. A Viking tapestry, Europe's oldest, was discovered here. It's now in the Jamtli museum (see 28), but a replica is on display at Överhogdals Forngård museum.
➜ Överhogdals Forngård, Överhogdal 588, 840 90 Ytterhogdal, +46 680 82100. www.forngarden.se
185km, 62.2668, 14.8055

16 SÖRTJÄRN
Small village stop at the confluence of the Ljusnan and Linan rivers.
198km, 62.3427, 14.6299

17 NEDERHÖGEN
Rural forest village stop on the pilgrim route to Nidaros (see Åre chapter). In the 17th century the inhabitants fled to the mountains and lived in caves during the 'Baltzarfejden' – a bloody local feud in the wider Kalmar War.
211km, 62.4105, 14.4287

18 RÖJAN
Halt in the forest a short walk from the Ljusnan river and a habitat where you can find the protected black vanilla orchid – the provincial flower of Jämtland.
219km, 62.4791, 14.3590

19 KVARNSJÖ
Idyllic stop by Kvarnsjö lake with good berry-picking, wild camping and swimming.
229km, 62.5657, 14.3721

20 ÅSARNA
Station in a village famous for its very successful cross-country skiing club. Northbound trains stop for meals at the Åsarna Ski Centre, while southbound trains halt near the Vildmarkscafe. Located by Grannen lake and the Ljungan river.
239km, 62.6472, 14.3745

21 SVENSTAVIK CENTRAL

Town at the end of Storsjön lake, the fifth-largest lake in Sweden, with an area of 464km² and a depth of 74m. Watch out for Storsjöodjuret, the legendary lake monster! Variety of places to eat and stay.

254km, 62.7671, 14.4363

22 HACKÅS

Village with one of Norrland's oldest churches. On the outskirts of Svenstavik with the possibility of wild camping.

275km, 62.9242, 14.5220

23 FÅKER

Little village on the edge of Näkten lake. The church is built on the site of an Iron Age sacrifice site, and 126 ancient iron bars were found here, indicative of the importance of the area around Storsjön during the Iron Age.

284km, 62.9931, 14.5745

24 TANDSBYN

Small stop in a community that started with the arrival of the railway. Not too far from Östersund (see 26), if you want to wild camp catch a bus from here to the central station.

294km, 62.9985, 14.7437

25 BRUNFLO

Small town on lake Storsjön with several places to eat and stay. Climb the clocktower, 1km from the town centre, for amazing views towards the mountains in the west.

306km, 63.0759, 14.8328

26 ÖSTERSUND CENTRAL

Main station in Östersund, which is the only city in Jämtland and its economic and political centre. There is a wide selection of places to eat and stay close to the station.

→ www.svenskaturistforeningen.se
320km, 63.1703, 14.6381

ÖSTERSUND TO GÄLLIVARE

27 ÖSTERSUND WEST

Second stop in small city of Östersund.
321km, 63.1784, 14.6312

28 JAMTLI

Special stop for the regional open-air museum of Jämtland and Härjedalen on the outskirts of Östersund. Interesting mixture of historical buildings, an indoor museum and temporary exhibitions. There's an STF hostel in the grounds of the museum.

→ Jamtli Museum, Museiplan, 831 31 Östersund, +46 631 50100. www.jamtli.com
STF Östersund, Stiftelsen Jamtli, Museiplan, 831 28 Östersund, +46 631 50300. www.svenskaturistforeningen.se
323km, 63.1928, 14.6366

29 LIT

Village at the confluence of Indalsälven and Hårkan rivers, with fantastic river views along the section of line after the station.
349km, 63.3185, 14.8566

13

32 MUNKFLOHÖGEN
Rural stop between forest and farmland. Named after a monk who drowned in a nearby spring when on his way to warn the monastery of the Black Death. The village and monastery died out in the 14th century.
383km, 63.5601, 14.9490

33 JÄMTLANDS SIKÅS
Village stop with a small food shop and sawmill. Northbound trains stop for pre-ordered traditional flatbread wraps.
401km, 63.6261, 15.2064

34 HALLVIKEN
Until 1770 this village was known as Hall and could only be reached via footpaths and bridleways. Between 1907 and 1912 the section of the Inlandsbanan from Östersund to Ulriksfors was built and the village adopted the new name of Hallviken.
419km, 63.7259, 15.4742

35 ULRIKSFORS
Village on the edge of Strömsund town, which was once connected to the Inlandsbanan by a branch line. Wild camp on the shore of Russfjärden lake or head into town for a variety of food and accommodation options.
436km, 63.8321, 15.6211

36 LÖVBERGA
Village at the end of Flåsjön lake, known to be a good area to see beavers. Good lakeside wild camping spot for wildlife watching.
456km, 63.9617, 15.8531

37 HOTING CAMPING
Small halt for a campsite on Hoting outskirts.
→ Hoting Camping, Västra Hoting 325, 830 80 Hoting, +46 671 10248. www.hotingscamping.se
486km, 64.1078, 16.1736

38 HOTING
Provincial town on the shore of Hotingsjön lake, with a variety of places to sleep and eat. Café Koppen at the station provides pre-ordered drinks and sandwiches.
488km, 64.1158, 16.2015

39 CAMPING
Halt on outskirts of Dorotea for campsite. Tent pitches, cabins and tipis for rent.
→ Doro Camping, Storgatan 1A, 917 31 Dorotea, +46 942 10238. www.dorocamping.com
508km, 64.2564, 16.3903

43

30 HÄGGENÅS
Local halt close to the site of one of Sweden's last places of execution. The last condemned criminal was a farmhand who had robbed a pedlar to get money to emigrate to America.
359km, 63.3857, 14.8799

31 NORDERÅSEN
By area the largest village in Jämtland – not many houses, but lots of space between them.
366km, 63.4349, 14.8291

40 DOROTEA

In 1713 the first settler moved to the Sami camp Svanavatten (Swanwaters), which grew to become the town of Bergvattnet. In 1799, it was renamed in honour of Queen Frederica Dorothea Wilhelmina. Lying on the bank of the Bergvattenån river there are various places to eat and sleep and an open air museum.

509km, 64.2582, 16.4074

41 MESELEFORS CAMPING

Halt for campsite on the bank of the Ångermanälven river.

→ Meselefors Camping, Meselefors 216, 912 90 Vilhelmina, +46 0940 25089. www.meselefors.com
541km, 64.4390, 16.7961

42 MESELEFORS

Rural forest halt by Meselet lake, with opportunities to wild camp by the water.

543km, 64.4429, 16.8170

43 VILHELMINA

Small church town lying between two lakes – Volgsjön and Baksjön. The town museum has an interesting collection telling the stories of the local Sami and the early settlers.

→ Vilhelmina Museum, Tingsgatan 1, 912 33 Vilhelmina, +46 940 144974. www.vilhelmina.se
565km, 64.6230, 16.6515

44 VILHELMINA NORRA

All trains stop at Bergmans fish and farm shop by the north shore of Vualtjere lake. Great view of the rapids between the lakes. Try the locally caught smoked fish.

→ Bergmans Fisk & Vilhelmina Gårdsbutik, Sågån 1, 912 92 Vilhelmina, +46 940 25090. www.mbergmansfisk.se
568km, 64.6463, 16.6136

45 VOJMÅN

Halt by the Vojmån river, a popular section for fishing and canoeing. Wild camp and catch trout or grayling for your dinner.

592km, 64.7920, 16.8163

46 STORUMAN

Small regional town with amenities at the southern end of Luspsjön lake, including a camping area at Badsjön lake in the centre.

→ Storumans Bad & Camping, Lokgränd 3, 923 31 Storuman, +46 951 14300. www.campingstoruman.se
633km, 65.0961, 17.1110

47 SANDSJÖNÄS

Village at the north end of Sandsjön lake with a long sandy beach. Lovely spot to wild camp or rent a boat and explore the lake.

670km, 65.2422, 17.6622

48 BLATTNICKSELE

Small village on bank of Vindelälven with a beautifully located lakeside campsite.

→ Blattnicksele Camping, 924 92 Blattnicksele, +46 952 20008. www.blattnickselecamping.se
682km, 65.3447, 17.5894

49 SORSELE

Quiet little town on the Vindelälven river, with several places to stay and eat. The Inlandsbanan Museum is located at the station, where you can take river boat trips.

705km, 65.5350, 17.5428 🚂🛏🍴🚆🚻

50 BURESJÖN

Farming and forestry community between the Gargån river and Buresjön lake. Waterside wild camping with great wild swimming.

725km, 65.5537, 17.8529 🚂⛺🏊

51 SLAGNÄS

Village by Slagnässjön lake. Visit or stay at the Båtsuoj Sami Centre, where you can learn about the local forest Sami, stay in a traditional kåta and forage for berries.

→ Båtsuoj Skogsamecenter, Gasahed 1, 930 91 Slagnäs, +46 70 6423166, www.batsuoj.se
741km, 65.5858, 18.1584 🚂🛏🍴🐾🏊

52 RENVIKEN

The English translation is 'reindeer bay', as herds congregate here in the open where there's a breeze to get some respite from the mosquitoes.

761km, 65.6454, 18.5250 🚂🐾🛶

53 AVAVIKEN

Village located on a spit of land between Asptjärnen and Åkerudden lakes. There was once a harbour transporting silver and lead from local mines to the Norwegian border.

769km, 65.6050, 18.6509 🚂⛺🚻

54 ARVIDSJAUR

Small town with usual amenities. Lappstaden Sami church village is one of the best-preserved in Sweden, with 80 huts and storage buildings dating from the 18th century.

794km, 65.5887, 19.1695 🚂🛏🍴🚻

55 MOSKOSEL

Northbound trains stop here for the navvy museum; find out about the men who built the Inlandsbanan. Food and takeaway.

842km, 65.8824, 19.4268 🚂🚻

56 PITEÄLVSBRON

Bridge over the rapids of the Piteälven river that is shared by both road and rail traffic. About 50km downstream at Storforsen (65.8500, 20.4061) the river falls dramatically over one of Europe's biggest rapids.

854km, 65.9873, 19.3593 🚂🏊

57 VARJISTRÄSK

Stop on the shore of Stor Varjisträsket lake – a great place to swim and pick berries.

866km, 66.0445, 19.5299 🛏🏊🛶⛺

58 KÅBDALIS

In the winter this is a small ski slope with lots of little cabins. Great views in the summer.

904km, 66.1526, 19.9888 🚂📷

59 KITAJAUR

Small village on old Sami site – meaning 'spring reindeer resting place when snowing'. Located on the Vitbäcken river.

908km, 66.1799, 19.9469 🚂⛺

60 ARCTIC CIRCLE

The train stops on the Arctic Circle so you can take pictures by the sign.

960km, 66.5565, 19.9188 🚂

61 JOKKMOKK

Town at the heart of the Laponia World Heritage area. Traditionally a meeting place for the Sami people. Fascinating Sami Centre and Mountain Museum – learn about the people whose land extends across four countries. Numerous places to eat and stay.

→ Svenskt Fjäll- och Samemuseum, Kyrkogatan 3, 962 23 Jokkmokk, +46 971 17070 , www.ajtte.com
966km, 66.6071, 19.8398 🚂🛏🍴🚻🐾

62 VAIKIJAUR

Northbound trains stop here for the Fjällglimten restaurant where you can buy local snacks and delicacies to take onboard.

974km, 66.6424, 19.8258 🚂🍴

63 PORJUS

Small village stop by the dam on the Stora Luleälven river that creates Porjusselet lake.

1,014km, 66.9566, 19.8035 🚂

64 AVVAKAJJO

Small isolated halt in the middle of a bog. It was built by railway employees for berry picking and fishing!

1,038km, 67.1255, 20.0258 🚂🛶

65 GÄLLIVARE

The end of the line. A mining town with gold, copper and iron ore workings. Many food and accommodation options as well as a mountain downtown (Dundret) with great hiking and views towards the north.

1,067km, 67.1336, 20.6506 🚂🛏🍴🚻📷

ÅRE FJÄLLEN

Our perfect week

→ **Toast** the sunset from the summit of Åreskutan with a glass of sparkling wine made from birch sap.

→ **Slide** down the granite slabs of the Ullån river into the bubbling pools below.

→ **Swim** below one of Sweden's most powerful waterfalls – there are several to choose from.

→ **Forage** for cloudberries around Mullfjället.

→ **Imagine** being a prehistoric elk hunter while exploring the Glösa rock carvings.

→ **Paddle** to a secluded beach on Ottsjön to camp for the night.

→ **Learn** about the history of mining in the area at the Fröå Mine.

→ **Follow** St Olav's pilgrim route along the river.

→ **Hunt** for gravel pyramids in the Vålådalen nature reserve.

→ **Burrow** underground in the Kvarnbäckslabyrinten cave system.

The local tourist authority describes this rugged and beautiful region as not just a place but 'a way of life'. The people who choose to live here have an obvious affinity with the landscape and nature on their doorstep.

Below Åre's mountains you will find powerful rivers and some of Sweden's biggest and most impressive waterfalls. These feed a network of lakes, which can be easily explored by kayak or canoe, or you can hike to other mountain streams and tarns, which offer incredible wild swimming. One such place is Ullån, near Åre, with its warm water, granite slides and bubbling pools.

Until the arrival of the railway at the end of the 19th century the community of Åre did not exist. The surrounding landscape had for centuries been an important reindeer grazing area for the Sami, and the only industry was a few mines and mountain farms. The trains suddenly made the mountains very accessible. The two villages of Totten and Mörviken grew to accommodate the influx of early mountain tourism, and the town of Åre was born.

The early visitors came for their health; they could walk up Åreskutan and breathe the fresh mountain air. With the subsequent growth of recreational skiing, the number of visitors grew until this became one of northern Europe's largest alpine ski areas. Despite all this development, the landscape is still largely much the same as it has been for thousands of years, and it's still a very important reindeer grazing area.

Historical traditions of self-sufficiency and the preserving of seasonal produce are still prevalent, and local cooking makes creative use of these techniques and the abundance of first-class ingredients. Hot-smoked Arctic char with cloudberry cream on unleavened 'thinbread' is one delicious example.

Make sure you take advantage of the allemansrätt (right to roam) and spend at least a few nights wild camping in the mountains. For the perfect post-wilderness treat, stock up on local organic ale and hire the floating sauna on Åresjön, which has an outboard motor so you can sail it off to your own secluded spot. If you like the outdoors you can't help liking the Åre way of life.

6

WILD SWIMMING

1 LAPPFORSEN

Waterfall on the Rutsälven where on hot days the water temperature can quickly reach 24°C. Sit on a ledge and let the warm water pour over you. If you follow the river downstream to Storvallforsen you'll also find some deep pools where you can swim against the current.

→ Follow Kolåsen Sjövägen W out of Kolåsen (63.7523, 12.9497) between lakes. When the road turns to follow the lake on its R, take the turning L that keeps parallel to the lake on the L. Follow this road for 4km, bearing L every time it forks, until it ends (63.7881, 12.8672). From here walk SW for about 1km to the river. You will hear the waterfall.

25 mins, 63.7845, 12.8582

2 NULLTJÄRN

Lake with a good-sized sandy beach and limpid water. Although normally very cold it can warm up quickly on a hot day. A tranquil spot to camp, swim and cook your local produce, with fantastic views of the surrounding mountains.

→ Follow route 644 west from Vålådalen, signposted Nulltjärnsgården. The beach is a short walk from the parking area at the end of the road.

5 mins, 63.1564, 12.8995

3 ÅRESJÖN FLOATING SAUNA

Hire a wood-fired sauna on a raft anchored on Åresjön at the eastern end of Åre, with amazing views and mountain lake water to cool off in. For something even more different, the raft can be fitted with an outboard motor so you can set off to find your own secluded bay or maybe just tour the lake for a few hours. Contact Explore Åre to make a booking.

→ Book through Explore Åre, +46 647 50885. www.exploreare.se

63.3942, 13.0869

4 ULLÅN

Known locally as Åre's natural adventure pool. The Ullån river flows over numerous smooth granite slabs, creating a series of natural slides that end in deep and bubbly pools. The further upstream you go, the steeper the river gets, with the slides becoming spectacular waterfalls; the deeper and calmer pools for swimming can be found downstream closer to the road bridge. In summer the water can get very warm.

→ Pull off and park by the bridge over the Ullån on the E14 (63.4044, 13.0237) then follow the path upstream along W bank.

30 mins, 63.4121, 13.0184

5 LILLÅDAMMEN

Hike up to Lillådammen for a swim in a mountain lake (63.4196, 13.1875), from the car park at Fröå Mines. On the way up you will pass Byxtjärnen, another small lake where you can also swim. The total length is 7km with a climb of 290m.

→ Trailhead is in the car park at Fröå Gruva (see 23). The route is clearly marked.221c.

2 hours, 63.4041, 13.2083

6 FRÖÅTJÄRN

Small mountain lake with plenty of places along the shoreline for wild swimming and foraging. Walk a circuit from here and finish with a cold, refreshing swim.

→ Take the E14 from Åre dir Östersund. Just outside town at Björnänge turn L and follow signs to Åre Björnen. In Björnen turn R signposted Gamla Fröåvägen at the crossroads after ski lifts. Follow until you see the lake on L.

63.3947, 13.1644

WATERFALLS & LAKES

7 TÄNNFORSEN

Sweden's biggest waterfall, with a total height of 32m and an average summer volume of 400 cubic metres per second. The spring floods of 1995 saw a record of 900 cubic metres per second. The falls form part of the Indalsälven and join the two lakes of Tännsjön (above) and Östra Noren (below). During the winter they freeze, creating dramatic ice formations.

→ Take the E14 west from Åre; after 13km cross the bridge over the Indalsälven and turn R at Staa. Follow signs for 8km to Tännforsen. From the parking area there are two paths that will take you to the base of the falls and several viewing points.

5 mins, 63.4452, 12.7402

8 RISTAFALLET

One of Sweden's most powerful waterfalls, on the Indalsälven just downstream of Åre. The falls are divided in two by a wooded island and the average summer volume is 400 cubic metres per second. The damp atmosphere around Ristafallet has created a very special ecosystem that is home to many rare lichens and mosses. In the winter, when the water freezes, you can walk out to the island and explore a hidden 20m ice cave.

→ Take the E14 out of Åre dir Östersund. After 18km at the village of Rista turn R and follow signs to Ristafallet. There's a marked path from the parking area.

10 mins, 63.3121, 13.3510

9 OTTSJÖN

Explore Ottsjön lake by canoe or kayak. Stop to cook lunch or set up camp on one of the many secluded beaches. Boats and equipment can be hired from the Fjäll Kajak Center. From their base it's a short paddle along the last stretch of the Vålån river and into the lake. Guided tours are also available.

→ ATI Mountain Experience, Östra Vålådalen 118, 830 12 Vålådalen, +46 647 35253. www.mountainexperience.se

63.1688, 13.0600

10 HANDÖLFORSARNA

The river Handölån flows out of a lake and through the village of Handöl as the longest waterfall in Sweden. At its most spectacular during the spring floods, the waterfall drops 125m over five separate sections. The average summer flow is around 50 cubic metres per second.

→ Park by the old soapstone works in Handöl (63.2498, 12.4482) and follow path to river.
5 mins, 63.2518, 12.4437

11 BRUDSLÖJAN

With a name meaning 'The Bride's Veil', this is the most spectacular of a series of waterfalls that spill quite literally over the Norwegian border. They are in a small canyon created during the last ice age, which links several small lakes. You can canoe or swim below the falls, and there are some great places to wild camp nearby.

→ Follow the E14 from Storlien towards the Norwegian border. Just before the border there's parking on both sides of the road (63.3278, 12.0577) with a small gateway marked 'Brudslöjan'. From here it's a walk of about 3km to the waterfall.
20 mins, 63.3270, 12.0465

HIKES

12 MULLFJÄLLET CIRCULAR WALK

A mountain trail with amazing views that begins with a demanding climb up a series of ski slopes. A beautiful valley with plenty of opportunities for berry picking will then take you to a hiking shelter at Forsaskalet.

→ The trailhead is in the car park at Åre Duved ski resort, just off the E14. The trail is clearly marked with the number 203 and loops back down to where you started. Distance 19km, ascent 590m.
6–7 hours, 63.3959, 12.9210

13 HIKE TO TEGEFORS

Easy walk from Åre to the spectacular Tegefors waterfall, where there's a hiking shelter and fireplace. Get a warming fire started and then go for a bracing swim below the cascades.

→ Trailhead is in Åre Torg, the square in the centre of the town. The route is clearly indicated with signs marked 218. Return the same way. Distance 12km, mainly level.
3 hours, 63.4003, 13.0783

14 ÅRESKUTAN CIRCULAR WALK

A fantastic circumnavigation of Åreskutan that you can do in one long day or split over two days, wild camping en route. The views in all directions are amazing.

→ Start at the base of the VM6 lift, a short (signposted) walk from Åre Torg in the town centre. Take the VM6, and then Hummel lifts, up as far as they go (Mörvikshummeln). Continue on foot, following the signs to

Stendalen. From here follow the trail marked 211 all the way around the mountain and back to Åre. Distance 25.5km, ascent 490m.
9 hours, 63.4025, 13.0772

15 THE TROLL TRAIL

A short, easy family hike which starts either at Åre Torg if you want to walk up to it, or Fjällgården if you take the funicular railway up from the square. Pine trees and dark green moss border this magical trail with troll figures to discover. Have a refreshing drink at Fjällgården before taking the railway back down to the square.

17

18

22

➔ Start at the funicular railway in Åre main square. Walk up to the base of the cable car (Kabin dal) and then eastwards past the VM6 lift along trail 212. Distance 1km, ascent 140m.

30 mins, 63.4006, 13.0788

NATURE & WILDLIFE

16 ÅRESKUTAN

Take the cable car from the centre of Åre and seven minutes later you will be 1,274m above sea level with breathtaking views of the beautiful mountains and lakes surrounding you (63.4309, 13.0932). Bring along a picnic and enjoy the view.

➔ Cable car base station: Kabinbanevägen, 830 13 Åre.

63.4022, 13.0766

17 ÄNNSJÖNS FÅGELSTATION

Very shallow lake, which is an important sanctuary and breeding area for a variety of raptors and waterfowl, including grouse and waders. Watch out for reindeer grazing the surrounding land. Start at the fågelstation (bird research station). From here paths lead to various hides and viewing points.

➔ Small sign L shortly after entering Handöl from the E14. Ännsjöns fågelstation, Handöl

563, 830 15 Duved, +46 647 72210. www.annsjon.org

63.2587, 12.4476

18 VÅLÅDALEN NATURE RESERVE

This nature reserve can be explored on foot or by canoe. Start at the visitor centre (Naturum Vålådalen), where you can learn about the wildlife you're likely to encounter in the season of your visit. When hiking in this area you're likely to come across strange-looking gravel pyramids. These were deposited when the glaciers melted at the end of the last ice age.

➔ Follow signs for Vålådalen from E14 12km SE of Åre for 29km. Naturum Vålådalen, Vålådalen 26, 830 12 Vålådalen, +46 647 35232. www.naturumvaladalen.se

63.1482, 12.9651

19 KVARNBÄCKSLABYRINTEN

A limestone cave located on the north side of Åreskutan (63.4641, 12.9286), consisting of two separate and active water systems. Both are a mixture of narrow passages and large chambers, and the upper of the two is wetter but has lots of spectacular marbled limestone. Do not try to explore the cave without a guide and proper equipment. JoPe

Fors & Fjäll in Undersåker provide guided tours.

→ JoPe Fors & Fjäll, Hosbacken 7, 830 10 Undersåker, +46 647 31465. www.jope.se 63.3163, 13.2672 🔲📷

20 MILLESTGÅRDEN

Elk farm where you can take a guided tour to meet the tame animals. Learn all about Europe's largest animal and why it's known as the king of the forest. There's also a restaurant serving local food, including cheese made from elk milk.

→ Signed about 2km W of Duved on the 638, Duvedsbyn 187, 830 15 Duved, +46 647 20035. www.millestgarden.se 63.3924, 12.8744 🍴📷

21 STORLIEN BLOMSTERSTIGEN

At the end of the 19th century Dr Ernst Westerlund set up a spa in Storlien for patients diagnosed with nervous illnesses. They would be sent to walk briskly up a path to the top of Skurdalshöjden. The doctor, who was a keen botanist, would sit on a bench and make sure the patients were walking fast enough as they passed. Grateful patients began to return and place wooden benches along the 6km route, and it became

known as the 'flower trail' because it was so rich in flora.

→ The path is well signposted from the gateway, and maps can be bought in the village. Near Vargvägen 2, 830 91 Storlien. www.blomsterstigen.com 60 mins, 63.3167, 12.1020 📷🏞️

CULTURE & HISTORY

22 NJARKA SAMELÄGER

Traditional Sami camp situated on a peninsula jutting into Haggsjön lake. Built and run by the Matsson family to educate visitors about the lives of the reindeer-herding Sami people. Learn about their culture, history and present circumstances and stay the night in one of their fantastic cabins or a traditional Sami kåta and enjoy the sauna.

→ Signed off E14 4km E of Duved. Häggsjönäs Njarka 111, 830 15 Duved, +46 76 7700779. www.njarka.com 63.5118, 12.6911 🚌🚲🏞️

23 FRÖÅ GRUVA

Copper mine that was active during three periods between 1744 and 1919. The water-works and buildings have now been restored, and you can learn about the history of mining

in the area. Three signposted walks of less than 5km start at the mine. Fröå day in mid-July sees lots of family activities taking place on site.

→ Take the E14 from Åre dir Östersund. Just outside town at Björnänge turn L and follow the signs for Fröå Gruva and Åre Björnen. Follow the road for 7km until you see the Fröå signs (830 13 Åre). www.froagruva.se 63.4041, 13.2083 🚌📷

24 HANDÖL

The village of Handöl is famous for having

the only soapstone quarry in Sweden. Since the 16th century stone from here has been used in the production of stoves due to its smoothness, workability, and great capacity for storing heat. In 1719 the survivors of the Carolean death march, on which over 3,000 soldiers froze to death, found their way here, and there is a memorial to commemorate this.

→ The village is signposted from the E14 about 40km west of Åre, at Enafors.
63.2592, 12.4426 ▣

ANCIENT & SACRED

25 ST OLAVSLEDEN FROM ÅRE OLD CHURCH
Part of the pilgrim route stretching from Selånger on the Swedish Baltic coast through the mountains to Trondheim on the Norwegian coast. The route follows the one taken by King Olav Haraldsson when he returned from exile in an attempt to convert Norway to Christianity.

→ Starting at the church (Kyrkvägen 8, 830 13 Åre), follow the route for a day in either direction from Åre as it follows the Indalsälven (Indal River). www.stolavsleden.com has maps and further information in English on the entire route.
63.3974, 13.0813 ✝

26 GLOSA ÄLGRIKET HÄLLRISTNINGAR
Well-preserved Stone Age rock carvings, estimated to be 6200–5500 years old, at least 3000 years older than the oldest carvings in southern Sweden (see Österlen for these). There are around 60 carvings, all depicting elks and believed to have been made by prehistoric trappers. The visitor centre and outdoor museum exhibits include a 5km trail to the elk-trapping pits.

→ Glösa is halfway between Åre and Östersund. Take route 666 off the E14 and then follow the signs. www.glosaalgriket.se
63.3817, 14.0272 ✝ ▣

SLOW FOOD

27 ÅRE BRYGGCOMPAGNI
Local microbrewery established in 2013 in the village of Huså. Their beers are brewed with water from Kallsjön (the Cold Lake) and are perfect after a hard day in the mountains. Visit to purchase, or call to arrange to be shown around.

→ Åre Bryggcompagni AB, Huså Bygatan 21, 830 05 Järpen, +46 735 002125. www.arebryggcompagni.se
63.4906, 13.1189 🍴

28 KRETSLOPPSHUSET
Organic café, restaurant and food shop in a fantastic garden setting. The name Kretsloppshuset means 'the circle of life house' in English, which reflects their holistic approach to food and cooking. Try the delicious lingonberry ketchup!

→ Kyrkvägen 5, 830 04 Mörsil, +46 647 665212. www.kretsloppshuset.com
63.3095, 13.6544 🍴

29 FÄVIKEN MAGASINET
Widely rated as one of the world's best – and most isolated – restaurants, Fäviken is housed in an 18th-century barn on a large hunting estate. It can only accommodate 24 diners each night, and guests can stay in basic rooms on site. The cuisine uses farmed, hunted or foraged local produce, prepared and cooked with traditional techniques.

→ Fäviken 216, 830 05 Järpen, +46 647 40177. www.favikenmagasinet.se
63.4352, 13.2932 🍴 🛏

30 FLAMMAN RESTAURANT
Listed in the restaurant White Guide as one of Sweden's best places to eat. Specialises in serving local food sourced from the surrounding forest, mountains, rivers and lakes. Bed and breakfast accommodation is also available. Try the sparkling wine made from birch sap!

→ Vintergatan 46, 830 19 Storlien, +46 647 70010. www.flamman.nu
63.3174, 12.0980 🍴 🛏

31 OTTSJÖ BRYGGHUS
Ottsjön microbrewery produces organic beer and cask ale, which is sold locally. Visit their pub in an old joinery where you can sample the beer and try local produce from a mainly vegetarian menu. Call to enquire about brewery open days.

→ Högåsvägen 35, 830 10 Undersåker, +46 70 3908610. www.ottsjobrygghus.se
63.2182, 13.0603 🍴

CAMP & STAY

32 COPPERHILL MOUNTAIN LODGE
Located high above Åre on Förberget, in an area once extensively mined for copper, this is an ideal place to recharge after some nights of wild camping. With many guests in outdoor gear having come straight off the mountain, you can't help but feel immediately at home here. Secure drying rooms are also available for tents and other kit. The restaurant is Sami-themed and

serves food prepared from local organic produce. Amazing views.

→ Signed from the E14 at Björnänge. Åre Björnen, 830 13 Åre, +46 647 14300. www.copperhill.se

63.3833, 13.1788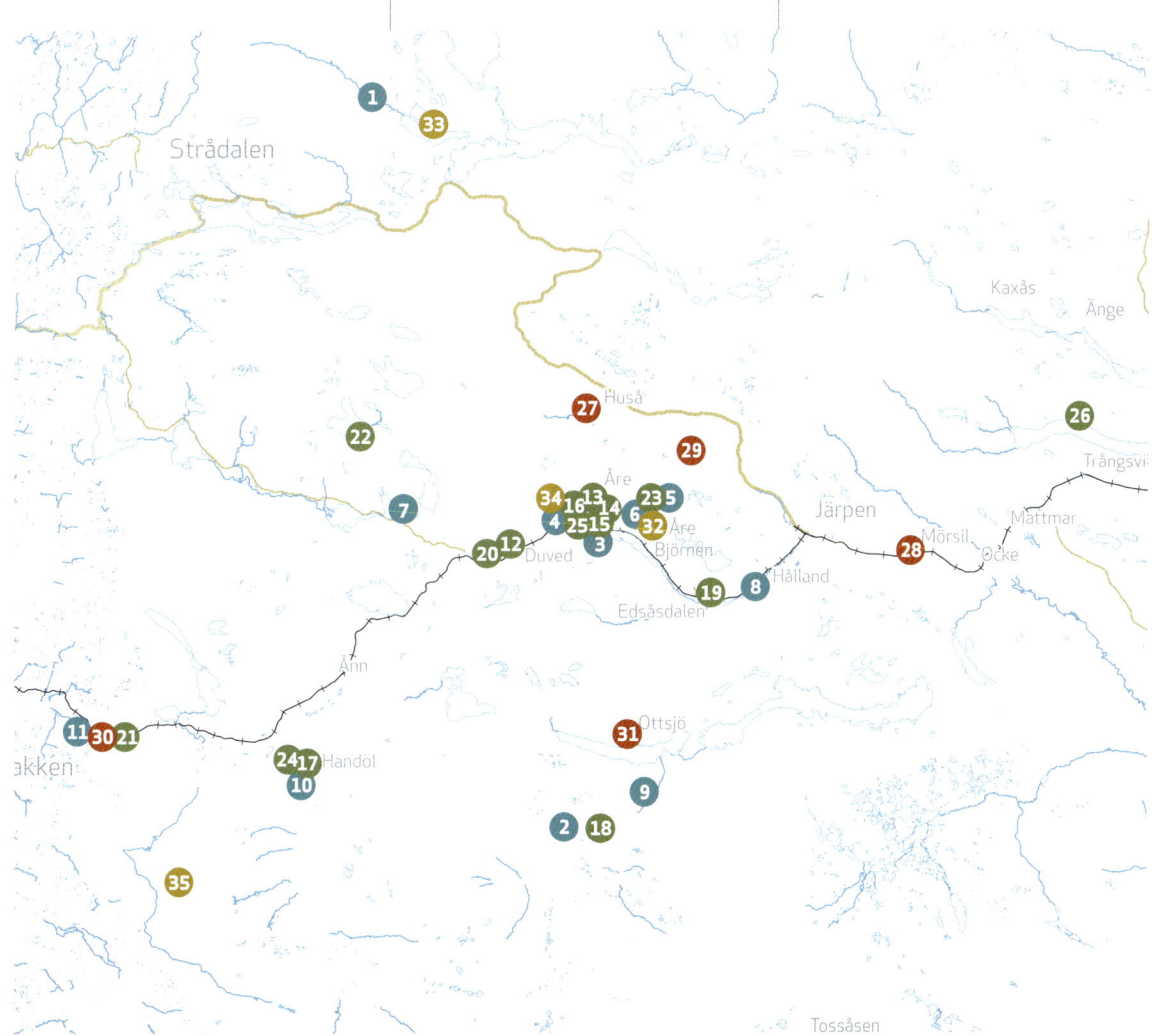

33 KOLÅSEN FJÄLLSTATION

Mountain Station run by the STF and ideally located to explore the Skäckerfjällen Nature Reserve on foot or by canoe. Open canoes and all equipment can be hired here. The food is organic and all local, with much coming from the garden and animals they keep.

→ From Järpen take route 336 N to Kallsedet, where Kolåsen is signposted. Kolåsens Fjällhotell, 830 05 Järpen, +46 647 81017.

www.kolasen.se

63.7507, 12.9597

34 BUUSTAMONS FJÄLLGÅRD

Small hotel and restaurant located at a height of 732m on the tree line in Ullådalen. In the cellar they have a distillery producing their own aquavit, using water from a mountain spring, which is flavoured with local herbs. The kitchen produces food from local produce with influences from mountainous regions throughout the world.

→ Bustamon is signed from the E14 just W of Åre. Follow the road up 4km and turn at the parking area. Buustamon 142, 830 13 Åre, +46 647 53175. www.buusta.se

63.4239, 13.0242

35 BLÅHAMMAREN FJÄLLSTATION

The highest-altitude STF mountain lodge, located 1,086m above sea level on the Norwegian border. Accessible only by foot in the summer and on skis in the winter, the views make it well worth the effort. Before bed you will likely be told the story of the 18th-century Carolean death march in the mountains nearby. Several hiking trails start here and head off in different directions.

→ Parking at Storulvån Fjällstation; follow signs from the E14 about 40km E of Åre (63.1691, 12.3622). From here there is a 12km marked path. www.svenskaturistforeningen.se

90 mins, 63.1856, 12.1742

HÖGAKUSTEN

Our perfect week

→ **Find** a beach 260m above the sea on Högklinten.

→ **Crawl** with a torch along the Skalberg caves.

→ **Hike** a section of the High Coast Trail.

→ **Lie** in the sun on warm rock at Rotsidan beach.

→ **Paddle** to Mjältön and find the cave.

→ **Pilot** a boat around the islands on the Ångermanälven river estuary.

→ **Feast** on waffles at the Skuleberget Toppstugan.

→ **Taste** some fermented herring, famously foul-smelling but then strangely addictive (drinking schnapps helps).

→ **Stay** overnight in a lighthouse on Högbonden.

→ **Take** a sauna and swim after an evening grill at Fjälludden.

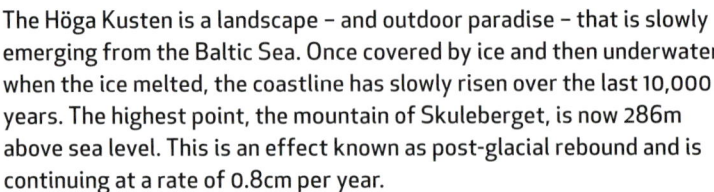

The Höga Kusten is a landscape – and outdoor paradise – that is slowly emerging from the Baltic Sea. Once covered by ice and then underwater when the ice melted, the coastline has slowly risen over the last 10,000 years. The highest point, the mountain of Skuleberget, is now 286m above sea level. This is an effect known as post-glacial rebound and is continuing at a rate of 0.8cm per year.

Until the end of the 19th century this magnificent stretch of coastline had no name, then it started to attract the attention of geologists and became known as Ångermanlands Höga Kusten – Ångermanland's High Coast.

During the 1960s the government wanted all Swedes to have access to meaningful leisure activities, and after a national survey of natural resources this area was chosen as one of three in the country deemed the best for facilitating an active outdoor life. This led eventually to a further project in the 1970s that saw the area being nominated as a UNESCO World Heritage site and changing its name to the now ubiquitous High Coast.

For many years a Swedish secret, the High Coast is now rapidly becoming recognised by outdoor enthusiasts from around the world as a real playground for all manner of outdoor activities. The nucleus of this growth is the exciting FriluftsByn (Outdoor Village) project at the foot of Skuleberget – the perfect base camp for your High Coast adventure.

Offshore you'll find many small and uninhabited islands that can easily be reached and explored by kayak. For the gastronomically adventurous there's the opportunity to try several different varieties of fermented herring at the annual premiere on the island from which it originated.

For the ultimate High Coast adventure, spend several days walking the 128km trail that links together many of the main landmarks. You can then spend a day resting your weary legs lying on slabs of warm dolerite rock on the beach at Rotsidan. Maybe then spend the night on the beach or head out to the island of Högbonden where you can sleep in an old lighthouse high on the cliffs, with the sea far below. Once you've been to the High Coast you will definitely want to come back.

COAST & ISLANDS

1 TRYSUNDA

Island in the High Coast archipelago that's widely considered one of the most beautiful in Sweden. The only harbour is at a well-preserved fishing village dating from the 16th century. Its church is decorated with amazing murals. The coastline of the rocky, forested island is characterised by shallow coves perfect for wild camping and swimming.

➜ In summer there's a ferry to Trysunda from the harbour in Köpmanholmen several times a day. For a current timetable see: www.ornskoldsvikshamn.se/turlistor
63.1403, 18.7967 ▣▣▣▣▣

2 BALESUDDEN

High peninsula that was once used as a location for a warning beacon but is now a nature reserve. Follow the paths to the top for fantastic view out to sea (63.1645, 18.7177). The footpath will also take you past Balestjärn, a magical lake with crystal-clear water through which you can see old tree trunks lying on the bottom. The path also takes you past a sandy cove with a barbecue area where you can stop to cook.

➜ The signposted footpath into the reserve starts from the main car park (also see map), just N of Sandlågan, and signposted from route 922 between Domsjö and Bjästa.
1 hour, 63.2010, 18.7019 ▣▣▣▣

3 NORRFÄLLSVIKEN

Coastal nature reserve that was once part of the sea bed and is now a vast area of lichen-covered cobble fields. It's nearly 5,000 years since the land emerged from the water, and it has risen a further 50m since then. Follow the 5km coastal path and you'll find a shelter where you can light a fire, with great views of the islands of Rävsön and Högbonden.

➜ At the tip of the Mjällom peninsula. From Nordingrå follow signs for Norrfällsviken. Drive through camping area to the car park.
30 mins, 62.9651, 18.5445 ▣▣▣

4 MJÄLTÖN

Island in the High Coast archipelago. It's the highest in Sweden, reaching 236m above sea level. Part of the island is a nature reserve, including the natural harbour of Baggviken. From here you can follow a path up to the highest point, from where the views are breathtaking. There's also a large cave that's well worth a visit. There are no regular sailings to the island, so you will need to

arrange to be dropped off and collected. Alternatively you can hire sea kayaks from FriluftsByn (see 23) and make the sheltered 40km return paddle there. They will assist you with the route.

➜ Charter boats from High Coast Sea, +46 613 20000. www.highcoastsea.com
63.0452, 18.5196 ▣▣▣▣

5 ROTSIDAN

A 4km section of coast comprised of smooth slabs of dark dolerite rock. The rock warms up in the sun, making it a relaxing place to swim or enjoy a picnic. There are a few marked areas where you are allowed to build a fire, but these are forbidden in all other areas in case they fracture the rock.

➜ From Nordingrå follow signs to Häggvik, Kåsta and then Fällsvik. From here there are signs to Rotsidan nature reserve and parking.
62.8483, 18.3831 ▣▣▣

6 STORÖN

Island and nature reserve at the southernmost tip of the High Coast, with a dramatic landscape and fascinating cultural history. For several hundred years there was an important fishing harbour on the east side of the island, although the rising of the land

9

meant the fishermen constantly had to clear stone from the entrance. Finally in the 1870s the sea won the battle, and the harbour became an idyllic lake cut off from the sea. At the northern end there's a cabin with two beds open to visitors to the reserve. Hörsångs campsite provides a ferry service out to the island.

→ Hörsångs Camping & Beach, Hörsång Gräta 904, 872 98 Noraström, +46 613 34105
62.7776, 18.2230

7 FJÄLLUDDEN

The forest industry company Holmen leases the land that forms a natural harbour and makes it available to the public. There is a barbecue area, cabin and sauna, reachable by road or sea. Perfect for a grill and swim.

→ From Örnsköldsvik drive S and E dir Gullvik then Åvika Brygga, and turn R at the signs to Genesön. At Genesön keep R and drive for around 2.8km to the end of the road and the rocky shore of Fjälludden.
63.2273, 18.7200

RIVERS & LAKES

8 TROLLTJÄRN

Idyllic small lake with a mirror-like surface,

overlooked by steep rock faces. The water is 12m deep. On the cliff below the northern viewpoint is a rock carving of two moose believed to date from the Neolithic period.

→ From the crossroads in the village of Lägsta head N dir Norrtjärn. Trolltjärns Naturreservat is signposted to R at 2km. The path to the lake is signposted from the parking area after 1.5km on R.
63.8402, 18.0556

9 ÅNGERMANÄLVEN

Hire a small motor boat for a day or longer to explore the Ångermanälven river estuary and its many islands. The High Coast is well known for its deep waters and is therefore an ideal place for a beginner to safely learn to drive a boat.

→ Frånö Båthamn, 872 43 Kramfors, +46 73 0282571. www.flowweb.net
62.9133, 17.8396

10 VÄSTANÅFALLET

A powerful cascading waterfall which is at its most impressive during the spring floods. At the base of the 90m falls are the remains of numerous industries that have exploited the power of the water over the centuries. There's a visitor centre with a café and

information on local history, flora and fauna.

→ Västanåfallet Nature Reserve is at the village of Viksjö along route 331, approximately 35km W of Härnösand. Follow signs to Naturreservatet Västanå.
5 mins, 62.7348, 17.4141

CULTURE & HISTORY

11 HEMSÖFASTNING

The impressive Hemsö fortress stands at the mouth of the Ångermanälven river estuary, just outside Härnösand on the island of Hemsön. Work began in 1953 on this warren of tunnels blasted out of solid rock. The once top-secret facility was designed not just for coastal artillery but to withstand a nuclear attack, with bunkers 40m below ground level and subterranean living quarters for 320 soldiers. During the Cold War it was one of Sweden's most important defence installations, but it was decommissioned in 1992 and is now a fascinating museum with the added bonus of amazing views.

→ Take route 729 N and E across the island from ferry and follow signs R after 4km. Härnösand Ö, 870 10 Ålandsbro, +46 70 5441320. www.hemsofastning.se
62.6943, 18.0877

12 MANNAMINNE

An open-air museum developed over 30 years by artist Anders Åberg and his wife Barbro as a 'gesamtkunstwerk'. The guiding principle in his work is to connect people's lives, work and activities in the past with the present – all with a view to an integrated and sustainable future. It is a constantly evolving collection of crafts, art, vehicles, buildings and culture from both Sweden and around the world; a fantasy land that will fascinate and enchant adults and children alike. During the summer there's also a quirky restaurant serving home-cooked local food.

➜ From the E4 follow signs for Nordingrå. After 13km turn R onto route 836, museum is shortly on L. Häggvik 109, 870 30 Nordingrå. +46 613 20290. www.mannaminne.se
62.9111, 18.3041 🖼️🍴

13 HÖGAKUSTENBRON

The High Coast Bridge is a colossal suspension bridge spanning the mouth of the Ångermanälven river. The 14th-largest in the world, it is both an impressive example of engineering and a perfect vantage point for views along the estuary.

➜ On the E4 25km N of Härnösand.
62.7976, 17.9385 🖼️

14 MURBERGET

The Västernorrland county museum has an extensive collection of exhibits that tell the story of this part of Sweden. An outdoor section focuses on life in the 19th and early 20th centuries, and at midsummer this village area comes alive with singing, dancing and period costumes. There are children's activities, local art and handicrafts and don't miss the delicious home-made cinnamon buns.

Länsmuseet Västernorrland, Murbergsvägen 31, 871 21 Härnösand, +46 611 88600. www.murberget.se
62.6451, 17.9236 🖼️🚲🐾🍴

15 GENE FORNBY

Reconstructed Iron Age farm as it would have looked around the year 500 BC, based on the finds from a nearby archaeological. excavation. It is believed that this was owned by a family of local importance. It would have originally been on the shoreline, but that is now 500m away. On weekdays in July there are guides, but at other times you can look around by yourself.

➜ Leave Örnsköldsvik dir Domsjö and after crossing the traffic lights in Sund turn L signed Gene. Gene Fornby is signed from here.
63.2497, 18.6954 🖼️🚗

16 SKULESKOGEN NATIONAL PARK

The crown jewel of the Höga Kusten is the 30km2 area at the highest point along the coast, designated as the Skuleskogen National Park in 1984. The visitor centre is a good place to start: they have maps, and several trails start from there. There are lots of fascinating geological features including the Slättdal crevice, which is a 100m long, 30m deep sheer-sided cleft in the rock. There are several hiking cabins. Wild camping is allowed during the summer at indicated sites as long as you do not stay in the same place for more than three nights.

➜ National park visitor centre: Naturum Höga Kusten, Skuleberget, 870 33 Docksta, +46 613 700200. www.naturumhogakusten.se
63.0727, 18.3558 🖼️🚶🏕️

17 BORGBERGET

Extensive hill fort believed to date to at least the Viking period (AD 800–1050). At 190m above sea level, it has breathtaking views both inland and out to sea. The remains of the vast stone ramparts are still visible, as are the foundations from two houses. No archaeological excavations have been made here, so little is known about it.

→ Leave the town of Bollstabruk to W on route 774 (Tunsjövägen). Within 2km turn R for 'Fornborg' (hill fort) and follow the signs to the start of the path up to the fort.
63.0124, 17.6222

LOCAL FOOD

18 SÅGVERKET

Hostel and restaurant in an old sawmill on the coast just north of Härnösand. The kitchen specialises in simple dishes made from scratch and – as much as possible – from local and organic ingredients. You can relax in a hammock in the garden, feed the chickens or maybe after dinner wander down to the water's edge with a drink.

→ Rö 303, 870 15 Utansjö, +46 611 64011.
www.sagverket.se
62.7149, 17.9757

19 SURSTRÖMMING

The island of Ulvön in the Örnsköldsviks archipelago is the place most Swedes think of as the birthplace of surströmming – fermented herring, a fish dish that smells really bad but actually tastes very good. Small herring are caught in the spring, salted and left to ferment in barrels. Surströmming is still produced on the island, and the third Thursday in August is always the 'premiere' of the season, with plenty of opportunities for tasting. Visit the island for a day or stay longer. The island website (www.ulvon.info) has details of accommodation and other activities on the island.

→ Several ferries a day in summer from harbour in Köpmanholmen. For timetable see www.ornskoldsvikshamn.se/turlistor
63.0460, 18.6528

20 SKULEBERGET TOPPSTUGAN

Ride the chairlift to the top of Skuleberget (294m above sea level) where you will have a fantastic view of the High Coast including the islands of Mjältön and Ulvön. The Toppstugan is the café at the top, where they use local produce to serve a variety of meals, drinks and snacks that you can enjoy on the sun terrace.

→ The Toppstugan is operated by FriluftsByn (see 23) and the chairlift station is a short signposted walk from there.
63.0753, 18.3495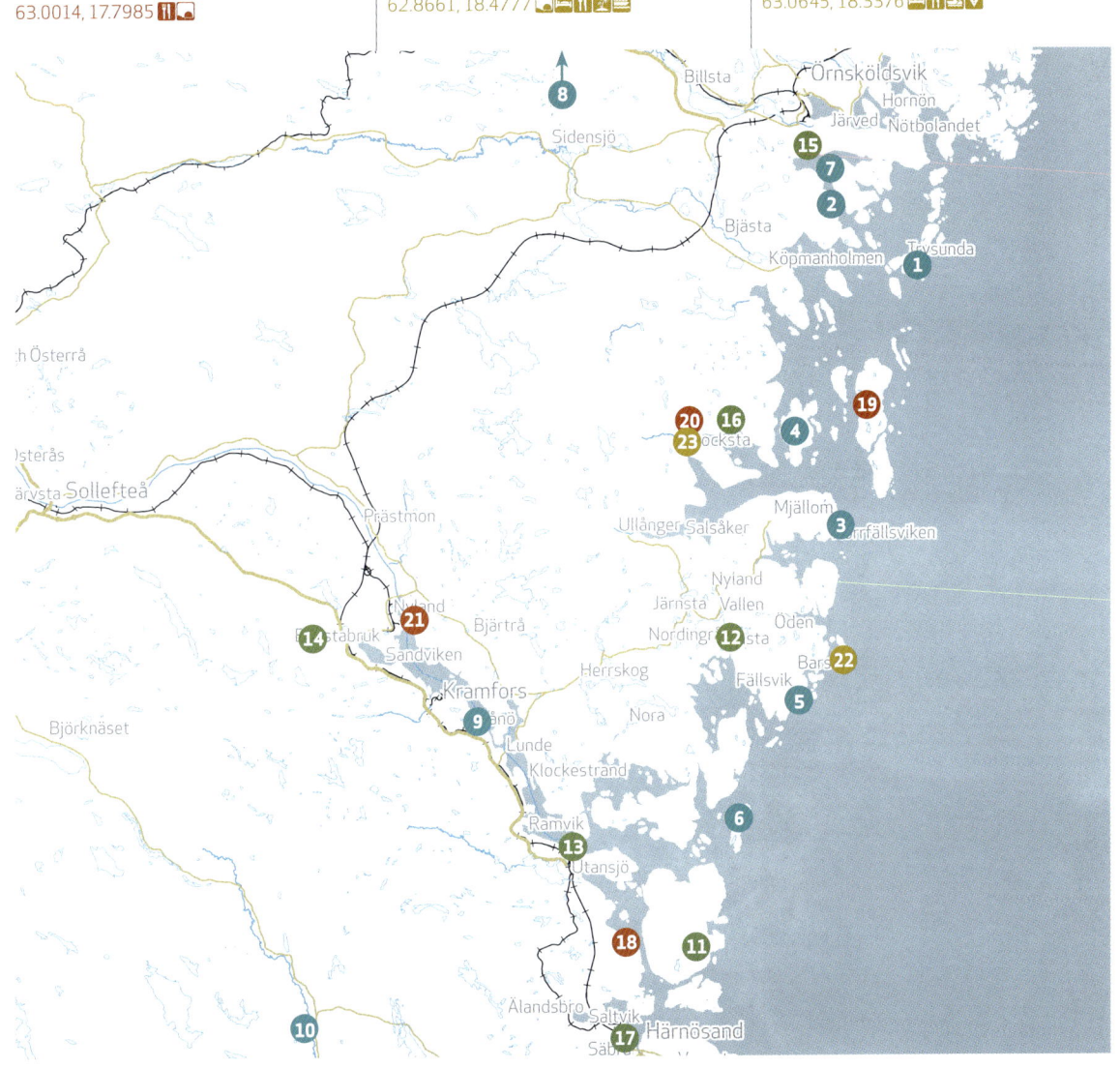

21 BOX DISTILLERY

The world's northernmost whisky distillery, on the bank of the Ångermanälven river. Based in an old power station, it uses water from a local spring and organically grown malted barley to produce a well-regarded single malt. There's a visitor centre and café, and guided tours and tastings are available.

→ Sörviken 140, 872 96 Bjärtrå, +46 612 53060. www.boxwhisky.se
63.0014, 17.7985

SLEEP

22 HÖGBONDEN FYR

Sweden's second-highest lighthouse, on the island nature reserve of Högbonden. The lighthouse keeper's cottage is now a hostel with amazing sea views. A café is open in high season – otherwise bring food and fuel with you as there's a grill area.

→ Boats operated by Höga Kusten Båtarna to Högbonden leave from harbours in Barsta and Bönhamn several times daily in high season. Högbonden Fyr & Vandrarhem: +46 613 23005. www.hogbondenfyr.se. Högakusten Båtarna, +46 613 10550. www.hkship.se
62.8661, 18.4777

23 FRILUFTSBYN

The outdoor village is a constantly evolving project run by a team who are passionate about the outdoors and the High Coast. Lying at the base of Skuleberget mountain it's situated in a landscape that's a veritable playground for anyone with an interest in outdoor adventures. The village organises activities and events, and has a variety of accommodation options. This is the perfect central location to choose as your base for exploring the rest of what the High Coast has to offer. Visit their website for a calendar of interesting events to include in your stay.

→ www.friluftsbyn.se
63.0645, 18.3376

DALA-FLODA

Our perfect week

→ **Paddle** to Harpikön and spend the night on a wild island.

→ **Try** to spot an elk from the Mejdåsen Observation Tower.

→ **Watch** the peregrine falcons returning to their nest on Djurmo Klack.

→ **Swim** and paddle down the Mossel stream until you reach the Västerdalälven.

→ **Catch** crayfish and cook them over an open fire.

→ **Discover** why so many Swedish houses are painted red at Falun Mine.

→ **Learn** to dance the 'huppleken' at the Komidsommarfest.

→ **Make** charcoal at Kvarna and use it to grill the fish you catch when rafting in Vansbro.

→ **Slow** down and explore ancient forest tracks on a wagon drawn by a North Swedish Horse.

→ **Eat** a farm breakfast at Wålstedts Trädgård.

If you have a picture in your head of Sweden then it will very likely be of Dalarna, which is often described as 'Sweden in miniature'. Located about three hours drive northwest of Stockholm, this is a highly accessible yet fairytale landscape, rich in both wildlife and heritage – perfect ingredients for an unforgettable adventure.

The village of Dala-Floda sits on the banks of the Västerdalälven (West Dala River) at the heart of southern Dalarna, where it is known as Dalarna's Garden of Eden. With its red-painted wooden houses it's the ideal base for forays into the forests and onto the lakes and rivers that characterise the area.

Visit at midsummer and you'll find yourself invited to join in as locals in brightly coloured traditional costumes gather around the village maypole. The girls dance around it wearing crowns of fresh flowers to the sound of traditional fiddle music. There follows much feasting and merriment until late into the night as the arrival of summer, light and nature is celebrated. On their way home, girls and young women are supposed to pick seven different species of flowers and lay them under their pillows to ensure that their future husbands appear to them in a dream.

Heading out into the forest you're likely to see a moose, and if you're lucky you may even catch sight of a wolf, lynx, wolverine or brown bear. You don't have to look hard to find a bountiful feast of wild berries and mushrooms, which can be enjoyed beside an open fire as you wild camp on the smooth granite or sandy beaches that form the shores of many of the lakes.

Returning after a few nights in the wilderness, you may feel like indulging yourself with a night at Värdshuset and a meal made with organic produce from Wålstedts farm. If afterwards you can't sleep, walk down to the lake and swim under the red sky of a midnight twilight – although the sun dips below the horizon, it is never truly dark in midsummer.

WILD SWIMMING

1 FLOSJÖN BADPLATS

Swimming area in Flosjön lake, a short walk from Dala-Floda village centre. During the summer the water temperature is often over 20°C and it's a great place to go to cool down at the end of a hot day. There is a floating platform with a diving board and a wooden jetty out to the deeper water.

→ Follow Flosjövägen N through the village, then Badvägen along the lake past the Värdshuset hotel until you reach the Flosjöbadet sign and parking area.
2 mins, 60.5156, 14.8087 🏊📷

2 MOSSEL

The Mossel stream runs from Lingtjärnen to join the Flosjöneret and then the Västerdalälven. Just after it runs under the bridge in the village of Mossel, it forms a deep pool where locals have put up a slide and swings: a perfect family swimming spot. As the water has run off the surface of a lake it's also normally very warm. For a fun family adventure, follow the stream downstream until it meets the main river.

→ From the ICA store on Stora vägen (E16) in Dala-Floda head W, dir Björbo. Take first R, signed Mossel, and continue about 1.5km to a bridge. The swimming spot is on the R.
60.5169, 14.7748 🏊📷

3 SÅNGEN

Sången lake is in the forest about 10km from Dala-Floda. With a long, sandy beach and shallow lagoon, it's easy to imagine you are by the sea here. Next to the beach is a hiking shelter with a fire pit and supply of logs, maintained in memory of a local fisherman. This is a great place to wild camp, forage, swim and fish.

→ Head from Dala-Floda towards Mossel. Just before the bridge turn R and follow 5.5km until you cross the (signposted) Sången creek. Take next L, signed Sången, and continue 5.5km. The forest track to the beach is at the top end of the lake.
5 mins, 60.5861, 14.7809 🏊📷🚶☀️🏕️

4 LÅNGSJÖN

Swimming spot on Långsjön, just outside of Dala-Floda. Next to the road, it's the ideal spot to stop and cool off quickly. There is a small jetty and a shelter.

→ From Dala-Floda head towards Mockfjärd. The lake is 6km along on the R.
2 mins, 60.5017, 14.8982 📷

5 LISSKAS BASTU

Community-run, traditional, wood-fired sauna built on stilts over Flosjön, so you can dive straight into the lake to cool off. Contact the committee to make a booking.

→ Sauna booking: Thomas Dolk, Syrholsvägen 22, 785 44 Dala-Floda, +46 705 602338. www.facebook.com/Syrholn
60.5158, 14.8089 📷

KAYAK & RAFT

6 HARPIKÖN KAYAK TRIP

Paddle from Flosjön badplats (see 1) in Dala-Floda to the island of Harpikön. This big island has a few summerhouses on its southern tip, but the rest is largely very wild with several small, secluded beaches and great places to pitch a tent. Pack everything you need in a kayak and spend a night wild camping by the water – perhaps take a skinny dip in the midnight twilight and dry off by a campfire.

→ Hire kayaks and equipment from Kajaktiv, they can also advise on other paddle trips in the area. Kajaktiv, Lissforsvägen 11, 785 44 Dala-Floda, +46 241 22361. www.kajaktiv.se
2.5 hours (one way), 60.5575, 14.8476 🚶☀️🏕️📷🛶🏊

7 VANSBRO RAFTING

Before the advent of road and rail transport in Sweden, the big rivers were used to float logs downstream to sawmills, with men travelling on rafts made from the logs. The Västerdalälven was one such river. In Vansbro you board a purpose-built raft and use the electric outboards to take you as far upstream as you want. From there you slowly drift back downstream with the current, Huckleberry Finn-style. Look out for moose and beavers, or maybe do a spot of fishing.

→ Meet them by the river behind the ST1 petrol station on Route E16 in Vansbro. +46 701 768383. www.vansbroaventyr.se 60.5044, 14.2292

8 LAKE RUNN KAYAKING

Runn is a 64km² lake between the towns of Falun and Borlänge, with more than 100 islands. Pack a canoe or kayak and head off on an expedition. Paddle adventures here can last from a few hours to several days. There are lots of spots to wild camp on the islands. Make your own route, or the tourist office in Falun has detailed maps of 13 suggested ones. They can also assist with the hire of canoes, kayaks or SUPs.

→ Start your trip at Roxnäs Udde in Falun. 60.5807, 15.6982

VIEWS & HIKES

9 FÄNFORSEN

A 600m-long rapid on the Västerdalälven river where the water spectacularly drops nearly 9m. The rapids are popular with kayakers, and several companies run white-water rafting trips here. Grab an ice cream from the restaurant in the rest area and follow the riverside path downstream.

→ Head for Fänforsen Rastplats on route 66 at the W end of Björbo. You'll hear and then see the rapids from here.

5 mins, 60.4633, 14.6838

10 MEJDÅSEN OBSERVATION TOWER

Located on a hill 2.5km from the village of Björbo, this recently renovated 400m-high tower was built in the 1940s by local forest owners for firewatching. It offers fantastic views from the mountains on the border with Norway in one direction and along the Västerdalälven valley in the other. Save this adventure for a clear day!

→ Stop at the Konsum supermarket in Björbo and pick up a free local map. Either drive via

gravel forest roads or walk S from Björbo (1hr).
10 mins, 60.4361, 14.7122

11 TROLLDALEN

Nature reserve set in a steep-sided and densely wooded valley. The Troll Valley was said to be the home of a group of trolls who once terrorised the nearby village of Björka. The trolls made a pact with the villagers that they would leave Trolldalen if any man could fell a big tree over seven Thursdays, with seven axe strikes per day. A local man succeeded, and the trolls have not been seen since. A natural stone arch high on a 40m cliff is known as the troll church and is also believed to be an entrance to their world. A main trail takes you through a wild flower meadow and in a circular route around the valley, which is rich in flora and fauna including several rare orchids. There are loads of bilberries to pick and a hiking shelter with a fireplace where you can stop to cook. Spend a day here foraging – and looking for signs of trolls.

→ Park by the level crossing in Björka and follow signs to Trolldalen.

25 mins to the reserve boundary,
60.5308, 15.0813

12 ÄPPELBO SAGOSTIG

Story trail in the forest near Äppelbo village, where if children look carefully they may spot some mythical creatures watching them. The path takes you through a landscape ripe with foraging opportunities, and depending on the time of year you will find various berries and mushrooms. The total length of the path is only 1.5km, but there's lots to keep you busy and a hiking shelter where you can make a fire and cook.

→ From the middle of Äppelbo, follow Ovanheden S to the hostel where the trail starts. Äppelbo Gemenskap & Vandrarhem, Älvgården, 780 54 Äppelbo.

1 hour, 60.4780, 14.0030

13 DJURMO KLACK

Nature reserve with a precipice giving fantastic views along the Dalälven (Dala river). A footpath marked Djurmo Klack takes you from the parking area up to the viewpoint at 400m (60.5561, 15.1801). There are two Bronze Age burial mounds to look out for and a variety of wildlife. The caves on the rock face are protected, as they are home to eagle owls and peregrine falcons. The information board in the parking area has a map of other trails in the reserve.

→ From Djurås head SE dir Djurmo. Turn L at sign Helgbo, Sifferbo, Stugby. Take first L and cross railway. Continue for 2km until you reach parking area and info board.
1.5 hours, 60.5612, 15.2047 🐾🏕️🚲📷✝️

14 ÄLVMÖTET

Promontory between the Västerdalälven (West Dala River) and Österdalälven (East Dala River) as they unite to form the Dalälven (Dala River). This confluence has long been seen by romantic locals as symbolic of a strong relationship, and many couples propose here.

→ Signed R from the E16 entering Djurås, shortly after the roundabout. Follow Älvuddsvägen L round the health centre and park in their car park.
10 mins, 60.5517, 15.1321 🏞️

CYCLE

15 VANSBRO DRESSIN

The draisine is a pedal-powered rail vehicle originally used by railway workers. They can be rented from Vansbro to travel as far as you want along an unused 30km section of the Inlandsbanan (Inland Railway) to Mora. A tandem takes two adults and two children, while a single takes two adults. Last used by trains in 1969, the track alongside Vansjön lake is slowly returning to nature, and you can stop by a sandy beach to relax in the sun with great views of the mountains. Take a proper picnic as you can definitely burn it off!

→ Collect your draisine key, instructions and map from the ST1 petrol station on Route E16 in Vansbro. +46 701 768383. www.vansbroaventyr.se
8 hours return trip for the entire section, 60.5086, 14.2305 🚲🚣

16 RÄLSLEDEN

Cycle or walk the Rälsleden, which follows the route of the old railway line between Falun and Rättvik. Starting at Stora Torget in Falun, it's 52.5km of easy cycling to Rättvik Station (60.8850, 15.1156). The route passes some great swimming spots, you can wild camp en route and there are plenty of places to stop for sandwiches or freshly baked pastries. Cycle there and back or get the bus back.

→ Start at Stora Torget, the main square in the centre of Falun town. The route is signposted and simple to follow.
6 hours (one way), 60.6074, 15.6300 🚴🏊🚲🏕️

18

HISTORY & CULTURE

17 KVARNA CULTURAL RESERVE

In Sweden there are a number of cultural reserves that have a purpose similar to nature reserves. The Kvarna reserve is in the forest on the edge of the village of Dala-Floda. Water from the Närsströmmen stream is used to power some working examples of 17th-century industrial machinery. During the summer, regular events are held where you can see the machinery in operation, help produce charcoal or listen to local folk music. There is also an outdoor fireplace where you can cook your own food, and plenty of berries and mushrooms can be foraged. A great place for kids to play, with lots of old buildings to explore and streams to dam. Spend several hours or a whole day here exploring.

➜ From the ICA store in the village centre take Stora vägen (E16) W, dir Björbo. Take the first R and follow signs.

5 mins, 60.5074, 14.7655

18 GAGNEF BY HORSE & CART

Explore Dala-Floda and further afield on ancient forest tracks while relaxing on a wagon drawn by a North Swedish Horse.

Your local guide will explain local history and traditions while you take in all the sights at an unhurried pace. Longer trips including overnight camps, and traditional campfire meals can be arranged.

➜ Contact Növarjan to book, at Ersaholsvägen 12, 78544 Dala-Floda, +46 70 2323707. www.novarjan.se

60.5002, 14.8018

19 DAFLO FESTIVALEN

Most summers in mid-July the Wålstedts farm hosts the DaFlo Festival, with artists from Sweden and around the world giving performances and workshops in music, dance and circus skills. Britta Wålstedt, who is a professional circus artist, brings her friends and colleagues back to her family farm for a weekend of world-class entertainment, raising money for a variety of children's projects.

➜ Wålstedts Trädgård, Hagen 13, 785 44 Dala-Floda, +46 730 534545. www.vidga.se

60.4861, 14.8315

20 FALU GRUVA

Falun Mine was once known as Sweden's treasure chest, due to its importance in

18

20

155

the copper trade. The metal from here was used for castle roofs, church steeples, coins and household utensils all over Europe, and the tailings from the mine are used in the red paint used on wooden houses across Sweden. No longer an active mine, it is now a protected UNESCO World Heritage Site. There is a fascinating museum, which gives an insight into not only this site but also into the industrial heritage of the wider region, and you can take an underground mine tour (wear sturdy shoes and warm clothes). You can easily spend a whole day here.

→ Falu Gruva, Gruvplatsen 1, 791 61 Falun, +46 23 782030. www.falugruva.se
60.6002, 15.6166 🚗🚌🍴🚻

21 ARVSELEN'S LEVANDE FÄBOD

Fäbod are Swedish pastures where farmers would take their animals to graze over the summer months. The lodgings are now mainly used as summerhouses, but Arvselen is an example that is still worked throughout the summer as it would have been during the 19th century. There is no running water or electricity here. Learn how the landscape used to be worked and enjoy butter and cheese produced from the fresh cows' and goats' milk. If you want the full experience you can stay overnight in the traditional wooden cowshed.

→ From Malung take the E45 dir Mora and after 3km 'levande fäbord' is signed from the L for Arvselen. Romarheden 312, 782 35 Malung, +46 70 6904489. www.arvselen.se
60.7392, 13.7875 🐄🚗🚲🛏🍴

22 KOMIDSOMMARFEST

The 'Cow Party' is celebrated every year on the second weekend of July. Traditionally young people would have met to celebrate midsummer up in the summer pastures where the girls were tending the cows. They then wanted to meet again when they returned to the village, and in Dala-Floda a dance was held on the old wooden bridge, which had a smooth surface for the rather wild local 'huppleken' dance. Since the beginning of the 20th century this has become an annual party, with a week of events leading up to a street market and a big dance in the evening on the Saturday and a concert in the church on the Sunday. The market is a great opportunity to taste local produce and buy local crafts.

→ The market is held along Kyrkbyvägen in Dala-Floda.
60.5072, 14.7979 🚶🚲🍴

23 KVARNSTENSBROTTET

Nature reserve and Sweden's oldest millstone quarry. A stone carved around AD 800 has been traced back to here. This was around the same time that the Vikings were establishing important trading routes to the east and copper was first mined in Falun. Millstones were known in the area as 'life's stones' due to their importance in food production, and those quarried here were mainly used to grind barley and rye. There are 1.5km of paths you can follow around the site, which is littered with broken stones from over the centuries.

→ Take route 66 south from Malung centre and look for turning on L signposted Kvarnstensbrottet within 2km. Follow signs from here for 4km.
25 mins, 60.6733, 13.7515 🚗🏞

24 ÄLGBERGET TRAINING CAMP

The remains of 'Läger 4 Älgberget' – a secret camp in the middle of the Swedish forest where during the Second World War, Norwegian refugees were trained to return home as paramilitary police once the occupying German forces had capitulated. When the tide of the war turned in favour of the Allies, it was also used to train Resistance fighters. Now reclaimed by the forest, the remote site is rich in both nature and history. Try to find the railway lines leading nowhere that were used to train saboteurs. Great foraging.

→ From the ICA store in Dala-Floda head W dir Björbo. Take first turning R and follow for 17km until you reach turning for Älgberget on R. The site is on both sides of the main road.
60.6042, 14.6096 🚗🏞🏕

ORGANIC FOOD & FORAGING

25 WÅLSTEDTS TRÄDGÅRD

Traditional Swedish family farm that has been organic for two generations. The farm has a restaurant serving home-cooked meals prepared from their own produce, where you can also take baking courses. They also have a wool spinnery where naturally dyed yarn is produced from rare breeds. Rent the cabin in their summer pasture – you'll need to walk, but will be given a more-than-sustaining picnic to help you on your way. The farm is located beside the Västerdalälven, where there's a wooden jetty you can use for a swim in the river.

→ Hagen 13, 785 44 Dala-Floda, +46 702 241163. www.walstedtsgard.se
60.4899, 14.8461 🛏🍴🐄🚴

26 GRANGÄRDE MUSTERI

Organic fruit farm where they press their berries on site to create juices full of flavour and vitamins. There is a farm shop where you can taste and purchase produce, as well as a café serving home-prepared local produce. A bottle of Tillmans freshly pressed juice is an ideal addition to your hamper when heading off for a forest or river adventure.

➔ Gamlavägen 67, 770 13 Grangärde,
+46 240 641067, www.grangardemusteri.se
60.2688, 14.9803 🍴

27 CAFÉ LILLFIKET

Small café specialising in organic and very local produce. It also serves as the local tourist information and through the summer hires out bicycles. Bring your map and plan your next adventure over a coffee and pastry.

➔ Stora vägen 47, 785 44 Dala-Floda,
+46 241 22300
60.5093, 14.8014 🍴🚴

28 CRAYFISHING

Crayfish have been caught and eaten in Sweden for centuries, and have become a fully fledged national institution with associated songs and parties. Fishing for them is tightly regulated due to the decline in numbers. In the Västerdalälven at Dala-Floda fishing is allowed for 24 hours on one weekend in mid-August. As crayfish are nocturnal, this involves spending a night by the river around a campfire. Peter Persson of Növarjan is a local guide and can organise everything you need, including traditional tips for preparation and cooking.

➔ Ersaholsvägen 12, 78544 Dala-Floda,
+46 70 2323707, www.novarjan.se
60.5061, 14.7988 🍴🛶🛷

ACCOMMODATION

29 VÄRDSHUSET

Small, environmentally focused hotel and restaurant with a view over Flosjön, producing award-winning food from local organic produce. One of the first restaurants in Sweden to receive organic certification. During the summer they harvest their own vegetables, herbs and salad leaves in their beautiful kitchen garden. Before dinner you can refresh yourself in the traditional sauna followed by a swim in the lake.

➔ Badvägen 6, 785 44 Dala-Floda,
+46 241 22050, www.dalafloda-vardshus.se
60.5132, 14.8088 🛏️🍴

157

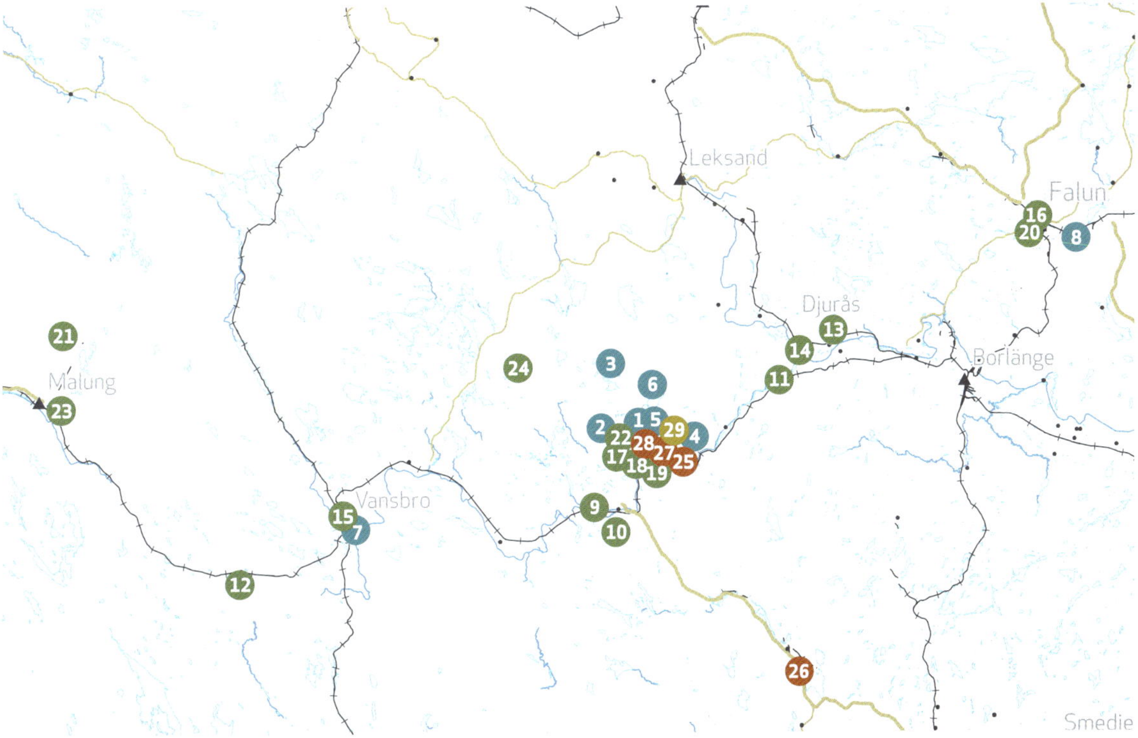

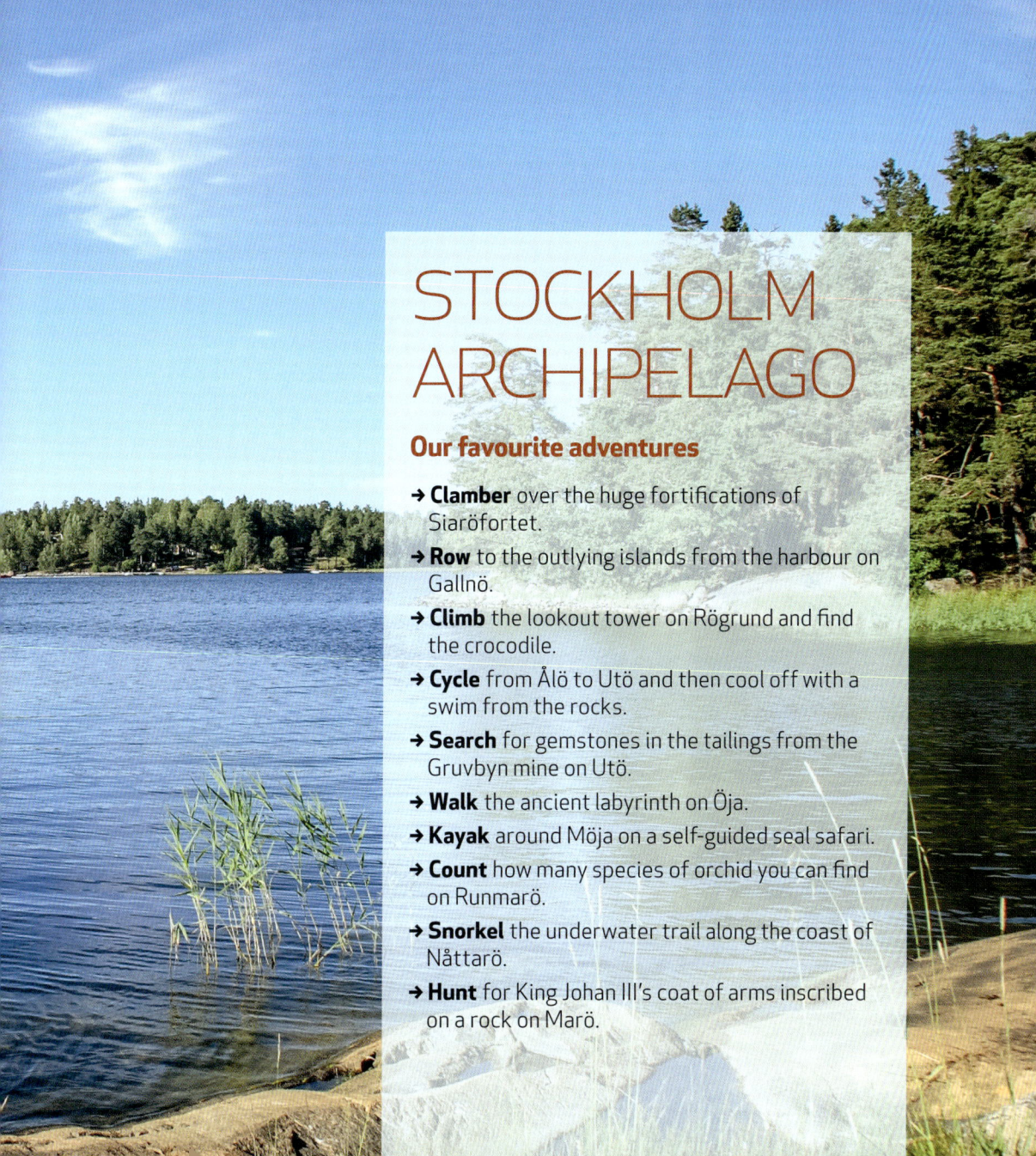

STOCKHOLM ARCHIPELAGO

Our favourite adventures

→ **Clamber** over the huge fortifications of Siaröfortet.

→ **Row** to the outlying islands from the harbour on Gallnö.

→ **Climb** the lookout tower on Rögrund and find the crocodile.

→ **Cycle** from Ålö to Utö and then cool off with a swim from the rocks.

→ **Search** for gemstones in the tailings from the Gruvbyn mine on Utö.

→ **Walk** the ancient labyrinth on Öja.

→ **Kayak** around Möja on a self-guided seal safari.

→ **Count** how many species of orchid you can find on Runmarö.

→ **Snorkel** the underwater trail along the coast of Nåttarö.

→ **Hunt** for King Johan III's coat of arms inscribed on a rock on Marö.

The Stockholm Archipelago comprises over 30,000 islands, islets and rocks – from Arholma in the north to Landsort in the south. Some of the islands are inhabited all year round, many have summerhouses but more still are uninhabited and waiting to be explored. Although many of the islands in the inner archipelago can be visited on day trips from Stockholm, this chapter focuses on a multi-day summer adventure in the outer archipelago.

The main ferry company is the state-owned Waxholmsbolaget, which runs a regular service on several different routes from the main city harbour at Strömkajen – the quay just in front of the Grand Hôtel close to Kungsträdgården in central Stockholm. They offer a five-day island-hopping pass that allows you unlimited travel from the time of first use. If you have longer, there's a 30-day pass instead.

The ferry network is divided into northern, central and southern routes. Although a pass gives you access to the entire network, choosing a specific route makes it easier to visit as many islands as possible, because the routes head in different directions. All pass the island of Vaxholm, known as the 'lock on Stockholm's gateway', where you can stop to explore the town and the impressive fortifications.

Once in the outer archipelago you can use a boat timetable to plan your route or simply make it up as you go along. Many of the islands have accommodation available, but during the summer it's advisable to plan and book this in advance. Thanks to the allemansrätt (right to roam) it's possible to wild camp throughout the archipelago, with the less populated islands offering a better choice of unobtrusive sites. Read the section on where you're allowed to camp in Sweden at the front of this book.

You can travel light, as there are grocery stores on some islands and often pubs or restaurants on the larger ones. Many of the larger islands also have places where you can rent bikes or kayaks, and Waxholmsbolaget boats will carry these, space permitting. In some places there are even rowing boats you can use for free to make your own way to smaller islands. The larger islands often have more than one quay so you can disembark at one jetty, explore that island and then catch a ferry to another island from a different jetty. For ticket information and timetables visit www.waxholmsbolaget.se.

NORTHERN ROUTE

IDYLLIC ISLANDS

1 SÖDERÖRA

Small island paradise in the northern archipelago. Used as the location for Saltkråkan in the 1960s *Pippi Longstocking* television series. The island has a history of boatbuilding, and the island boatmen were (allegedly) once very proficient alcohol smugglers!

59.6315, 19.0242

2 LJUSTERÖ

Once two islands, now one of the largest islands in the middle archipelago. In the 19th century it was a popular place for wealthy people and artists to have a summer residence. Today many people live here all year round, and there's a wide variety of amenities and activities available. Grocery store on island.

59.5071, 18.5972

3 GRÄSKÖ

Like many other islands in the archipelago, Gräskö was for a long time used as a pasture island. Sheep and cows would be brought on boats in the spring, and then they would be rounded up in the autumn, having had an almost feral existence for several months. There are now about 30 full-time residents with a variety of mainly boat-related occupations. Grocery store on island.

59.6812, 19.0228

4 ARHOLMA

Island looking out to the north with a Cold War coastal battery that is now a museum. Living on the last outpost before the open sea, the people of Arholma traditionally made a living by piloting ships through the archipelago. The island is now better known for its hostelries and great beaches. Grocery store on island.

59.8535, 19.1261

5 NORRÖRA

Idyllic island where a lot of the 1960s *Pippi Longstocking* television series (re-edited as films for the English-language market) was filmed. Not much has changed since then!

59.6441, 19.0377

6 RÖDLÖGA

This island is the furthest to the east you can go without having your own boat. A network of paths will take you through a mixture of red granite, woodland and wild rose bushes to all the best swimming spots. Grocery store on island.

59.5919, 19.1654

7 SVARTLÖGA

Svartlöga appears like a black line on the horizon, which is how it gets its name – 'svart' is black in Swedish. A varied landscape of woodland and meadows with excellent opportunities for swimming and walking. It also has the world's smallest post office.

59.5724, 19.0488

NATURE & WILDLIFE

8 FEJAN

Once used as a quarantine station when cholera swept across Europe at the end of the 19th century. The buildings were used in 1944 as a transit camp when 30,000 Estonians fled Soviet occupation and crossed the Baltic in small boats. Kayaks can be hired, which are great for a seal safari. Grocery store on island.

59.7384, 19.1648

9 ÄNGSÖ

Island that is also a Swedish national park. It has one of the best-preserved forests in the archipelago, with rare trees, bushes and flowers such as cowslip and wood anemones. Many birds nest here, and ospreys and eagles can be seen. As recently at the 17th century Ängsö consisted of two islands separated by a narrow sound. The bottom of the sound has since risen from the sea to join the islands with a green meadow known as Stormier. Wild camping is not allowed here.

59.6230, 18.7629 🚤🚶🌼

10 LIDÖ

The southern half of the island is mainly open farmland, while the north is virgin forest. The majority of the trees are spruce, but in the area around the manor house there are several heritage trees of different broadleaf species. There is also a rich bird life. Grocery store on island.

59.7793, 19.0839 🚤🍴⛺🚤

11 GISSLINGÖ

Forest- and moss-covered rocky island with several boggy areas. The most easterly of the larger islands in the archipelago, only separated from the island of Korsö to the south by a small sound. The northern part of the island is a nature reserve and wild camping is not allowed there. Good berry picking.

59.7753, 19.1818 🚤⛺

12 TJOCKÖ

Beautiful island covered with a mixture of spruce and broadleaf woodland. Lots of great spots for picking berries and mushrooms. It wasn't always a popular place, as the local population were once infamous for their wrecking activities. This is how the neighbouring island of Rovholmen (Robber Island) got its name. Grocery store on island.

59.7469, 19.1383 🚤🍴⛺🚤

13 TYVÖ

Island currently owned by a foundation set up in memory of the brother and sister who once farmed the island. Although there are about 60 homes, the northern part was controlled by the military for many years and so is completely undeveloped. Small footpaths criss-cross the island, giving access to the wilder areas.

59.7757, 19.1345 🚤🚤

18

14 YXLAN

Long and narrow island with a steep, rocky coastline on the western side and a landscape that varies between broadleaf and coniferous forest. Much less cultivated than its more fertile neighbour Blidö. Grocery store on island.

59.6115, 18.8467 🛥️🍴⛺💧

15 VETTERSÖ

Mixture of oak and pine woodland, cliffs and meadows that were once cultivated farmland. There are now around 100 permanent homes on the island and the numerous adjacent smaller islands.

59.5666, 18.6999 🛥️🍴⛺💧

16 SKÄLBOTTNA

The north-eastern half of the island is a nature reserve and bird sanctuary. Covered by relatively young pine forest, the interior of the island has a lot of boggy areas. Meadows that had been allowed to become overgrown are now being restored. Norrviken bathing area has a lovely sandy bottom, and in the autumn there are some fantastic spots for mushroom picking.

59.5621, 18.7931 🛥️💧⛺

17 IDÖ

Time has stood still on this island, which has no permanent population. In May it bursts into bloom with carpets of wood anemones, wild garlic and primroses.

59.8034, 19.1294 🛥️🐕➕⛺

HISTORY

18 SIARÖFORTET

Impressive island fortress commissioned in 1914 in response to the perceived threat from the east. The intention was that it would be the first defence for any naval forces heading towards Stockholm. Demiliatarised since 1959, the various installations can now be visited as an interesting heritage site. Great for children.

59.5557, 18.6241 🍴💺🏠

19 MARÖ

Old sources suggest that the island was once inhabited by monks and known as Munkskär (Monk Rock). On a rock surface an inscription of the coat of arms of the future king Johan III can be found. Dating from 1561, this is believed to be the second-oldest inscription in the archipelago.

59.6993, 19.0561 🛥️

31

9

20 BLIDÖ

One of the largest islands in the northern archipelago. The protected strait between Yxlan and Blidö has always attracted sailors, and the island is first mentioned in King Valdemar's logbook from the 13th century. The transport of sand from the archipelago into Stockholm for use in construction was a local industry until well into the early 20th century. Grocery store on island.

59.6336, 18.9467

CENTRAL ROUTE

BEACHES & SWIMMING

21 GRINDA

Popular and busy destination for day-trippers from Stockholm. A trail takes you around the island to all the main viewpoints and swimming spots. The island farm is open to visitors. Grocery store on island.

59.4108, 18.5636

22 GÄLLNÖ

Gällnö is a typical central-archipelago island with lush meadows, pastures and a shoreline that alternates between steep cliffs and beaches. Farmed since the Middle Ages, with exceptionally well-preserved farmland and buildings. Rowing boats can be used freely to row between the adjacent islands of Karklö and Hjälmö. Grocery store on island.

59.3951, 18.6515

23 FINNHAMN

Group of islands connected by a narrow isthmus to the main island where almost all the buildings can be found. A varied landscape consisting of forests dominated by oak and hazel, with open areas of farmland. The coastline is a mixture of cliffs, secluded coves and small, sandy beaches. In the evenings you may see an eagle owl. Grocery store on main island.

59.4776, 18.8166

24 EDÖ

Edö and Edö Ö are two islands separated by a narrow sound. The southern coastline has numerous jetties and holiday homes, while the north is more wooded and rocky. There are many meadows on the higher ground.

59.4698, 18.6467

25 NAMDÖ

Island with several villages, farms and lovely beaches. Hire bikes to explore. Around the

28

main island are close to 100 additional islets, rocks and skerries. Towards the open sea you can find some of the most beautiful islands in the central archipelago, such as Biskopsö, Bullerö, Gillinge, Jungfruskär and Långviksskär. Grocery store on island.
59.1934, 18.6910

26 GRANHOLMEN
Small island with about 15 summerhouses, previously known as West Granholm with the neighbouring island of Edlunda known as East Granholm. Not much space for wild camping.
59.3764, 18.3044

27 FÅGLARÖ
Typical archipelago landscape, which until the 1950s had a working farm. An attractive mix of broadleaf woodland, pine forest and meadows fringed by a coastline with some beautiful beaches.
59.4689, 18.4651

REALLY WILD ISLANDS

28 HARÖ
Probably inhabited since the Middle Ages, with the earliest known map from the 1640s.

The traditional industries were fishing and seal hunting. The current village is not in its original location – it had to move because the island rose and the old harbour was no longer navigable. The island is rocky and wooded with several lakes.
59.3304, 18.8832

29 HASSELÖ
Hasselö and the adjacent island of Hasselkobben are slightly off the beaten track, with few amenities and rugged shorelines. With only a few summerhouses, it's perfect for a Robinson Crusoe experience.
59.3151, 18.8277

30 EKNÖ
Small, rocky island that's had no permanent residents since the last inhabitant left in 1875.
59.3002, 18.8653

BOAT & KAYAK

31 MÖJA
The inhabitants of this idyllic island used to row out to the fishing points in the outer archipelago in August and then not return

29

31

38

until January. Hire kayaks here to explore. The adjacent island of Berg is home to what is probably the world's shortest railway, just 102m long. Grocery store on island.
59.4239, 18.8853 🛏🍴⛺🛶⛴

32 RÖGRUND
Island owned by the Archipelago Foundation with magnificent views from the look-out tower located at the highest point. On the headland is a larger-than-life concrete crocodile. Kayaks are available for hire.
59.1656, 18.5877 🛏🍴⛺🛶⛴

33 INGMARSÖ
Mixture of permanent residences and holiday homes. The interior has both forest and pastures with a network of paths of gravel tracks. Kayaks can be hired for exploring the surrounding smaller islands and skerries. Grocery store on island.
59.4728, 18.7603 🛏🍴⛺🛶⛴

34 NORRA STAVSUDDA
Northern Stavsudda is the main island of the Stavsudda group. Kayaks can be rented here, and there are several boatyards, one of which unusually builds hovercraft that are used worldwide by rescue teams. There's

more space for wild camping on the other islands in the group. Grocery store on island.
59.4085, 18.7741 🛏🍴⛺🛶⛴🚣

35 KARKLÖ
Separated from the island of Gällnö by a narrow sound; rowing boats can be borrowed to make the crossing. There's a grocery store on Gällnö.
59.4146, 18.6330 🛏⛺🛶⛴

36 SANDÖN
Popular – and therefore often very busy – yachting island close to the open sea. In July an annual regatta is held at Sandhamn. Try the 'sailors' buns' at the island bakery. Grocery store on island.
59.2816, 18.9133 🛏🍴⛺⛴

HISTORY & CULTURE

37 HUSARÖ
Home to pilots from the 15th century until 1912, when the pilot station was closed. There's a small pilot museum on the island. During the Great Northern War in 1719, the Russians burned down the island's buildings and much of its forest.
59.5058, 18.8477 🛏⛺⛴

35

37

40

38 SVARTSÖ

Mixture of open agricultural land and virgin forest scattered with crystal-clear lakes. The old mission house at Ahlsvik is now a museum. Grocery store on island.

59.4522, 18.6844

NATURE & WILDLIFE

39 LÅDNA

Island that is largely part of the nature reserve of Hjälmö-Lådna. This means it's farmed in a traditional manner in order to preserve the unique archipelago environment. Walk south to the strait between Lådna and Lådnaön, where you can borrow a rowing boat to row over to Lådnaön.

59.4308, 18.7085

40 RUNMARÖ

One of the largest islands in the archipelago, with several villages in a landscape of mixed woodland. Over 27 different varieties of orchid can also be found here. As with many other islands in the area, it was once home to many pilots who guided ships into port in Stockholm. Bikes are available for hire. Grocery store on island.

59.2756, 18.7680

ACCOMMODATION

41 STORA KALHOLMEN

Small, wooded island with great swimming spots. The only building is a youth hostel, which also has a wood-fired sauna.

59.4558, 18.8263

SOUTHERN ROUTE

BEACHES & SWIMMING

42 NÅTTARÖ

A landscape that is best described as a giant sandpit! The island has great beaches and an unusual snorkelling trail where you can learn about the marine environment of the Baltic Sea. On the east coast you can find several caves. Grocery store on island.

58.8716, 18.1199

43 RÅNÖ

Island with a fantastic swimming spot at Hästholmsviken that has smooth rocks and a very shallow, sandy bottom. A circular 7.5km trail follows the shoreline. Watch moose and deer, and in late summer pick berries and mushrooms. Grocery store on island.

58.9300, 18.1826

39

44 ÅLÖ

Separated from the island of Utö by a very narrow strait that can be crossed via a bridge. Largely uninhabited, with rugged cliffs and a large sandy beach called Storsand. You can hire bikes from the restaurant at the quayside to cycle to Utö, where you can then leave them.

58.9178, 18.2107

45 ASPÖ

In Stockholm's archipelago there are three islands named Aspö – all of them are in the southern part and all of them are on the Waxholmsbolaget timetable! This one has numerous walking trails through the forests and between the summerhouses. There are plenty of small coves and beaches.

58.9007, 18.1545

46 FIVERSÄTRAÖ

Rocky and lightly forested island with lots of summer houses. It can be hard to find a suitable and unobtrusive place for wild camping here. The coast is formed mainly of smooth granite slabs.

59.0764, 18.5182

47 KYMMENDÖ

The model for the fictional island of Hemsö in the novel *The People of Hemsö*, by novelist and playwright August Strindberg. A mixture of forest and pasture with numerous bays and beaches. Grocery store on island.

59.1130, 18.5040

48 HUVUDSKÄR

Small, rocky island in an area that for many hundreds of years was very important for fishermen. On the island is a lighthouse that has been solar-powered and remotely controlled by the Swedish Maritime Administration since 1992. There are some grassy areas for wild camping to the east of the island.

58.9630, 18.5700

Remember the semaphore!

If you want a ferry to stop and collect you from a jetty then you need to swivel the round semaphore sign to the vertical position. This signals to the crew that you want them to stop. When it's dark you need to use a torch to signal.

KAYAK & FISH

49 FJÄRDLÅNG

Trails criss-cross the island, with the highest point being 36m above sea level and offering great views from the cliffs. Kayaks, rowing boats and fishing equipment can all be hired. Grocery store on island.

59.0473, 18.5227

WILDLIFE & NATURE

50 ÖJA

Island at the southern tip of the archipelago. The main village and its lighthouse are known as Landsort. The flora and fauna are unlike anything elsewhere in the archipelago, including trees such as whitebeam and yew. On the coast footpath you'll discover coastal defences from over several centuries, a plague graveyard and a 3000-year-old stone labyrinth that the fishermen would walk for good luck before heading to sea.

58.7514, 17.8648

HISTORY & CULTURE

51 UTÖ

The northern part of Utö and the surrounding islands is a nature reserve. Close to the reserve is the old iron-ore mine of Gruvbyn, the start point for a cultural trail. The landscape is predominantly coniferous forest and pasture with a rocky shoreline. Around the old mine tailings it's possible to find iron pyrites, blue tourmaline and red garnets. The mining came to an end in 1879 to be replaced by forestry, and the main industry now is tourism. Bikes are available for hire. Grocery store on island.

58.9366, 18.2528

52 ORNÖ

Largest island in the southern archipelago. Good to explore by bikes, which can be hired. Forested and rocky with numerous lakes – the deepest is called Stunnträsk and is said to harbour organisms that have lived there since the last glaciation. There's a museum on the island and several ancient burial sites. Until 1997 this was a secret military area, and foreign citizens were not allowed access – there are still some prohibited areas, which are clearly marked. Kayaks can be hired. Grocery store on island.

59.0545, 18.4020

53 DALARÖ

Connected to the mainland via a bridge, the island of Dalarö has very strong maritime and military connections and is now a hub for travel in the archipelago. In the 19th century a popular resort developed, which was largely destroyed by fire in 1890 and has subsequently been redeveloped but many historical buildings remain. Although the western end of the island is very built up, the east is more rural. The smaller surrounding islands offer better wild camping.

59.1341, 18.4077

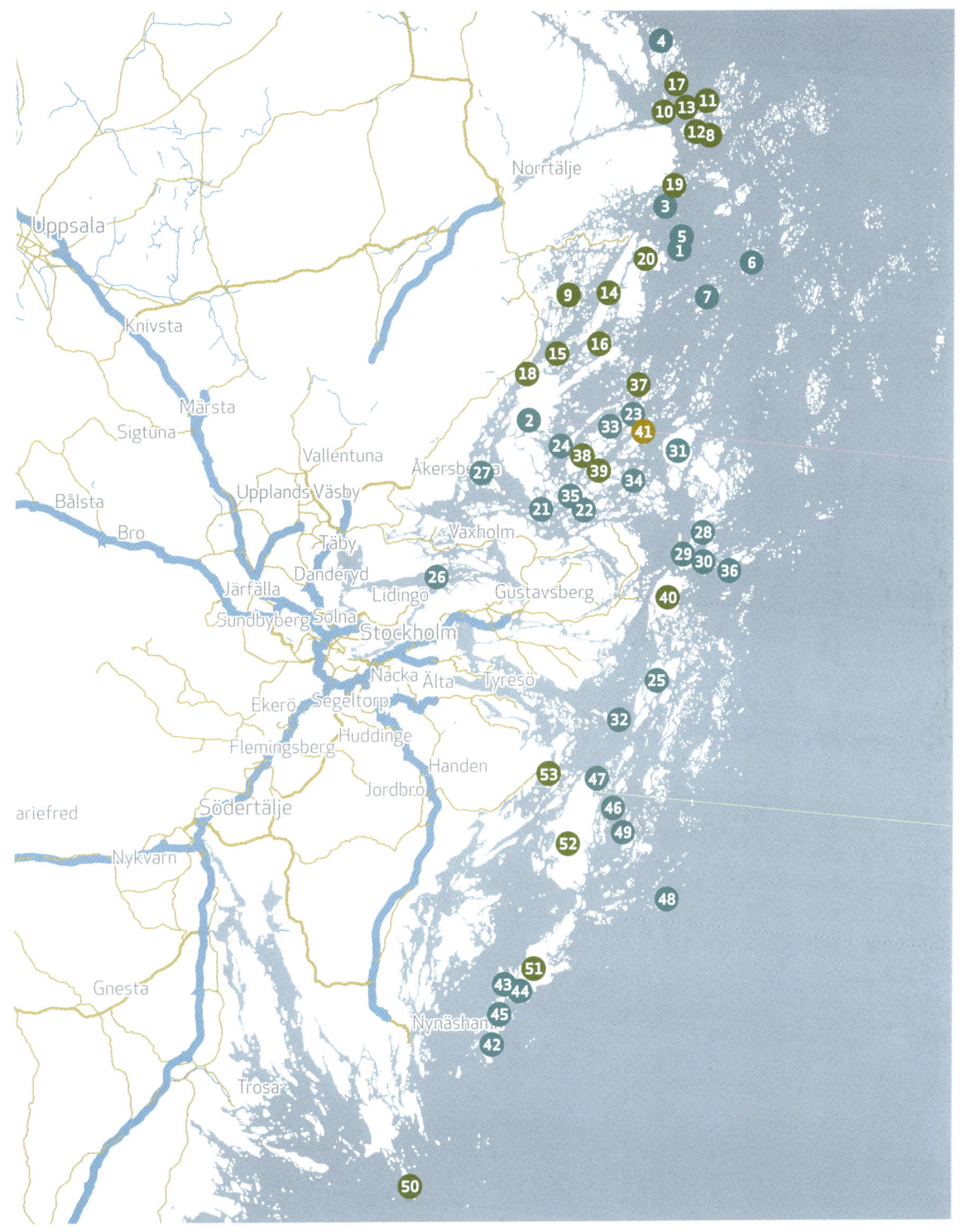

TJÖRN

Our perfect week

→ **Circumnavigate** a small island by kayak – there are plenty to choose from!

→ **Wild** camp on a remote skerry.

→ **Learn** how to pickle herring at Sillebua.

→ **Look** for trolls at Sankt Olovs Valar.

→ **Count** the steps on the path up to the viewpoint at Tjörnehuvud.

→ **Paddle** to a seafood restaurant.

→ **Search** for interesting finds amongst the driftwood on Toftö.

→ **Find** the herbs traditionally used to spice herring on Flatholmen.

→ **Dive** from a granite cliff at one of the many fantastic bathing spots.

→ **Taste** the Tjörnkagan local bread at Sundsby Säteri.

An impressive suspension bridge over the Stenungsund connects Tjörn to the mainland. It is Sweden's sixth-largest island, located in a labyrinthine archipelago of thousands of smaller islands and skerries just north of Gothenburg.

This is a coastal landscape that is best explored by kayak. No previous experience is necessary, as the waters are generally very sheltered and in most places you can easily hug the shore in shallow water. Join the seals in picking a route between the smooth granite boulders that characterise the shoreline. If you hire your boats and equipment from Kajaktiv (see 15) then you can be sure that you'll get exactly what you need as well as any necessary safety instruction and advice.

Paddle between the main islands just offshore and wild camp in spectacular locations. Camping on a small island with your tent pitched on warm flat granite is a unique experience. If you've not camped on rock before, it's simple – you can use small boulders to anchor the tent, and a geodesic design makes things much easier. Resupply at the small harbour villages or stop at the numerous eateries, which are often located directly on the quayside.

The villages on the main island can get quite busy during the summer, but if you head along the coast or out into the archipelago you'll find an abundance of idyllic retreats. Before heading off on your explorations, make time to visit the maritime and herring-pickling museums to get an idea of the historical importance of this area.

Although never far from the sea, inland you'll find wildflower meadows and an agricultural landscape dotted with remains from the Stone Age, Bronze Age and Viking period. From the heights of the ancient beacon at Vetteberget you can see as far as Denmark on a clear day.

Leave the trappings of 21st century life behind and arrange for the boat taxi to drop you off on a remote island for the night. Watch the boats sail by, forage for berries and dry off after swimming by lying on the warm rock. Bring a smörgåsbord of local seafood and enjoy it under a fiery sunset.

8

BEACHES & SEA SWIMMING

1 STOCKEVIK

Bathing area with a jetty, cliffs and diving board. In summer, swimming lessons for children are available.

→ From Skärhamn head S and take R at the sign to Stockevik. Follow road to the parking area beyond the jetty. Swimming spot is 300m further.

5 mins, 57.9598, 11.5478

2 RÖRA

Swim and dive from smooth granite rocks in the bay, or just lie in the sun. The rock stays warm long into the evening and is great for late picnics.

→ From route 723 at Kållekärr, turn N just by Statoil and follow the signs to Rörastrand, being sure to bear R when you first see the water. From the parking area it's a 300m walk.

5 mins, 58.0580, 11.6198

3 LILLA ASKERÖN

Small, sandy beach with a jetty and rocks to dive from. Great for small children.

→ Head over the Skåpesunds bridge from Tjörn to Orust. Turn R at the sign marked

Askeröarna. The bathing area can be seen on R after the first bridge; there is parking further along before the second bridge.

5 mins, 58.0871, 11.7192

4 KÅREVIK

Perfect place for teaching children to swim. Sandy, shallow beach with grassy areas to sit. Also a jetty and diving board for the more adventurous.

→ From Rönnäng, take Kyrkvägen, then turn R just after the church. Kåreviksvägen, 471 41 Rönnäng.

57.9341, 11.5915

5 TUBBEVIKEN

A couple of springboards and some steps back up from the steep granite. Perfect for an early morning swim.

→ In Skärhamn follow Hamngaten N then turn L onto Strandvägen and enclosed swimming area with parking.

5 mins, 57.9948, 11.5461

6 GRÅSKÄRSBADET

Sandy beach where you can swim out to a wooden boardwalk along the edge of a small granite cliff with a high-diving board. A jetty

forms a small lagoon, creating a great place for young children to play in.

→ Follow the signs from Hamngaten to the Nordiska Akvarellmuseet at the S end of Skärhamn. The bathing area is next to the museum.

57.9867, 11.5400

ISLANDS & KAYAKING

7 ÅSTOL

Very small (0.15km²) island south of Rönnäng with a working harbour mainly landing crayfish, crab and lobster. The island has a very strong connection with the fishing industry, and there's a memorial garden for fishermen lost at sea. Find a place along the shore to wild camp then stroll to the quayside to stock up on fresh seafood for a sunset smörgåsbord.

→ Ferry to Åstol leaves hourly from Rönnäng. 57.9224, 11.5848

8 KLÄDESHOLMEN

Two small islands, Klädesholmen and Koholmen, but known collectively as Klädesholmen. Despite their size (0.29km²) nearly half of all the pickled herring in Sweden originates from here. Traditionally

the herring was spiced according to a family recipe and then cured in tins or small barrels. Some of the companies here are now in their fifth generation. If you circumnavigate the islands by kayak you'll find several good sites to wild camp – or explore the labyrinth of surrounding skerries, as many have great hidden spots perfect for a single tent. Feast of course on pickled herring!

→ Klädesholmen is connected to Tjörn by a bridge on Route 169 to Bleket.
57.9487, 11.5457 🛶 🏃 ⛺ 🍴

9 STORA DYRÖN

Island of 0.24km² lying south-east of Rönnäng. The coastline is largely steep, smooth granite but with plenty of opportunities to wild camp. A 5km trail goes round the island, and you will likely meet the wild mouflon sheep that graze there. From the high ground there are fantastic views of Pater Noster, Marstrand and Åstol. On the west side of the island you'll find the remains of a Stone Age village and a Bronze Age cairn. Unlike the surrounding islands, the predominant industry here was farming, with the islanders only resorting to fishing when there was a poor harvest. The main village has a few small shops for provisions.

→ Ferry to Stora Dyrön leaves hourly from Rönnäng.
57.9301, 11.6128 🛶 🏃 ⛺ 🛶

10 TJÖRNEKALV

In Swedish a 'kalv' (calf) is the name given to a small island next to a big island. In this instance Tjörnekalv is 1.5km² and lies just off the coast of Tjörn at Rönnäng. Like many of the other islands in the area it was once very active in the fishing industry, and in the 18th century the islanders were employed in several salteries and herring oil boilers, now long gone. There are lots of great places to wild camp along the coastline with an abundance of berries and mushrooms for foraging – the island is home to over 245 different plant species.

→ Ferry to Tjörnekalv leaves hourly from Rönnäng.
57.9334, 11.5675 🛶 🏃 🛶

11 HÄRÖN

Island nature reserve of 7km² that is one of the best-preserved agricultural landscapes in Sweden. The majority of the land is still managed using traditional techniques. Camping is only allowed in signposted areas, and there are several marked trails

around the island. The seasonal Magasinet restaurant is a must for any seafood connoisseur – and you can even arrive there by kayak!

➜ There's a regular ferry service to Härön from Kyrkesund. Magasinet, 471 90 Kyrkesund, +46 304 664020. www.magasinetharon.com/engelska/ 58.0207, 11.5034 🛶🏊🏕🍴

12 STIGFJORDEN

Large area of shallow, sheltered water between the islands of Tjörn and Orust. Much of the area is a nature reserve, and in the spring and autumn it's an important feeding area for thousands of ducks, geese, swans and other waterfowl. With around 100 islands and skerries to explore by kayak, there are almost limitless opportunities for spectacular wild camping.

➜ On a map Stigfjorden is marked as the area almost entirely enclosed between Tjörn and Orust. 58.0773, 11.6062 🛶🏊🏕🐾

13 FLATHOLMEN

During the golden age of herring fishing this island had over 100 permanent residents. Now only a few people live there, and only during the summer months, and there is no mains electricity. The main island is 0.5km² and there are also numerous outlying skerries to explore, with plenty of opportunities to wild camp – mainly on smooth granite. You can find many of the herbs that were once used for spicing the herring – for example swallowwort, wild parsley, wormwood, viper's bugloss and creeping bellflower.

➜ Paddle out to Flatholmen from Stockevik. 57.9637, 11.5168 🛶🏊🏕🐾

14 TOFTÖ

Interesting island of 0.35km² lying just off Tjorn, north west of Skärhamn. The three deep bays on the west side of the island naturally collect flotsam and jetsam, and in hard times the islanders were said to deliberately lure ships onto the rocks here with false lights. When a storm was brewing many of the poor would pray to God to bless the shore with a wreck, which could provide very lucrative loot. See if you can find the spot where coastal fires were once lit – the traces of fire are still visible.

➜ There's a ferry service to Toftö from Skärhamn. 57.9958, 11.5288 🛶🏊📷

15 KAJAKTIV

Kayak hire for your explorations on the sea around Tjörn. The staff can advise you on what trips are best for complete beginners and make sure that you have a suitable boat and equipment. Instruction, safety briefings and guiding are also available. Paddlers with previous experience can get advice on more challenging trips.

→ Kajaktiv Tjörn, Bleketvägen 42, 471 96 Bleket, +46 72 2060767. www.kajaktivtjorn.se
57.9494, 11.5670 ⬛

16 BOAT TAXI

If you want to explore some of the islands without having to paddle yourself, you can book the boat taxi for up to eight people. They also offer day cruises and seal safaris. Perhaps arrange to be dropped off on a remote island for a night!

→ Tjörns Skärgårdsturer, St Olofs väg 3, 471 90 Kyrkesund, +46 733 411855. www.skargardsturer.se
58.0163, 11.5174 ⬛

HISTORY & CULTURE

17 PILANE GRAVFÄLT

Unusual mixture of the remains of Stone Age homesteads, Iron Age graves and modern sculptures, all set in undulating flower meadows. An interesting area to explore, with over 90 graves and rich meadow flora.

→ Follow signs to Kyrkesund from route 169. Go through Kållekärr and after 3km turn R at the roundabout. Follow the road for 4.5km and look for the sign for 'Pilane gravfält' on L.
15 mins, 58.0247, 11.5665 ⬛⬛

18 STYRDALEN DÖSEN

Fantastic dolmen, easy to find next to a small lane. Four uprights support the capstone to form a tiny square chamber. The capstone also has several cup marks.

→ Head north from Kållekärr for 2km then turn R (E) on a small gravel road dir Valla. The dolmen is on the S side of the road after 1.5km.
5 mins, 58.0361, 11.6946 ⬛

19 SJÖFARTSMUSEET

Small maritime museum that will help you understand the importance of Tjörn to Sweden's seafaring legacy.

→ Postvägen 26, 471 32 Skärhamn, +46 733 670677. www.deseglade.se
57.9900, 11.5468 ⬛

20 SILLEBUA

An old herring-pickling factory that now tells the story of the islands' most important industry and the golden period of production between 1860 and 1960.

→ Car park on R just before crossing from Koholmen to Klädesholmen. Walk on 200m to end of road and L to find museum. Sillgränd 8, 471 51 Klädesholmen, +46 304 673004. www.kladesholmen.com
5 mins, 57.9448, 11.5433 ⬛⬛

21 HAMNEBERGET

Viewpoint overlooking the harbour at Skärhamn. There's also a Bronze Age cairn, believed to be the grave of some important person from the area. This is signified by its vantage point, although the water level would have been much higher then.

→ Rocky outcrop with obvious water tower overlooking Skärhamn.
15 mins, 57.9918, 11.5507 ⬛⬛✝

22 TJÖRNEHUVUD

Headland with fantastic views over Marstrand, Åstol, Dyrön, Tjörnekalv and Klädesholmen. The path is steep and has lots of steps but is well worth the effort!

→ The signposted path starts at Hotel Bergabo, Kyrkvägen 22, 471 41 Rönnäng.
1 hour, 57.9343, 11.5807 ⬛⬛

23 SANKT OLOVS VALAR

On the hilltop south-east of the village of Kyrkesund is St Olaf's Beacon. Legend says the cairns are four trolls that were turned into stone by Olaf. Later canonised, he was King Olaf II of Norway from 1015–28. If you're not afraid of trolls, the views are fantastic.

→ From Kyrkesund walk up the rocky outcrop SE of the village towards the large radio mast.
30 mins, 58.0156, 11.5194 ⬛⬛✝⬛⬛

24 VETTEBERGET

The highest point on Tjörn – in good weather you can see Skagen in Denmark. At the top is a Bronze Age cairn where a knife and sword dating from around 1000 BC were excavated. During the Viking period there was a beacon located here to warn of approaching enemies. The path up is 2km, ascent 116m.

→ Follow route 169 dir Rönnäng. At the crossing with the road to Skärhamn and the Nordiska Akvarellmuseet, turn L onto the gravel road, Vetterbergsvägen. Follow to the parking area and signs for the walk.
45 mins, 57.9602, 11.6066 ✝⬛⬛

25 PATER NOSTER

Lighthouse on a group of islands far out in the archipelago. Returning seamen would pray for assistance in spotting a landmark they could recognise. These prayers would be said in Latin: "Pater Noster, qui est in caelis…" and so the islands got their name. The old lighthouse keeper's cottage is now a café and guesthouse.

→ Ferries for Pater Noster leave from Rönnäng. Kayaking here is only suitable for experienced paddlers.

57.8961, 11.4658

26 ÅSTOLS RÖKERI

Traditional island fish smokery famous for its seafood restaurant, shop and music. Guided tours are also available. Located on the quayside of the tiny island of Åstol, so you can arrive by kayak or take the ferry from Rönnäng.

→ Hamnen 4, 471 44 Åstol, +46 704 153495. www.astolsrokeri.se

57.9248, 11.5891

27 SUNDSBY SÄTERI

Old manor house owned by the community and now run as a café with kitchen garden. Try the Tjörnkagan local bread. The grounds are a fantastic wild playground for children and host numerous cultural events.

→ Sundsby Säteri, 471 73 Hjälteby, +46 304 666300. www.sundsbygardscafe.se

58.0701, 11.6889

28 SALT OCH SILL

Floating seafood restaurant and hotel with unique sea views. The kitchen sources its ingredients from local fishermen, whose boats you can see sailing by while you eat.

→ Klädesholmen, 471 51 Tjörn, +46 304 673480. www.saltosill.se

57.9500, 11.5495

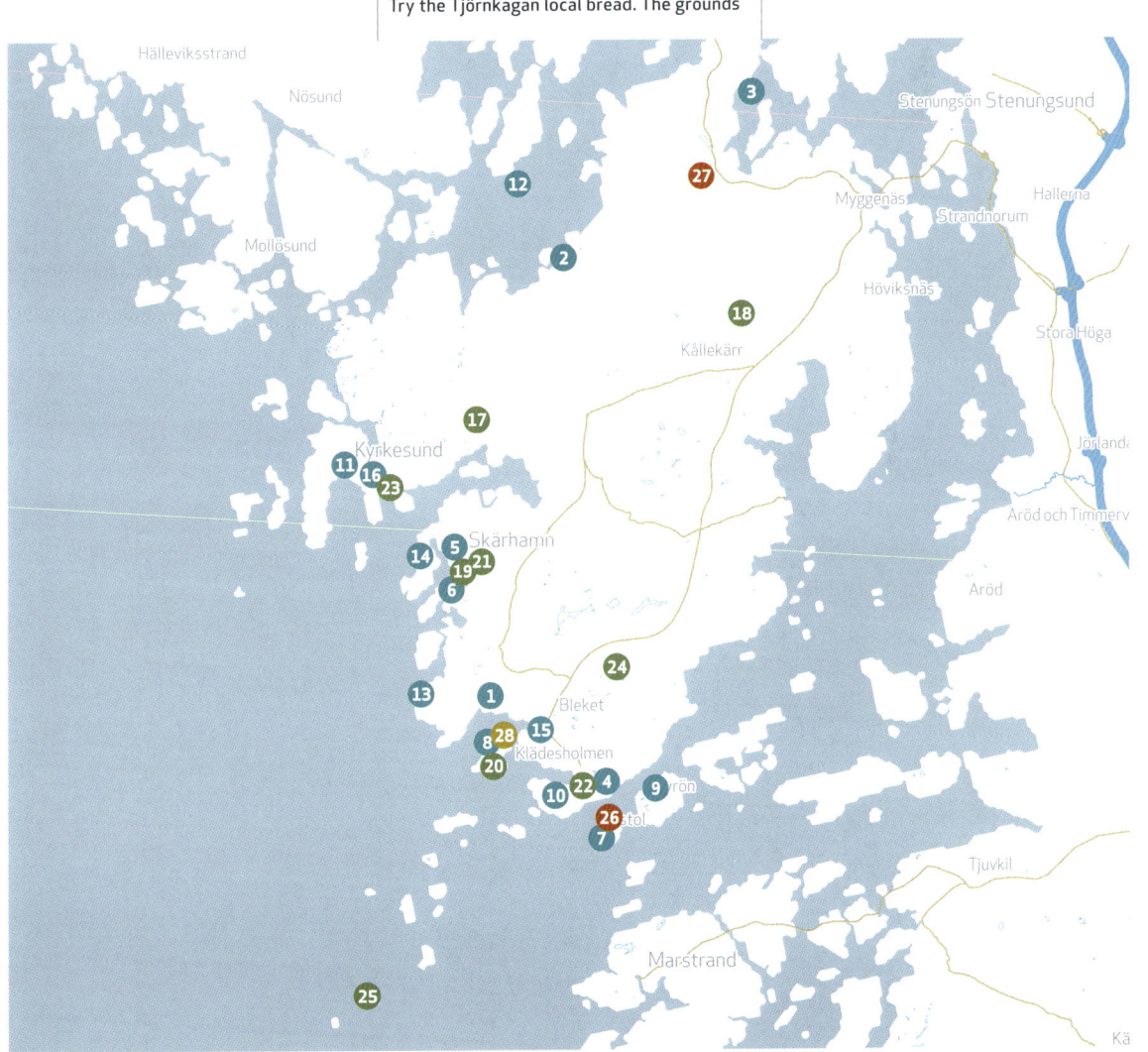

ÖSTERLEN

Our perfect week

→ **Watch** the sunset or sunrise while sitting against one of the 59 standing stones that make up the Ales Stenar stone ship.

→ **Choose** some fish straight from a boat in Simrishamn harbour to cook for dinner.

→ **Lie** on your back and watch a golden eagle soar overhead in Fyledalen.

→ **Gather** your thoughts gazing out to sea in the meditation space at Dag Hammarskjölds Backåkra.

→ **Take** a dip in the Priest's Bathtub.

→ **Examine** the rock carvings at Järrestads Hällristningar and ponder their significance.

→ **Find** as many tree species as you can at Kiviks Esperöds Arboretum.

→ **Skinny** dip on a remote stretch of beach (there's over 60km to choose from) and dry in the sun.

→ **Taste** the cider at Kiviks Musteri.

→ **Read** a *Wallander* book 'on location'.

This is the south eastern corner of Skåne (Scania) and a landscape packed full of colour and history. Yellow fields of rape with bright red poppies on the margins contrast against deep blue skies. Bronze and Stone Age rock carvings can be found in abundance, and on the slopes overlooking the sea at Kåseberga is a vast stone ship some believe to have been a type of sun calendar.

Perhaps the perfect way to see Österlen is to make a slow tour by bike. Start off heading east along the coast from Ystad. You can make frequent stops to swim in the Baltic from fine, white-sand beaches, and at the end of the day camp in the dunes, or maybe at an organic farm where you can cook over an open fire or even stay in an old circus wagon.

This area was once part of Denmark, and this is obvious as you pass through the villages with their small thatched cottages and occasional windmills. The farmland, apple orchards and small fishing harbours mean that if you stop to buy food it's unlikely to have travelled far to reach your plate. Seafood is of course a speciality in the region.

When you reach the end of the Österlen section of coastline, head back inland, stopping to visit the small waterfalls that characterise the wooded valleys you pass on the way. If you're a fan of Nordic Noir and Henning Mankell's *Wallander* novels, the places will be very familiar to you as names and filming locations for the television series. Rest your weary legs by finishing off with a tour of Ystad on a vintage fire engine, and have a few more locations pointed out.

On a hot day it's easy to imagine that you're by the Mediterranean in parts of Österlen, until you go for a swim to cool off – the Baltic is very good for that!

2

BEACHES

1 KNÄBÄCKSHUSEN BEACH

The original village of Knäbäckshusen was moved to its current location in the mid-1950s to make room for a firing range. A path takes you past the 17 original houses and over a small heath to a small wooden fishermen's chapel. From here a series of steps bring you down to a tree-fringed, sandy beach. A great place to cool off and swim on a hot day.

→ Park on Knäbäckshusen road in the village and follow the marked path to the beach.
25 mins, 55.6412, 14.2742

2 YSTADS SANDSKOG

Long white-sand beach on the outskirts of Ystad, fringed by pine forest and sand dunes. The trees were planted on the recommendation of famous botanist Carl Linnaeus who visited the town in 1749. Make your base here to explore the town or find your own spot in the dunes and go swimming.

→ Follow route 9 out of Ystad dir Simrishamn, and look for the signs for Ystads Sandskog on R as you leave town.
5 mins, 55.4357, 13.8985

3 PRÄSTENS BADKAR

Unusual circular formation on the beach known as The Priest's Bathtub, after a priest was said to have used it to take a bath – presumably a very austere and brief one! Most likely a "sand volcano" formed over 500 million years ago when the sea floor in this region was still seismically active.

→ Park on Häradsuddsvägen in Vik and then walk south along the beach.
20 mins, 55.6127, 14.2975

4 SANDHAMMAREN

Typical long and sandy Österlen beach that has often been described as one of Sweden's best. Named after the notorious sand bar lying off the coast, where many ships once ran aground. For this reason there are four lighthouses and a lifeboat station here, which date from the 19th century and are now open to visitors. The area also has Sweden's most southerly herd of elk. Great swimming.

→ Follow the coast road (Kustvägen) E from Kåseberga. Sandhammaren is signposted R after 7km.
5 mins, 55.3863, 14.1958

RESERVES & NATIONAL PARKS

5 KIVIKS ESPERÖDS ARBORETUM

An arboretum with the feel of a secret garden. Established by a sea captain in the 1920s in the grounds of a manor house, then abandoned and overgrown for many years until the present owner took over in 1985. There are over 3,000 trees from all around the world. Entrance is free of charge, and guided tours are available.

→ Signed turn off route 9 at the S end of Kivik, 400m on R at bend. Kiviks Esperöds Herrgård, 277 31 Kivik, +46 414 71261. www.kiviksesperodarboretet.se
5 minutes, 55.6782, 14.2399

6 HAVÄNG

Idyllic spot where the river Verkeån runs into the sea, and a great safe place for children to play in the warmer river water. The lime in the soil and the dry climate have together created one of Sweden's rarest habitats – sandy steppe. Overlooking the beach is Havängsdösen Neolithic stone circle, long hidden under the sand until uncovered during a severe storm in 1843.

→ Signed from route 9 5km N of Kivik. Park in the car park by the STF hostel and follow signs

to the beach. Skepparsgården, Haväng, 277 37 Kivik.

20 mins, 55.7244, 14.1926

7 FYLEDALEN

A biologically and geologically interesting valley that is now a nature reserve. Large numbers of birds of prey gather here: look out for kites, hawks, buzzards and golden eagles. Readers of the *Wallander* books will be familiar with the area, as it features in a few stories.

→ Take turn for Lyckås off route 19 just S of Tomelilla then follow Fyledalsvägen through the valley. R, signed Tomelilla, just before 5km has large area almost immediately on L to park and walk.

15 mins, 55.5474, 13.8680

8 CHRISTINEHOFS EKOPARK

Eco-park developed in the grounds of the 18th-century Christinehof stately home. The gardens often run activities such as tree climbing for children. You can follow the network of paths from the main house to Alunbruket, an old potash alum works. Potash alum was used for dyeing yarn, tanning hides and finishing the surface of paper for writing on. Refresh yourself at

Scania's oldest coffee house, enjoy their delicious salads or stay in one of the historic estate houses.

→ Signed from route 19, 13km S of Kivik. Entrance over cattle grid after 5km where road bends sharp L. Christinehofs Slott, 273 57 Brösarp, +46 417 26370. www.christinehofsekopark.se

55.7179, 13.9607

9 FRISEBODA NATURE RESERVE

Sparse pine forest running down through dunes to a fine sand beach. Plenty of space to find somewhere secluded to swim – the southern section is an unofficial naturist area. There are several small trails leading along the coast, but no marked paths. From the parking area it's a short walk to the sea. The cottages along the beach were originally used by eel fishermen.

→ Between Brösarp and Degeberga on route 19 look for signs E for 'Friseboda naturreservat och strövområde'.

20 mins, 55.8088, 14.2066

10 STENSHUVUD NATIONAL PARK

National park with 386 hectares of broadleaf forest, heath and sand flats, overlooked by the 97m-high headland of Stenshuvud. From

its summit you can see the Danish island of Bornholm far out in the Baltic. As well as the most diverse array of animal species in a Swedish national park, there are also several Stone and Bronze Age monuments. Follow one of the marked trails through the park and finish with a swim from the long sand beach.

→ Signed from route 9 S of Kivik. Stenshuvuds Nationalpark, 277 35 Kivik, +46 414 70882. www.stenshuvud.se

55.6560, 14.2685 🅿️🍽️🐕🔆🌳♿️

11 HALLAMÖLLA

Scania's highest waterfalls have a combined drop of about 23m. Alongside the falls is an old water mill dating back to the 15th century, which is still operated by volunteers on Sundays during the summer. Take a refreshing dip in the water below the bottom pool and you may well find yourself being watched by a kingfisher.

→ From route 19 take turning for Christinehofs Slott. After 2km, Hallamölla is signed R. Hallamölla, 273 01 Tomelilla, +46 414 91071.

55.7082, 14.0180 🅿️🏊♿️

12 STRÄNTEMÖLLA NATURRESERVAT

Nature reserve in the magnificent hilly landscape south of Rörum. The stream here has cut down into the bedrock and formed a series of spectacular small waterfalls. Sträntemölla mill is one of the oldest watermills in the country and was working until the 1960s. The mill pond and infrastructure are still in place. The wooded valley also has a rich variety of flora and fauna, and the sign board in the car park has maps for several walks along the stream.

→ From Rörum take the road signed Vemmerlöv. Parking on R after 1km.

20 mins, 55.6196, 14.2332 🚶🐕♿️

PEDAL POWER

13 FYLEDALEN DRESSIN

The draisine is a pedal-powered rail vehicle originally used by railway workers. Hire one in Tomelilla for a 19km (return) journey exploring a section of disused railway line along the Fyledalen valley. Expect to burn some calories, so bring along a substantial picnic! The trip starts and finishes at a level crossing by the Folkhögskolan (college) in Tomelilla.

→ Äventyr på Österlen, Stafettgatan 2, 273 35 Tomelilla, +46 417 10252. www.dressin.se

4 hours round trip, 55.5518, 13.9386 🚗🚲🔽

14 RAVLUNDA CYKEL

Bicycle hire serving the entire Österlen area. They have a huge selection of bikes and accessories, including both traditional and mountain bikes, tandems and children's bikes, trailers and seats. If you are planning to tour the area by bike, they can arrange to meet you at your start and finish points and advise you on the best choice of routes. For day trips they can also provide a picnic basket of local food.

→ Vitabyvägen 9, 277 37 Kivik, +46 73 9720548, www.ravlundacykel.se
55.7119, 14.1528 ▶🚲🔽

SACRED & ANCIENT

15 ALES STENAR

Sweden's largest stone ship, believed to date from about AD 600. Situated high on a ridge overlooking the Baltic, this fascinating monument consists of 59 raised stone blocks, and is an impressive 67m long and 19m wide. The function of the site is still under debate: it is generally regarded as a burial monument, but some believe that, like Stonehenge, it functioned as a sun calendar. The sun sets at the northwest point at summer solstice, and rises at the opposite tip during the winter solstice, making it a special place to watch the sunrise or sunset, especially at a solstice.

→ From the coast road (Kustvägen) E of Ystad turn S for Kåseberga and park at football field immediately on R. The path to Ales Stenar is signposted.
30 mins, 55.3825, 14.0547 🏞️✝️

16 HORSAHALLEN HÄLLRISTNINGAR

A mixture of rock carvings and standing stones concentrated in a small area overlooking the sea on the outskirts of Simrishamn. The site was also once a quarry and around 250 carvings now remain; 50 of them are of axes, the rest mainly a mixture of ships, wheeled crosses, cup marks, people, weapons and animals. They are believed to be connected to a Bronze Age worship of the passage of the sun.

→ Just off Branteviksvägen on the outskirts of Simrishamn. Heading S, look for a parking area L and a wide, signed path to the site R.
5 mins, 55.5368, 14.3544 ✝️

17 BRAGESTENARNA HÄLLRISTNINGAR

Small rock-carving site just south of Gislöv village, located in a rich prehistoric landscape. The symbols can be difficult

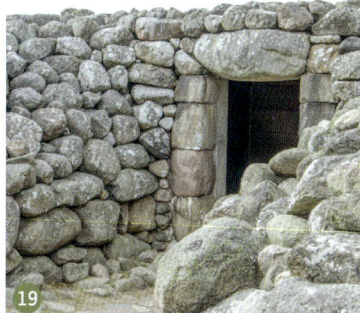

to make out in midday sun so a visit when the light slants low across the stones is recommended.

→ Head out of Gislöv S towards Skillinge. Once out of the village take the first turning L and the site is immediately on L.
5 mins, 55.5017, 14.2965 ⚰

18 JÄRRESTADS HÄLLRISTNINGAR

Skåne's most figure-rich Bronze Age rock carving, a large, polished granite slab decorated with over 550 images and 700 cup marks. The main figure is in the shape of a stylised bird, and is known as The Dancer. This is a very special place, in a quiet and rural location where you can also wild camp.

→ From Järrestad head N dir Gladsax on Vilhelmsbergsvägen. About 1km after crossing the railway, look for an unmarked track L. It's advisable to check the exact location on a map.
5 mins, 55.5502, 14.2791 ⚰⛰

19 KUNGAGRAVEN

Bronze Age tomb known as The King's Grave. Until 1748, stone from the site was taken for building, but two farmers then came across the burial chamber and dug it out – it's claimed they found a significant amount of treasure. The outside of the tomb has since been reconstructed, and you can enter the burial chamber, which has a stone coffin decorated with carvings of ships, horses and people. The tomb is in the garden of a café and has a small entrance charge.

→ Park in front of the Sågmöllan café. Bredarörsvägen 18, 277 30 Kivik, +46 70 6328829. www.kiviksgraven.se
55.6826, 14.2340 ⚰⛰

HISTORY & CULTURE

20 YSTAD WALLANDER TOUR

A guided tour of Ystad on a vintage fire truck. Fans of Henning Mankell's *Wallander* series will enjoy this tour of the locations featured in the books and films. Even if you've never read the books or seen the screen versions it is still an informative and unusual tour of the town, and children will love the fire truck.

→ Starts at Stortorget, but book through Ystad Tourist Office: St Knuts torg, 271 43 Ystad, +46 411 577681.
55.4296, 13.8199

21 DAG HAMMARSKJÖLDS BACKÅKRA

Summer residence of former head of the UN and Nobel Prize winner Dag Hammarskjöld, who was killed in a plane crash in September 1961. The farm is now a museum of his peace work. Situated in a secluded location overlooking the sea is a meditation space where you can gather your thoughts and enjoy the view. The rock inside the circle has the inscription PAX (peace).

→ Follow the coast road (Kustvägen) E from Kåseberga. Signposted R after 5km. Backåkravägen 73, 271 77 Löderup, +46 411 526010.

5 mins, 55.3885, 14.1309 ▣▣

22 GLIMMINGEHUS

Best-preserved medieval stronghold in Scandinavia, built at the beginning of the 16th century when the area formed a vital part of the Kingdom of Denmark. It is now a living museum of the Middle Ages with a variety of historical events and exhibitions taking place throughout the year. Children will love exploring the many defensive arrangements, which include false doors, dead-end corridors and a variety of death traps.

→ Signed from road 1km N of Glivarp village. 276 56 Hammenhög, +46 414 18620.

55.5010, 14.2309 ▣▣

23 LINDGRENS LÄNGA

A former forester's home that's been restored to house a museum where you can learn about the nature and culture of the Haväng area. A visit will help you to understand more of what you come across during your own explorations. In the area around the museum there are lots of standing stones.

→ Follow sign for Haväng from route 9 by Ravlunda and look for half-timbered, thatched house on L after 2km. Haväng, 277 37 Kivik, +46 414 74016. www.havangsmuseiforening.se

10 mins, 55.7200, 14.1895 ▣

24 SJÖRÄDDNINGS MUSEET

Lifeboat museum located in the old lifeboat station on the quay in Kåseberga. Learn about the perilous history of local seafarers and fishermen.

→ Follow Ales väg to the harbour. Kåseberga, 271 78 Löderup, +46 411 527009. www.sjoraddningsmuseet.se

55.3837, 14.0635 ▣▣

SLOW FOOD

25 KÅSEBERGA FISK AB

Fish smokery by the harbour in the tiny fishing village of Kåseberga. Local herring and Norwegian salmon are smoked in the traditional style using alder wood chips. Make some selections for a picnic and walk from here to Ales Stenar (25 mins, signposted, see 15) to watch the sun set.

→ Ales väg 34, 271 78 Löderup, +46 411 527180. www.kasebergafisk.se

55.3828, 14.0615 ▮▮

26 FISH FROM THE BOATS

Simrishamn is Sweden's largest fishing harbour in terms of the weight of fish landed. During the summer you can buy a variety of fresh fish direct from the small local boats. There will be a sign with days and times by the tourist information office, which is in the Marine Centre on the quayside.

→ Tourist Information Centre, Marint Centrum, Varvsgatan 2, 272 36, +46 414 819800.

55.5564, 14.3560 ▮▮

27 TÅNGDALA LÖNNKROG

Pizzeria in the garden of local artist Peter Ohman. The wood-fired oven started life as part of an art installation and is now a popular summer eatery. The wild garden is furnished with a quirky collection of furniture and the atmosphere and the food are both rather special. Call first to check when it's open.

→ Svinaberga 138, 277 35 Kivik, +46 414 24646.

55.6437, 14.2252 ▮▮

28 KIVIKS MUSTERI

Fruit and cider farm established in 1888, growing apples and a variety of berries to make cider, juice and other produce. Join a guided tour of the orchards and museum to learn about the history of cider making in the region. The shop sells many different varieties of cider and juice – perfect refreshments to add to your picnic hamper as you continue your explorations along the coast.

→ Karakåsvägen 45, 277 35 Kivik, +46 414 71900. www.kiviksmusteri.se

55.6740, 14.2658 ▮▮

29 NINNIS TRÄDGÅRD

Organic permaculture garden offering accommodation in a single cabin for two or a camping place in the garden, with the opportunity to cook food over an open fire. Fresh vegetables and eggs are available throughout the summer. A great base from which to explore the area.

→ Gladsaxvägen 21, Baskemölla, 272 94 Simrishamn, +46 414 26116. Ninnistradgard.blogspot.com
55.5902, 14.3108

30 KÖRSBÄRSGÅRDEN B&B

Peaceful bed and breakfast on a small farm surrounded by wildflower meadows. Guests also have access to a kitchen, lounge and sauna.

→ Eskerödsvägen 188, 297 95 Degeberga, +46 443 51544. www.korsbarsgarden.com
55.7930, 14.1181

31 ECOTOPIA

Alternative centre offering a variety of courses in sustainability and self-sufficiency. Accommodation is in a variety of small eco cabins and they welcome guests staying for more than one night to move and try another.

→ Ecotopia på Österlen, Bondrum 1334, 273 92 Skåne Tranås, +46 417 23034. www.ecotopia.se
55.6654, 14.0330

32 OLD CIRCUS WAGON

An old wooden circus touring wagon tastefully converted into self-catering accommodation. Located rurally in the little village of Östra Hoby, with a windmill as the closest neighbour and surrounded by fruit trees.

→ Östra Hoby, 27636 Borrby, +46 761 262932. www.millnwagon.com
55.4690, 14.2379

ICELAND

SOUTH WEST ICELAND & REYKJAVÍK

Our perfect week

→ **Hike** up a steaming valley and swim in the river that flows down it.

→ **Watch** a geyser spout boiling water 40 metres up into the air.

→ **Swim** between two continental plates at Þingvellir National Park.

→ **Visit** an abandoned and reputedly haunted fishing village.

→ **Bake** bread in lava from a 1973 eruption on Heimaey.

→ **Learn** about early settlers in the Reykjavík settlement museum and the National Museum.

→ **Sneak** through a crack in a cliff and stand under a waterfall at Gljúfrafoss.

→ **Walk** behind the curtain of falling water at Seljalandsfoss.

→ **Soak** in a secret pool surrounded by mountains.

→ **Warm** your tired feet after a day of walking in a footbath on the shore.

Following the path over the ridge, you pass some turquoise-blue circular pools, and the steam from them momentarily obscures the path. As it clears, you want to pinch yourself: before you is a lush green valley with the ochre-coloured rocks of a geothermal area at its head. Flowing down the middle of the valley, complete with pools and tiny rapids, is a stream with clouds of steam rising above it. This is Reykjadalur – the 'steamy valley' – and as you soak in one of its hot pools, you definitely won't want to leave.

Flying to Iceland will bring you to the main airport at Keflavík on the Reykjanes peninsula. Iceland (which has no military) was a founder member of NATO and until 2006 this airport was also a US naval airbase; the US Navy functioned as the Iceland Defence Force. Crossing the surrounding lava field on the 50km drive from here to Reykjavík, you might well be considering the possibility that you have landed by mistake on another planet. NASA obviously appreciated this landscape's potential: prior to the first manned mission to the moon, Neil Armstrong and Buzz Aldrin were sent to Iceland for training.

This chapter covers the entire south-west quadrant of Iceland, including the Reykjanes peninsula and the Vestmannaeyjar islands off the south coast. If your trip is a short one, then your explorations are likely to be centred on this area. With its hugely diverse and spectacular landscapes, along with fascinating stories associated with them, you'll always wish you had more time. Summer visitors are helped on that score as they can take advantage of 24-hour daylight.

If you want to see more of the country then Route 1, a ring road around the entire country, will take you through all the other areas in this book. Branch off to coastal towns and villages, or head inland on summer roads up into the highlands. Wherever you choose to go, there's plenty to explore.

Get yourself copies of some of the Icelandic Sagas and immerse yourself in stories from a thousand years ago. There's nothing better to read while sitting in a hot spring, looking out over a landscape that has changed very little since then.

HOT SPRINGS

1 SELJAVELLIR

Nestled in a narrow valley below the infamous Eyjafjallajökull volcano, this is the oldest swimming pool in Iceland. It was built by members of a youth movement in 1923 at a time when the majority of Icelanders worked in the fishing industry but left school without ever learning to swim. The pool itself is set into the side of a mountain and although some hot water seeps from the rock face, the majority is piped in from a nearby spring. It is 25m by 10m, has a very basic changing room and is run by volunteers. There is no charge. Swim lengths in a very spectacular environment.

→ Turn off the R1 onto the R242 (63.5355, -19.6378) signposted Raufarfell. Keep driving until the end of the road to find a parking area. Ignore the sign for Seljavellir. From the parking area walk on a rough path for approx 20 mins towards the bottom of the valley and the pool will come into view.

20 mins, 63.5592, -19.6224

2 BORHOLA KERLINGAFJÖLLUM

Hot pool on the edge of a river in a remote valley location. The water comes from a borehole originally drilled as a heating source for the neighbouring Kerlingarfjöll Mountain Resort. The various accommodation options include camping, if you want to stay. In English, Kerlingarfjöll is 'Woman's Mountain' and according to local legend it was once a female troll.

→ Starting at Laugarvatn (64.2153, -20.7317) travel NE on the R37 for 25km until the road meets the R35. Turn L onto the R35 (becomes the F35) and travel for a further 70km. Take a R turn onto the F347, continuing for approx 8km until the road stops at the resort. Pool is beside the river. +354 664 7000. www.kerlingarfjoll.is

64.6550, -19.2753

3 HVERAVELLIR

Riverside hot pool in one of Iceland's best-known geothermal areas with numerous beautiful springs and Martian-like volcanic features. The 18th-century Icelandic outlaw Fjalla-Eyvindur fled here to live in the wilderness with his wife, reputedly cooking food in the boiling water. There are various facilities in the immediate area, including a hut by the pool.

→ Starting at Laugarbraut (64.2153, -20.7317) travel NE on the R37 for 25km until the road meets the R35. Turn L onto the R35 (becomes the F35) and continue for a further 90km. Turn L onto the F735, Hveravellir is signed from here.

10 mins, 64.8660, -19.5534

4 GEYSIR

Geothermal area where you'll see several spouting hot springs including the world-famous Geysir, which lends its name to the English word for this phenomenon. It once spouted to a height of around 60m but is currently not very active. The nearby Strokkur is far more obliging and regularly reaches a height of around 40m, erupting at roughly 10-minute intervals. The visitor centre has lots of interesting information about the history and geology of the area.

→ Starting at Laugarbraut (64.2153, -20.7317) travel NE on the R37 for 25km until the road meets the R35. Turn L onto the R35 and continue for a further 5.5km until you reach the Hótel Geysir (64.3101, -20.2997). Take the next L, the F333, and find Geysir on L 300m up this road.

5 mins, 64.3139, -20.2995

5 MARTEINSLAUG

Small spring that can accommodate 3–5

people. Very close to Geysir (see above) for those who prefer watching boiling water spout while soaking at a considerably safer water temperature. Try not to move around too much: the bottom is muddy and algae can make it quite slippery. The water temperature varies from 39–43°C depending on where you are in the pool.

➜ As for Geysir, but continue on the F333 for a further 1.5km and then park by the church. Walk 100m E into the Sældarskora valley and find the spring by the stream.
10 mins, 64.3269, -20.2824

6 KÚALAUG

Small rectangular pool framed by lush green vegetation, and about 1km from Marteinslaug so you can combine the two.

➜ As for Marteinslaug (see 5) but turn L immediately before the church. Continue for another 1,500m then after crossing a bridge, park by a turning to the R. From here, walk 100m SE. For precise location consult a local map.
10 mins, 64.3286, -20.2720

7 LAUGARVATN FONTANA

Spa built over a natural hot spring on the shore of Laugarvatn lake. Relax in a variety of steam rooms and pools of different temperatures then jump into the lake to cool off. In the steam rooms you can hear and smell the water boiling in the spring below. Unique, with a very natural feel and the added bonus of fantastic views across the lake. Try the geothermally baked rye bread in the café.

➜ Hverabraut 1, 840 Laugarvatn, +354 486 1400. www.fontana.is
64.2153, -20.7317

8 VÍGðALAUG

Just before the hot stream runs into Laugarvatn lake, you'll find this small rock-ringed pool. Legend says that when Iceland converted to Christianity in the year 1000, the chieftains from the north demanded to be baptised in the cold water of the old parliament at Þingvellir but were brought to this hot pool instead.

➜ Located on the shore of the lake in the small town of Laugarvatn (60km E of Reykjavik) and close to Laugarvatn Fontana (see 7).
64.2162, -20.7315

9 REYKJADALUR

Hot stream running through the lush green Reykjadalur, which means 'steamy valley' and is a very accurate description of what

to expect. The further upstream you walk, the hotter the water gets and there are numerous pools where people have built small dams with rocks. When the path crosses the stream you'll see some turquoise hot pools, but these are too hot for bathing. A truly fantastical experience.

→ Turn off the R1 at Hveragerði (63.9952, -21.1930) and follow the Breiðamörk road until the car park at the end. Park here and follow the obvious path for approx 3km to Reykjadalur.
40 mins, 64.0321, -21.2156

10 KRÝSUVÍK

Geothermal area where the sulphur-rich,ochre-coloured earth makes a striking contrast with turquoise-blue boiling water. The water here is too hot for swimming but the landscape is full of volcanic features, including mudpots and steaming vents. Keep to the marked path and follow the safety instructions.

→ Start at Grindavik town (63.8418, -22.4374), travel 23km E on the R427, then turn L onto the F42. Carry on for 6km to the parking area. The pools are just off the road to R.
5 mins, 63.8947, -22.0512

11 SKÁTALAUG

Hot but slightly muddy pool fed by a pipe from a nearby spring and set in a moorland landscape. The temperature is around 34°C. Big enough to accommodate lots of people although there's nowhere to change. Not far from the road, so perfect if you need a break from driving.

→ Follow directions for Krýsuvík (see 10) but carry on for a further 1km to find the pool off the road to the L
10 mins, 63.9039, -22.0432

12 KVIKA

Created by the artist Ólöf Nordal, this small pool on the outskirts of Reykjavík is intended to be a place where local people can relax and unwind. Known in English as the 'Foot Bath', it accommodates just one person, but you're meant to sit around it warming your feet. Perfect after a day of hiking.

→ Located approx 10km from the centre of Reykjavik. Take the R49 NW out of town, then turn L onto Eiðsgrandi, continuing until you reach the end of the headland.
5 mins, 64.1624, -22.0084

13 HVALFJARÐARLAUG

Small and cosy stone-built hot tub on the shore next to a steaming stream with views across Hvalfjörður. The hot water is fed into the tub via a hose from a spring. By moving the hose in or out of the water you can regulate the temperature. Nice place for a picnic.

→ Approx 30km NE of Reykjavík. Take the R1 and after 25km turn R onto the R47 for a further 20km. Turn L when you get to Hvammsvík and find the tub on the E-facing coast near the end of the headland.

5 mins, 64.3737, -21.5639 ⬛🖼

14 ENGLANDSHVERIR

Large pool in the Lundareykjadalur valley fed by a small hot spring. Although situated close to a road, it's hidden from view. You can also swim beneath the bridge in the main Tunguá river, but it's not as warm.

→ Starting at the village of Kleppjárnsreykir (64.6562, -21.4034), Head SW on the R50 for 13.5km. Turn L onto the R52 and continue for a further 23km. Park by the hut beside the river. The pool is about 50m from the hut on the other side of the river.

64.4921, -21.1769 ⬛

15 KROSSLAUG

Small yet very cosy pool that can accommodate 4–5 people. The water is reputed to have healing powers and the temperature is 42°C. Beautiful surroundings in a small plantation.

→ 1.8km NW of Englandshverir (see 14) along the R52. Park in the layby to R of the road and follow the path through the metal gate.

50m, 64.4947, -21.1753 ⬛✝

16 SNORRALAUG

Reykholt was the home of Snorri Sturluson, a 12th-century Icelandic poet and politician, and this was his pool – hence its name. In his writings, Sturluson described bathing in his pool, which he accessed from his house via a tunnel ending in an external door in the bank. The pool itself is circular and lined with stone. Fed by a spring, the temperature fluctuates so do check before jumping in. If you can read Icelandic, don't miss the library here with a collection of Sturluson's work. Soak and imagine life back in the Middle Ages.

→ From village of Kleppjárnsreykir (64.6562, -21.4034), head N on the R50 for 0.5km, then turn R onto the R518 and continue E for 5km. The spring is in the small village of Reykholt.

64.6640, -21.2911 ⬛🚻

17 BLUE LAGOON

A name synonymous with Iceland and one of its top tourist attractions. The Blue Lagoon, an overspill pool for a geothermal power station, has been transformed into a world-famous spa facility. When sea water that has been naturally heated 2,000m underground surfaces here, it's rich in minerals and a distinctive milky-blue colour. The silica mud at the bottom of the pool has proven skin benefits and can be used as a face pack. Onsite hotel and the usual spa treatments, but book in advance if you plan to visit.

➔ Signposted off the R43, 3.5km N of Grindavík. +354 420 8800. www.bluelagoon.com

63.8798, -22.4481

18 BRIMKETILL

'Surf kettle' is the rough translation, and it's apt for a pool that has been sculpted out of the lava coast by the action of the waves. Legend says that it was once regularly occupied by a female troll called Oddný, when it was known as Oddnýjarlaug (the Pool of Oddný). You won't be sharing the pool with a troll but don't bet on a balmy seashore soak as the temperature is not very reliable. A beautiful feature nevertheless, and well worth a visit.

➔ On the R425 10km W of Grindavík, find a track (63.8213, -22.6023) on the seaward side of the road. Pull in here and a small wooden sign set back from the road indicates the direction to walk. Approx 250m.

10 mins, 63.8192, -22.6031

19 GUNNUHVER

Geothermal area that's far too hot for bathing, but home to Iceland's biggest and boiling mud pot with an impressive diameter of 20m. Legend says that it's named after a female ghost who haunted the place 400 years ago until the local priest tricked her into falling into the spring. There are viewing platforms from where you can look down at the gurgling and steaming mud.

➔ Follow the R425 W from Grindavík for 13km to the junction with the Gunnuhver road on L. Continue along this heading SW for 1.5km and you'll see (and smell) the geothermal area on your right. Car park beside the road.

5 mins, 63.8185, -22.6862

20 GAMLA LAUGIN

Large pool built in 1891 that served as the local baths and where local women would once have washed clothes. The hot water is drawn from a geothermal spring and has a

21

perfect temperature of 38–40°C. Between
1909 and 1947 swimming lessons were also
held here until a new pool was built close by
in Flúðir village, and the old pool was then
largely forgotten. Restored very recently,
the pool retains a very natural feel with a
small adjacent geyser erupting on cue every
five minutes. Changing rooms with showers
and an eating area have been added, and
although modern they are discreet. Its
English name is the 'Secret Lagoon'.

➜ 0.5 km from Flúðir. Hvammsvegur, 845
Flúðir, +354 861 0237. www.secretlagoon.is
64.1378, -20.3099 🄿🄿🄿

21 HRUNALAUG

Very beautiful natural hot spring located
in a lush green gully with a stone-walled
pool and the remains of an old stone
shed. Unfortunately this very small and
special site on private land has received an
unsustainable number of visitors in recent
years, so at some point access may need
to be restricted. Please, before visiting,
research the current situation online
and once there, pay heed to any signs,
particularly about not camping.

➜ From the junction of the R344 and
R345 just NE of Flúðir, follow the R345

(Kaldbaksvegur) and take the next L turn.
Continue for 400m and park just past the
cattle grid in a small parking area (64.1340,
-20.2571) then follow obvious 150m path to
the spring.
5 mins, 64.1328, -20.2551 🄿

22 STRÚTSLAUG

Also known as Holmsarbotnalaug, this is
a geothermal pool in the South Highlands,
north of Mýrdalsjökull glacier and close to
the Torfajökull glacier volcano. The pool
itself is located next to a cold-water river
and you can easily jump between the two. It
is advisable not to move around too much
in the pool itself or you'll stir up the muddy
bottom. There are no facilities here, but
you're surrounded by green meadows with
plenty of flat areas for wild camping. The
perfect place if you want to soak in solitude.

➜ Drive 20km SW from Kirkjubæjarklaustur
on the R1, turn R onto the F208, then L onto
the F210 for a further 35km. The spring is
located approx 7km NW off the road; for a
precise location consult a local map.
1 hour, 63.8703, -18.9461 🄿🄿

23 LANDMANNALAUGAR

Follow a wooden boardwalk, which brings
you to a platform by a steaming pool. From
here you swim in the pool towards the point
where the hot water emerges from beneath
the lava. Once you have found a spot with
a temperature you find comfortable, relax
and enjoy the hot water, which is reputed
to have various healing properties. Lockers
and changing rooms on site. This is also a
starting point for the Laugavegur hiking trail
and during the main tourist season it can be
quite busy. If you plan to do any hiking, buy a
local map which will also show you where the
mountain huts are en-route. Try to visit early
in the morning or later at night before other
visitors arrive.

➜ Head SW from Kirkjubæjarklaustur on
the R1 for 20km, then turn L onto the F208.
After a further 55km, turn L onto the F224 for
1.5km. The springs are signposted and a little
further on, before the road ends, you'll come
to the Brenisteinsalda campsite.
15 mins, 63.9923, -19.0596 🄿

WATERFALLS

24 GULLFOSS

Spectacular waterfall on the mighty Hvítá

river, which plunges 32m over two successive drops into a deep crevice. Seen from a distance, you're under the illusion that the river simply disappears into the ground.

→ From the Hôtel Geysir (see 4) on the R35, turn off L onto the R35, continuing for 9 km until you see a R turn signposted to Gullfoss. Park at the Gullfoss Café (64.3260, -20.1316) and the waterfall is an easy 0.5km walk.

10 mins, 64.3274, -20.1214 Ⓥ

25 GLYMUR

Second highest waterfall in Iceland, dropping 198m into an extremely majestic, mossy green canyon. The hike in is also very special but can be quite demanding. Bring a map.

→ Turn off the R47 onto the R5001 (Litlibotn) at the head of Botnsvogur (64.3854, -21.3550) and follow it to the parking area 200m before the end of the road. From here it's a 2.5km walk along a choice of two trails which join just before the falls.

1 hour, 64.3910, -21.2520 Ⓥ ⛰ 🏔

26 HRAUNFOSSAR AND BARNAFOSS

Two very different waterfalls on the Hvítá river within shouting distance of each other. Barnafoss ('Children's Waterfall') rushes down where the river forces its way through

a narrow gorge. Downstream, Hraunfossar ('Lava Falls') emerges from under moss-covered lava along a 900m stretch of the riverbank and tumbles into the main river.

→ Starting at the junction of the R50 and R518 (64.6636, -21.3919) N of Kleppjárnsreykir, follow the R518 for 23km to find a car park on L. From here it's a very short walk to the viewing area.

5 mins, 64.7029, -20.9772 Ⓥ

27 SKÓGAFOSS

Breathtaking waterfall and one of Iceland's biggest with a drop of 60m and a width of 25m. Water thunders down over what was once a sea cliff, but there is now a 5km plain to cross below the falls before the Skógá river reaches the coast.

→ Head W from Kirkjubæjarklaustur on the R1 and after 100km you'll see a signpost N to Skógafoss (63.5200, -19.5087). From the parking area it's a 300m walk.

10 mins, 63.5321, -19.5116 Ⓥ

28 SELJALANDSFOSS

Walk behind the huge curtain of water at this fall, which plunges 60m over an undercut former sea cliff. A remarkable and very unusual perspective.

➜ From the junction of the R1 and R249 W of Holt, find a R turn after 700m and arrive at a car park. Waterfall is a 250m walk.
100m, 63.6154, -19.9883 🔽 🖼

29 GLJÚFRAFOSS

A short distance from Seljalandsfoss (see 28) the waterfall of Gljúfrabúi, literally 'the one who lives in the canyon' has drilled an extraordinary cylindrical chamber into the rock. You can climb inside, via a small crack in the outside cliff face, and enter the mossy chamber for a very special and personal audience with Gljúfrabúi.

➜ Follow directions for Seljalandsfoss (see 28) but continue on the R249 for a further 900m then turn R and park and walk 100m.
10 mins, 63.6208, -19.9859 🔽

30 SELATANGAR

This fishing village, first established in the Middle Ages but abandoned in the 19th century, is rumoured to be haunted. Explore the ruined homes made from 'bricks' hewn out of lava rock.

➜ From Grindavík take the R427 E for 13km then see a blue heritage sign on R signposted to Selatangar. 600m signposted walk.
15 mins, 63.8380, -22.2407 🚻

NATIONAL PARKS & HIKES

31 ÞINGVELLIR NATIONAL PARK

The first Icelandic parliament, the Althing, was established here and continued to be held as an open-air assembly from 930 until 1798. As well as its historical importance, the area is significant geologically as it lies in a rift valley at the crest of the Mid-Atlantic Ridge. The national park was founded in 1930 to celebrate the 1000th anniversary of the Althing and in 2004 it also became a World Heritage Site. The visitor centre has lots of information about the park and surrounding area, and there are numerous marked footpaths. Delve into Iceland's fascinating history in a truly magnificent landscape.

➜ Starting at the junction of the R1 and R36, just N of the town of Mosfellsbaer, travel 30km along the R36. Þingvellir is signed to the R.
64.2557, -21.1300 🚻 ♿ ➜

32 LAUGAVEGUR

Hiking trail that connects the nature reserves of Landmannalaugar and Þórsmörk, covering a distance of 55km. The journey over mixed terrain, passing canyons, volcanoes and glaciers, is very definitely a

unique experience and normally done over 4–5 days. Wild camping is not allowed on the protected reserves but accommodation is available in six huts along the route. The huts and trails are maintained by Ferðafélag Íslands (Iceland Touring Association) and details are on the website.

➔ Between Landmannalaugar (63.9923, -19.0596) and Þórsmörk (63.6912, -19.5392). Contact Ferðafélag Íslands to book huts: www.fi.is/en

4 days, 63.6912, -19.5392 🏠▼

33 SILFRA LAKE SNORKELLING

Silfra, on the edge of Þingvallavatn lake, is a water-filled fissure between the North American and Eurasian continental plates. It's possible to dive or snorkel along it and the underwater visibility is amazing – you can see up to 70m away. The water, which has a constant temperature of 2–4°C, originates from the Langjökull glacier and has taken 30–100 years to reach the lake. During this time it has filtered through 50km of porous lava rock – an unforgettable experience. 2km up the valley is the famous gorge of Fjaðrárgljúfur.

➔ Follow directions to Þingvellir National Park (see 31) and stop in the main parking area. It is a

short signposted walk from here. To book guided snorkelling or diving visit: www.dive.is

64.2553, -21.1169 🤿

34 MIÐLÍNA

Cross a bridge over the huge fissure marking the boundary between two continents – the same rift you can swim along at Silfra, (see 33). It's located in the middle of a vast lava field.

➔ From Sandvík head N on the R425. After 7km take signposted road on R leading to a car park. Walk 215m on a marked footpath.

5 mins, 63.8683, -22.6755 🥾

35 ÞJÓÐMINJASAFN ÍSLANDS

This is Iceland's National Museum where you'll find out much more about this fascinating country's history, from the time of the first settlers right up to the present day.

➔ Suðurgötu 41, 101 Reykjavík, +354 530 2200. www.nationalmuseum.is

64.1420, -21.9477 🏛️💚

36 LANDNÁMSSÝNINGIN

Compelling exhibition chronicling the settlement of Iceland by Vikings from

mainland Scandinavia. The centrepiece is an excavated 10th-century farmhouse with a collection of associated artefacts. All around the exhibition, computer graphics show how Reykjavík would have looked at the time the farm was occupied.

➔ Aðalstræti 16, 101 Reykjavík, +354 411 6370. www.reykjavikcitymuseum.is

64.1473, -21.9427 🏛️💚

37 VESTMANNAEYJAR

A spectacular group of islands, of which Heimaey is the largest, lying 12km off the

south coast of the mainland. Most of the islands have steep cliffs so it was traditional for the islanders to supplement their fishing catch by hunting seabirds and collecting eggs. In 1627 the islands were attacked by pirates working for the Ottoman Empire and many islanders from Heimaey were transported as slaves. As a result, a law was passed making it legal to kill any Turks found on Icelandic territory. No Turks were put to death, but when the continued existence of this law was discovered in the 1970s, it was quickly repealed.

→ Ferries to Vestmannaeyjar leave from Landeyjahöfn (63.5339, -20.1331). For ferry times and booking contact: +354 4812800. www.herjolfur.is
63.4377, -20.2673

38 SÓLHEIMASANDUR BEACH

Lying on a remote black-sand beach is the largely intact hulk of a US Navy DC-3 plane that crash landed (luckily with no casualties) in 1973, allegedly because it ran out of fuel. An unusual photo opportunity for your Iceland album.

→ From Vik travel W on the R1 for 25km to find a gravel layby with a track and cattle grid heading off towards the sea (63.4912, -19.3630). Follow track for 4km to the plane.
63.4591, -19.3648

FIRE & ICE

39 HEKLA

An active volcano (correctly known as a stratovolcano), Hekla last erupted in February 2000. Over the last millennium it produced around 8 cubic km of lava – one of the largest volumes from any volcano in the world.

→ From the R1 and R26 junction (63.8793, -20.5023), NW of Hella, take the R26 for 18km. See Hekla to the SE 4km away. If you want to get closer you will need a guide. www.mountainguides.is
63.9903, -19.6731

40 EYJAFJALLAJÖKULL

When it erupted in 2010, this volcano created chaos for air travellers and its name proved a major challenge for news presenters worldwide. The pronunciation is something like 'Eh-ya-fyat-la-yuh-cuttle'.

→ Off the R1, 40km W of Vik is an information centre (63.5430, -19.6679). The volcano is 12km N of here. If you want a closer look you will need a guide: www.mountainguides.is
63.6198, -19.5997

41 ELDFELL

A volcano that emerged from a fissure on Heimaey in the Vestmannaeyjar (see 37) and erupted in 1973, forcing the evacuation of the island for six months. The 'new' cone is 200m high and the residential areas that were covered in ash are known as the 'Pompeii of the North'. Visit the island museum to learn about the eruption and its effects – bread continues to be baked using the heat trapped under the solid lava.

→ In the Vestmannaeyjar 1.5km SE from where the ferry docks. (See 37 for ferry.)
63.4325, -20.2474

WILD FOOD

42 ÞRÍR FRAKKAR

Restaurant in Reykjavík serving traditional Icelandic food. This is where you should head if you want to try some of Iceland's more unusual foods such as puffin, auk, whale, reindeer, horse, or rotten shark.

→ Central Reykjavík: Baldursgata 14, 101 Reykjavík, +354 552 3939. www.3frakkar.com
64.1423, -21.9338

43 GRAENA KANNAN CAFÉ

Organic café located in a greenhouse in what is considered to be the world's oldest eco-village. Founded as a community in 1930 with the idea of giving individuals of various backgrounds the opportunity to work, live and socialise together. Many of the residents have special needs and as well as the café there is an organic bakery, creative art workshops, a guesthouse and several horticultural projects. Have a look around and learn about the interesting work done here.

→ Located on Route 354 approx 30km NE of Selfoss: Sólheimar, 801 Selfoss, +354 4804400. www.solheimar.is
64.0659, -20.6448

SLEEP WILD

44 VOLCANO HOTEL

One of the smallest hotels in Iceland, situated close to the Katla volcano and Mýrdalsjökull glacier. Handy stop if you're travelling around Iceland on Route 1. Guests can enjoy the house speciality – locally sourced Arctic char – for dinner (make sure you book in advance).

→ Located 11km W of Vik on Route 1. Ketilsstaðaskóli, 871 Vík, Mýrdal, +354 4861200. www.volcanohotel.is
63.4366, -19.1637

45 HAPPY CAMPERS

Rent a custom-built camper van designed for Icelandic roads. All the vehicles are as environmentally friendly as possible and for every vehicle they own, 2,000 trees are planted. Your package will include all you need to cook, eat, sleep and travel.

→ 7km E of Keflavík Airport: 21 Stapabraut, 260 Keflavík, +354 578 7860. www.happycampers.is
63.9705, -22.5095 🚐

46 HOTEL GLYMUR

Friendly hotel set in a spectacular location overlooking the Whale Fjord. A mixture of classic hotel accommodation and cabins with a hot tub on the veranda.

→ 25km E of Akranes: Hvalfjarðarsveit, 301 Saurbaer, +354 430 3100. www.hotelglymur.is
64.4139, -21.6311 🛏️🍴

47 HOTEL RANGÁ

Quirky hotel situated in the middle of nowhere by the Rangá river. Every room is themed after a continent and in the lobby is a real stuffed polar bear called Hrammur. The restaurant serves local specialities such as smoked puffin, lamb and wild salmon.

→ Located approx 9km E of Hella, just off Route 1: Suðurlandsvegur, 851 Hella, +354 487 5700. www.hotelranga.is
63.7805, -20.3014 🛏️🍴

48 FROST OG FUNI

Boutique hotel on the edge of the Varmá river in the steamy Hveragerði geothermal area. The slow food is sourced from local organic farms. Relax after dinner in one of the natural spring-fed hot tubs.

→ 40km E of Reykjavík on Route 1 in the town of Hveragerði: Hverhamar, 810 Hveragerði, +354 483 4959. www.frostogfuni.is
64.0060, -21.1839 🛏️🍴♨️

49 ÞAKGIL CAMPSITE

Amazing camping area in a flat valley bottom surrounded by spectacular jagged rock slopes. Eat your meals in a cave fitted with a wood-burning stove and lit by candles in wall-mounted holders. Basic cabins are also available. Well protected from the wind.

→ From Vik head E on Route 1 for 5km. Turn N onto Kerlingardalsvegur for 16km until the end of the road. Höfðabrekkuafrétti, 871 Vík, +354 893 4889. www.thakgil.is
63.5302, -18.8881 🏕️🍴♨️🏔️

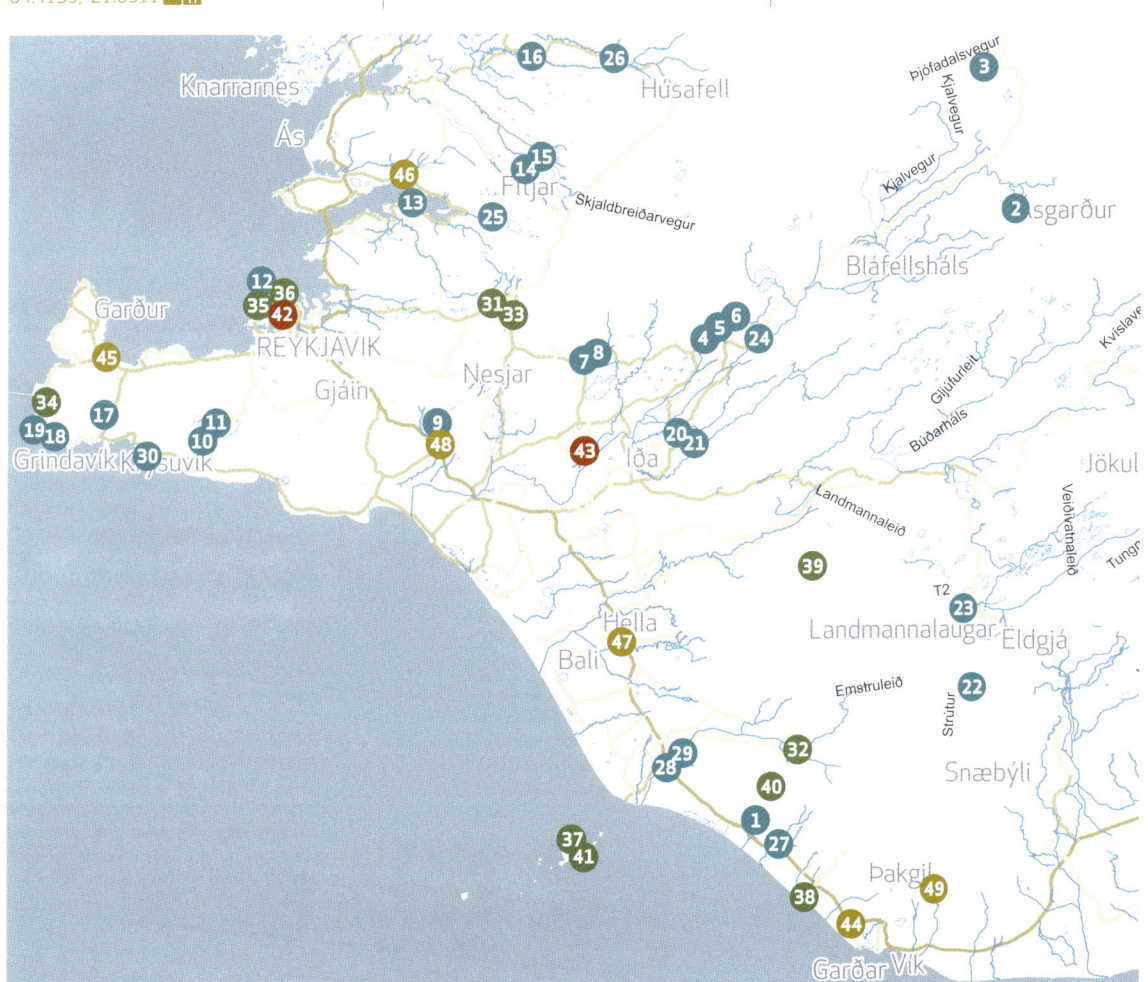

NORTH WEST ICELAND

Our perfect week

→ **Experience** the unique gait of the Icelandic ponies whilst on a trek into a remote valley.

→ **Get** chills up your spine at the sight of the necropants in the Witchcraft Museum.

→ **Find** out about Icelandic independence from Denmark at Hrafnseyri.

→ **Journey** to the centre of the earth with Jules Verne at Snæfellsjökull.

→ **Watch** for whales offshore and fish for dinner on your way back to Dalvík.

→ **Get** up close to an inquisitive puffin at the top of the Látrabjarg bird cliffs.

→ **Merge** with the mountains in the Hofsós infinity pool.

→ **Heal** yourself in the miraculous water of the Gvendarlaug hot spring.

→ **Learn** all about the Arctic Fox at the centre in Súðavík.

→ **Imagine** the stack of Hvítserkur as a troll or maybe a dragon… you decide.

Sitting in the warm water of the Hellulaug hot spring among the rocks on the foreshore, you gaze out along the rugged beach at tree trunks washed ashore after being carried out to sea off Siberia. It's well past midnight but the fiery red sky reflects off the sea to imbue everything with a warm glow. It's easy to imagine that a 10th-century Viking settler might well have enjoyed the very same experience.

The area defined in this guide as north west Iceland stretches from the Snæfellsnes Peninsula with its glacier-covered volcano to the area around the Skagafjörður bay, characterised by its many farms. In this rich agricultural area horses vastly outnumber humans.

In the far north-west is the especially rugged and remote coastline of the Westfjords, connected to the mainland by a narrow isthmus of land. This landscape of tiny fishing villages and abandoned remote farms is testament to social change because many young people have chosen to move to Reykjavík for work. If you're looking for solitude in a harsh yet very beautiful landscape then you will fall in love with this area.

The Route 1 ring road will take you through much of this region, although it bypasses the Westfjords which have their own spectacular ring road known as Route 2. Away from the main roads, summer mountain roads and hiking routes snake through truly spectacular terrain, often far from civilisation. One of the very best ways to explore is on horseback along trails that have been ridden for centuries and well before any road network was developed. Your pure-breed mounts will also be directly descended from the very first horses brought to Iceland by early settlers from mainland Scandinavia, over 1,000 years ago.

Wherever your explorations take you, you can be assured that you'll never be far from the restorative waters of a hot spring, and with 24-hour daylight during the summer months, time is unlikely to be an issue.

HOT SPRINGS

1 LÝSUHÓLSLAUG

Community swimming pool where you'll find two hot tubs filled with naturally heated mineral water from a spring, with no chemicals added. The water here is believed to be very good for the skin. Check the website for current opening times.

→ Starting at the coastal village of Grundarfjörður (64.9268, -23.2568) head W on the R54 for 41km. After you pass the second of two lakes, turn L onto the R5714. Follow it for 1.8km. Cross the bridge and take the next turning on R. +354 433 9917. www.facebook.com/lysuholslaug/
64.8460, -23.3374 🏊

2 STJÁNI

Sunken tank about 3 sq m with water piped from a hot spring. With the mountains on one side and flat coastal plain on the other, it's a great place for a refreshing soak if you're passing through the area.

→ Follow directions for Lýsuhólslaug (see 1) but do not cross the bridge. Instead, just before the bridge turn R onto a track. Park here and see the pool in front of you.
64.8415, -23.2172 🏊

3 LANDBROTALAUG

Very snug and (in the right company) romantic stone-built hot tub fed by a hot spring in the middle of nowhere behind an abandoned farm. There's a second larger pool, but it's very shallow. Beside the tub is a stone windbreak so you're well protected and on a clear day you have lovely views of the distant mountains.

→ Continue on the R54 past the junction with the R55 (see Sturlungalaug below) for 1.3km. Park by the track on L and follow it for 500m to the spring.
15 mins, 64.8322, -22.3184 🏞🏔📷

4 STURLUNGALAUG

Hot pool in an area of flat grassland close to a rocky outcrop. Nice and warm but quite murky and sometimes with a fair amount of algae. In the middle of nowhere.

→ From the junction of the R54 and the R55 (64.8252, -22.2742) SW of Búðardalur, follow the R55 for 4km until you see a track on L signposted 'Syðri Rauðamelur'. Follow this for about 6.5km through a couple of gates. When the road forks take R fork to the end to find the pool.
64.8701, -22.2838 🏞🏔

5 GRAFARLAUG

Hot spring-fed 12.5m pool that has recently been renovated. It now has one full-length section for swimming and two 'hot tub' sections. There's a very basic changing shed. Lovely views along the wide Reykjadal valley.

→ From the junction of the R1 and the R60, SE of Búðardalur, continue on the R60 for about 20km then turn R onto a gravel road (64.9695, -21.5513). Continue for 2.2km to parking area.
64.9610, -21.5166 🏊

6 HVERABORG

Geothermal area located in the Tvídægra moorland beside the Sika river where hot water rises up into two pots for bathing. These have been built up with rocks and there are rough stone walls for windbreaks. The pools are about 2m in diameter and have a temperature of 37°C. Well worth the walk.

→ From Laugarbakki village (65.3237, -20.8855) travel 25km S on the R1. Turn L onto smaller R701 before the bridge at the end of the lake. Turn L just before the next bridge onto a track on R. Follow this alongside the river until it ends after 11km (65.0507, -20.9503). Continue on foot for 5km. Springs are on the river edge with a hut on E slope.
1 hour, 64.9984, -20.9317 🏞🏔🏔

7 GUÐRÚNARLAUG

Lovely stone-built hot tub on the slopes behind Hotel Edda with a small wooden changing room. Visit early in the morning or late at night to have it all to yourself.

➜ From Búðardalur village (65.6864, -23.6006) travel 16km N on the R60, then turn L onto the smaller R58 (Saelingsdalsvegur). Continue for 2.5km to Hotel Edda. Hot tub is on the slope.
65.2465, -21.8048 ♨

8 LAUGALAND

Small pool naturally heated by a hot spring at the remote farm of Laugaland in the Skjaldfannardalur valley. This is the start of a well-known horse-riding route that crosses the Drangajökull glacier. Ask the very friendly farmer for permission to relax in the water. The birthplace of the well-known and popular Icelandic poet Steinn Steinarr (1908–58).

➜ Follow the R607 (Reykhólasveitarvegur) from its junction with the R60 until the end. Continue driving along the track (Laugaland) until it finishes at the farm with the same name.
5 mins, 65.5125, -22.3040 ♨ 📷

9 HELLULAUG

The natural hot tub Hellulaug is about 500m from Hótel Flókalundur, but hidden among the rocks on the foreshore. At high tide you can jump into the sea to cool off. To the west of Hellulaug below the ruins of the old Hella farm is a further turf pool that's been restored. The water temperature is around 38°C. Great sea views.

➜ 2km SW of Flókalundur village (65.5766, -23.1656), just off the R62, on the shore on the opposite side of the river mouth to village.
10 mins, 65.5726, -23.1721 ♨ 📷

10 REYKJAFJARÐARLAUG

Very basic swimming pool measuring 16m by 10m that's kept at a temperature of 32°C by a hot spring. Also a small hot tub beside the pool with a temperature of 45°C. There is a changing room, but no shower. Stunning views over the fjord and out to sea.

➜ From the village of Bíldudalur (65.6864, -23.6006), travel S on the R63 for approx 19km. Park by the road. The pool is in an inlet at the head of the fjord.
65.6231, -23.4703 ♨ 📷

11 BRÚARPOTTURINN

Very small concrete-walled pool, about the size of a bathtub, lying beside a river and next to a road bridge. Makes a refreshing stop-off for weary drivers.

→ From the village of Tálknafjörður (65.62674, -23.82302), head 5km NW on the R617. The pool is on the L of the road on the far side of the bridge over the Laugardals river.
65.6568, -23.9113

12 POLLURINN

Located on the hillside close to Tálknafjörður are three artificial pools that are naturally heated by a hot spring. In the largest one the water is about 46°C. The smaller pools are a bit cooler and there's a wooden changing hut. Amazing views over the fjord and very close to Brúarpotturinn (see 11).

→ From the village Tálknafjörður (65.6267, -23.8230), head 5km NW on road 617. Cross the bridge over the Laugardals river, continue for 0.5km, then take the first R turn. Head up the track and after 200m you'll see the pool.
65.6601, -23.9147

13 GALTAHRYGGJARLAUG

Small stone-lined hot spring in the middle of a meadow. Sit in water at 40°C surrounded by lush green grass and wild flowers. There's a small wooden changing hut.

→ Head SE from Ögure on the R61 then turn off R onto the R633 (approx 130km from Ísafjörður). Look out for signs to the Hotel Heydalur on the R. The spring is a brief signposted walk from the hotel.
10 mins, 65.8481, -22.6633

14 HÖRGSHLÍÐÐARLAUG

Artificial pool located on the shore of the Mjóifjörður (Narrow Fjord) where spectacular waterfalls cascade from the cliffs. The water for the pool comes from a hot spring, and there are hoses of hot and cold water you can move to adjust the temperature (normally around 40°C). There's a small changing room and you should ask permission from the farmer at Hörgshlíð (just down the road) before bathing. Great views along the fjord.

→ Follow directions to Galtahryggjarlaug (see 13) but stay on the R633 past the hotel turning, continuing on it just past the head of Mjóifjörður where you take the first L onto a smaller, unnamed road. The pool is on the shoreline beside the road about 2km from the head of the fjord.
65.8315, -22.6297

15 GJÖRVIDALSLAUG

Small and cosy pool with a little changing hut. The hot water, a balmy 42°C, is channelled to the pool from the spring 5m away. Ask at the farm for permission before bathing.

→ From the junction the R61 and F66, take the F66 heading S and then the next R to the farm at Múli. The spring is on the hillside overlooking the farm.
10 mins, 65.8243, -22.4442

16 NAUTEYRARLAUG
Another small pool with a little changing hut. The hot water has been fed directly to the pool by a pipe from the spring for a few years now. Borehole drilling in the area had accidentally stopped the natural flow. The temperature is around 42–43°C.
→ From the town of Hólmavík (65.7016, -21.6860), head N on R61. After 45km turn R onto the R635, and travel a further 6km. The spring is to the L of the road approx 500m after the bridge over the Hafnardalsá river.
65.9368, -22.3732

17 GVENDARLAUG
Two natural springs that are believed to have healing powers. The main pool has been used since medieval times and is also a protected archaeological site. It's one of several that were blessed by Bishop Guðmundur the Good (1160–1237). Relax in the hot water and soothe away any aches and pains. Adjacent is the second spring and a modern pool.

→ Starting at Hólmavík (65.7016, -21.6860), head N on the R61 for 10km then turn R onto the R643. Continue for a further 10km, then turn L onto a 1km-long track. The spring is at the end of the road.
65.7815, -21.5671

18 HOT TUBS AT DRANGSNES
Three timber-clad hot tubs on the shoreline overlooking the sea and fed by a hot spring. The original is an old fish container donated by a local fish farmer, while the other two are purpose-built hot tubs with seats. The temperature in the fish tub is 40°C and slightly cooler in the other two. Great views.
→ The hot springs are located on the shoreline in the small hamlet of Drangsnes on the R645 (65.6894, -21.4423).
65.6882, -21.4523

19 GRETTISLAUG
Two stone pools beside the sea with a drystone wall as a windbreak. The temperature is about 42–43°C and you can always jump into the sea to cool down. In *Grettir's Saga*, the outlaw Grettir Ásmundarson is said to have bathed here after swimming to the mainland from the island of Drangey, 7.5km offshore.

→ Starting at Saudarkroki (65.7425, -19.6434), head N on the R748 for 15km to reach Grettislaug. The spring is located on the harbour, which is on the E side of the headland.
65.8823, -19.7365 🏊

20 BISKUPSLAUG

Small stone-lined pool encircled by lush grass with great views of the surrounding mountains. Ask permission from the farmer at Reykir before bathing.

→ Starting at Saudarkroki (65.7425, -19.6434), head E on the R75. After 14km turn L onto the R76 for a further 5km, before turning R onto the R767. Stay on this road for 13km, passing Hólar, and turn L onto the smaller R768. Follow this road to the end (approx 4km) to arrive at the spring.
65.6600, -19.0864 🏊

21 HOFSÓS INFINITY POOL

Designed by the architect of the Blue Lagoon (see SW Iceland 17), the Hofsós infinity pool is built into the hillside above the sea, looking across to the island of Drangey. It's 25m by 10.5m and there are changing facilities and showers. The panoramic views from here are magnificent. Many Americans and Canadians of Icelandic descent travel to the town to visit the Emigration Centre by the seafront, which documents the stories of those who left to settle in North America.

→ Within walking distance of Hofsós village centre (65.8960, -19.4125). Signposted.
15 mins, 65.8960, -19.4124 🏊🏞

22 KROSSNES

Swimming pool in an especially wild and dramatic location on a beach in the remote Westfjords. Natural hot springs feed the pool, which is only metres from the North Atlantic. The timber-clad pool itself is raised off the ground and there are changing facilities. This is a swim you'll never forget.

→ Follow the R643 past Urðartindur Guest House, round the head of Norðfjörður (66.0505, -21.5659) to where it becomes the Krossneslaug road. Continue for 4km, round the headland. On your R find a signpost for the pool.
66.0563, -21.5085 🏊🏞🏄

23 HÁKARLAVOGUR

Large semi-natural hot tub set among the rocks on the shore and contained by a small wall on one side. The hot water comes from a spring which seeps into the pool through the rocks. A beautiful location with views along the rugged shoreline and out to sea.

→ From the village of Gjögur on the R643 follow the road to the airport (Flugvallarvegur Gjögri) and continue on the track around the end of the runway. Park on the L where the track divides. The pool is immediately on the R.
5 mins, 65.9981, -21.3175 ⬜📷

NATURE & WILDLIFE

24 LÁTRABJARG BIRD CLIFFS

Promontory with towering cliffs that is the westernmost point on Iceland. The sheer rock is an important nesting site and home to a colony of millions of seabirds. Species you'll see here include puffins, razorbills and guillemots. There's a path running along the cliff top, but the best view is from near the parking area. Don't forget your binoculars.
→ From the village of Flókalundur (65.5766, -23.1656), head W on the R62. After 43km turn L onto the R612 and follow it until the road ends at the cliffs and parking area.
65.5026, -24.5317 📷🚗

25 SÚÐAVÍK ARCTIC FOX CENTRE

Research centre in the village of Súðavík (R161) focusing on the Arctic fox, Iceland's only native terrestrial mammal. Learn about its biology and history as well as its relationship with humans since the days of the first settlers. Foxes living on the coast of Iceland mainly hunt birds, but they will also take seal pups as well as berries and seaweed.
→ Eyrardalur, 420 Súðavík, +354 456 4922, www.arcticfoxcentre.com
66.0305, -22.9917 🐾

26 DALVÍK WHALE WATCHING

Leave by boat from Dalvík, south of Ólafsfjörður on the Eyjafjörður, the longest fjord on the Icelandic coast, to look for whales. The most common species are humpback and minke whales, dolphins and harbour porpoises. Try a spot of sea fishing on your way back.
→ Book online: www.arcticseatours.is
65.9721, -18.5290 🚗🎫🚤

27 SNÆFELLSJÖKULL NATIONAL PARK

The 'jewel of West Iceland', the Snæfellsjökull National Park takes its name from the most famous volcano in Iceland and the glacier that covers it. Here you'll find numerous sites of historical, geological and biological interest, including the glacier itself and spectacular lava formations. On a clear day you can see the glacier from Reykjavík, 200km away. Snæfellsjökull is better known to readers of Jules Verne as the gateway to the centre of the earth.

"That is Snæfellsjökull a mountain about five thousand feet in height, one of the most remarkable in the whole island, and certainly doomed to be the most celebrated in the world, for through its crater we shall reach the centre of the earth". Where will your adventure in the National Park take you?
→ Start at the visitor centre, on the L of Hellnavegur (R5730) as you drive down the hill into Hellnar. www.ust.is/snaefellsjokull
64.7999, -23.7831 🚗📷⛺🛖🏔

HISTORY & CULTURE

28 HRAFNSEYRI

The birthplace of Jón Sigurðsson, a scholar and MP who led the Icelandic campaign for self-rule during the 19th century. At the informative small museum here, you'll find out how Iceland was once governed from Denmark and learn about Sigurðsson's efforts to change the constitution to achieve greater independence. Open summer months only. There's also a great little café: Safn Jóns Sigurðsonar, Hrafnseyri, 471 Þingeyri, +356 456 8260. www.hrafnseyri.is
→ Approx 48km N of the village of Flókalundur (65.5766, -23.1656), just off the R60.
65.7599, -23.4518 🏛🍴

29 WITCHCRAFT MUSEUM

A fascinating but also slightly chilling museum of Icelandic witchcraft. Witches here were traditionally male and the majority of the occult practices were generally based on old Viking superstitions. The artefacts range from pieces of wood carved with runes to spells and a rather macabre pair of 'necropants'. Made out of the skin of a dead man that had been peeled off from the waist down, these trousers were worn to bring wealth as part of a spell. This also involved keeping a coin (stolen from a poor widow) and a magic symbol (nábrókarstafur) in the scrotum to draw more money inside.
→ Strandagaldur, Höfðagata 8-10, 510 Hólmavík, +354 897 6525, www.galdrasyning.is
65.7069, -21.6666 🏛

30 HORSE RIDING IN ICELAND

Bred from the ponies taken to Iceland by settlers from mainland Scandinavia in the ninth and tenth centuries, Icelandic horses are unique and the law forbids the import of other horses in order to preserve the bloodline. Icelanders are very proud of these small horses which have a unique way of moving (a gait) called a tölt. This gait is an innate ability, which they can do at any pace, and it makes them sure-footed and comfortable to ride at speed. The horse was for many centuries a vital means of transport and until relatively recently many farmers travelled on horseback on a daily basis. There are several traditional riding routes across Iceland and riders come from all over the world for trekking. There's no better way to see the most wild and remote parts of the country.

→ Icelandic Horse offer a variety of tours: Hestasport, Vegamót, 560 Varmahlíð, +354 453 8383, www.riding.is
65.5514, -19.4512

ROCK & ICE

31 HVÍTSERKUR

A 15m-high basalt stack just off the eastern shore of the Vatnsnes peninsula. Its name means 'White Shirt', probably because of its guano coating courtesy of the many seabirds nesting on the rock. From different angles the stack can resemble various animals – in particular a dragon with its head down, drinking. Observe the numerous seabirds and possibly catch sight of seals.

→ At the junction of the R1 and R711 E of Laugarbakki, head N on R711 for 30km. After passing the mouth of Sigríðarstaðavatn (with sea on R), you'll see Hvítserkur and the car park.
65.6063, -20.6357

LOCAL FOOD

32 TJÖRUHÚSIÐ

Amazing seafood restaurant set in a traditional timber house next to the harbour. The house specialities are all-you-can-eat skate, monkfish, cod cheeks, or whatever else the boats have landed that day. If you're travelling on the R60 stop to walk up an appetite on the stunning Holt Beach (66.0181, -23.4366) (see p204).

→ By the harbour in Ísafjörður, Neðstakaupstað, 400 Ísafjörður, +354 456 4419
66.0682, -23.1264

33 PÁLÍNA'S FLOWER KITCHEN

Small restaurant attached to a boutique hotel. The kitchen fuses traditional Icelandic cuisine with contemporary techniques. Flowers, herbs and berries from the garden are used along with local lamb and fish. Signature dishes include Arctic char tartar, puffin with blueberries and violet ice cream.

→ Located 50km NE of Sauðárkrókur on the edge of Skagafjörður: Lónkot Rural Resort, 566 Hofsós, +354 453 7432. www.lonkot.is
66.0045, -19.4035

ACCOMMODATION

34 HOTEL BÚÐIR

Elegant boutique hotel sitting at the edge of the Snæfellsjökull Park with impressive views of the glacier and Búðir estuary. The restaurant specialises in local lamb and fish.

→ Far E Snæfellsnes peninsula: 356 Snæfellsbær, +354 435 6700. www.hotelbudir.is
64.8335, -23.5491

35 BRIMNES CABINS

Timber self-catering cabins with individual hot tubs located on a scenic road around the Troll Peninsula linking Skagafjörður in the west with Eyjafjörður in the east.

→ In Ólafsfjörður village: Bylgjubyggð 2, 625 Ólafsfjörður, +354 466 2400. www.brimnes.is
66.0694, -18.6549

36 FISHERMAN GUESTHOUSE

Small guesthouse with a café specialising in seafood from locally landed fish. They will pick you up from the airport in Ísafjörður. Great buffet breakfast.

→ Aðalgata 14, 430 Suðureyri, +354 450 9000. www.fisherman.is
66.1302, -23.5279

NORTHEAST ICELAND

Our perfect week

→ **Discover** how a farmer eked out a living in an old turf-roofed homestead.

→ **Learn** about whales in Icelandic waters at the Húsavík Whale Museum.

→ **Straddle** the Arctic Circle on the island of Grímsey.

→ **Smell** the sulphur in the air at one of the dramatic volcanic areas.

→ **Soak** in the Ostakarið cheese tub after a day of sea whale watching.

→ **Hike** some of the traditional Sprengisandur highland route and camp by a hot spring.

→ **Watch** rainbows form in the spray below Europe's most powerful waterfall, Dettifoss.

→ **Explore** the magical caves and arches in the fairytale surroundings of Dimmuborgir.

→ **Pamper** yourself with a massage at Mývatn Nature Baths.

→ **Swim** in Hell at Víti – not a boiling-hot but a pleasantly warm crater lake.

During the summer months the mountain roads heading into the interior of north east Iceland are finally clear of snow and open to traffic. Heading inland from Route 1 you'll find yourself navigating through ochre-coloured, steamy volcanic regions and over remote plateaus of black volcanic sand. You will also come across mighty, glacial rivers that have carved deep canyons across the landscape. In their rush to the sea, these glacial rivers are interrupted at intervals by immense and hugely spectacular waterfalls. One you shouldn't miss is Dettifoss, the most powerful in Europe. And as you travel, the horizon is dominated by the peaks of the highlands, intermittently illuminated by sunlight reflecting off the numerous glaciers.

The area defined in this guide as north east Iceland starts by Akureyri, the regional capital of the north and Iceland's second city. It then stretches around the coast to Seyðisfjörður, not far from Egilsstaðir, the main town in the east. Seyðisfjörður will be your point of arrival if you bring a vehicle on the Smyril Line ferry from Denmark.

Hot springs are dotted throughout this landscape, so whether you're exploring the coast or venturing inland towards the highlands, you'll never be far from a relaxing, hot soak. At the Mývatn Nature Baths you can even get a massage as well. In the area around Lake Mývatn, lush green vegetation on one side contrasts with the sulphurous landscape of a very active volcanic area on the other. Although at first glance a barren landscape, it's an oasis of birdlife and the lava islands are home to numerous nesting species.

Of all the many waterfalls you'll encounter, the 30-metre wide and shallow horseshoe-shaped Goðafoss (Waterfall of the Gods), on the Skjálfandafljót river, is likely to make the greatest impression on you. It certainly encapsulates the vast scale and immense power of nature in Iceland. This is a landscape that, time and again, will leave you feeling both awed and inspired, eager to press on and experience everything it has to offer.

HOT SPRINGS

1 MÝVATN NATURE BATHS

On the lower slopes of Dalfjall is Iceland's first (built in 1969) geothermal power station. The spa, developed here in 2004, is along the lines of the better-known Blue Lagoon (see SW Iceland 17) but smaller and set against a backdrop of ochre-coloured hills. Sulphur gives them their distinctive hue and it's also in the water, so remove any copper or silver jewellery before bathing. The milky-blue water is drawn from up to 25m underground, where it's heated to a very comfortable 38–40°C. Saunas are also available and there's a café.

→ From Reykjahlíð village (65.6419, -16.911) head E on R1 for 2.5km. Take 2nd R, baths are 1km down the track. Jarðbaðshólar 660 Mývatn, +354 464 4411. www.myvatnnaturebaths.is
65.6311, -16.8482

2 NÁMAFJALL HVERIR

Geothermal area south of Námaskarð on the east side of Námafjall mountain, with desert-like terrain. The light-yellow colour comes from sulphur, which was once mined here and exported all over the world. There are several springs and mud pots, but some are potentially dangerous so follow the current safety signs to find those that are safe for bathing. A fascinating area to explore.

→ From Reykjahlíð village (65.6419, -16.911) head E on R1 for 5km then turn R. Námafjall is 300m down the track. Parking available. 4km NE of Mývatn Nature Baths.
65.6417, -16.8076

3 STÓRAGJÁ

Breathtakingly beautiful subterranean hot spring at the bottom of a steaming lava fissure. At the time of writing Stóragjá had a safe temperature, but swimming is not recommended due to algae growth. Make sure you read the signs and follow the up-to-date advice about bathing before considering entering the water.

→ Park by road at the junction of Route 1 and Route 848 in Reykjahlíð and follow marked path.
10 mins, 65.6386, -16.9099

4 KALDBAKSLAUG

Steaming lake with comfortably warm water that, at approximately 6m wide and 180m long, is big enough for a decent swim. Unusually for a hot spring, you'll see fish in the water here. Combine with a visit to nearby Ostakariðin (see 5), a short walk along the road from Húsavík.

→ Head 3km S from the town of Húsavík on the R85. Park on rough ground on L of road. Lake is approx 50m off to L.
66.0157, -17.3575

5 OSTAKARIÐ

In translation the Icelandic name means 'Cheese Tub', which is appropriate for a hot tub made from a big metal tank once used in a cheese factory. Situated on a small hill overlooking Húsavík, a harbour town popular for whale-watching, the tub was constructed by a group of local people. It's free to use, but you're encouraged to leave a donation towards its upkeep. Big enough to accommodate 15–20 people, the water comes from a hot spring and there's a thermostatic mixing tap so you can adjust the temperature. Panels slide into position for use as windbreaks if needed, otherwise there are amazing sea views while you bathe. The perfect end to a day of whale-watching.

→ Approx 0.5km N of Húsavík. From the centre of town, take the road Höfðavegur NW past all the houses until you come to the first unmarked road, where you turn R. Take the L fork approx 200m down this track. Park on L.
66.0548, -17.3521

6 HÓLSGERÐISLAUG

Hot spring in a reasonably remote and very beautiful valley just south of Akureyri. The pool is surrounded by neatly stacked rocks on one side and lush green vegetation on the other. Room for ten people, at a push. Hólakirkja, nearby, is the site of one of the oldest churches in Iceland – the current building dates from the 19th century.

➔ Head S on the R821 from Akureyri. Approx 33km, S of the village of Hrafnagil, park at the side of road on L. Pool is 100m off road to L.
65.3027, -18.2558 ♨

7 LAUGAFELL

Hot springs, 25km west of the well-known Sprengisandur route through the highlands, where you'll find numerous hot pools – even the river flows warm! Basic geothermally heated hiking huts are close to the pools. Combine with a multi-day highlands hike, making this one of your overnight stops.

➔ Laugafell is very remote, situated off the F821, approx 4km S of the junction with F881.
65.0270, -18.3315 ♨🥾🏔

8 VÍTI

Very warm geothermal lake at the bottom of a huge crater that formed during a massive volcanic eruption at the start of the famous Mývatn fires in 1724 – a period of sustained volcanic activity in the area. In English, *víti* means 'hell' because people believed the nether regions lay under the ground. There are two lakes here (Öskjuvatn is the other one) but it's the green water of Víti that makes it popular for bathing. Don't swim on a still day as carbon dioxide can collect on the surface. Very remote and beautiful.

➔ At R1 and F905 junction, head S on F905 for 55km then take the F910 to Drekagil (20km). Cross two small fords then take F894 (8 km) to the car park at Vikraborgir. Be careful as the sloping path can be very slippery.
30 mins, 65.0469, -16.7259 🏞🏔

FIRE & WATER

9 LAKE MÝVATN

Fourth-largest natural lake in Iceland, teeming with fish and water birds, set in a landscape dominated by volcanic landforms. It was created by a large eruption 2,300 years ago when lava flowed down the valley of the Laxá river and into an existing lake. Some of the sediment trapped below the lake then caused explosions of steam, creating what are known as pseudocraters or rootless vents. Seen on the shore of the lake and also forming several of its islands, these are classic formations, and those on the south shore at Skútustaðir are protected as national monuments. The lake's name comes from the Icelandic *mý* (midge) and *vatn* (lake) and there are indeed a lot of midges around in the summer.

→ Lake Mývatn lies close to the village of Reykjahlíð (65.6419, -16.911) on the R1. 65.6039, -16.9961 🐎

10 GOÐAFOSS

The name of this very impressive 'Waterfall of the Gods' (English translation) originates from the actions of Þorgeir Þorkelsson at the very end of the 10th century. He was a law-speaker in Iceland's Althing (early parliament) and also a pagan priest and chieftain. After converting to Christianity, he threw the idols of his gods into these falls. The Skjálfandafljót river plunges down from a height of around 12m, forming a large horseshoe over an area 30m wide. One of Iceland's most spectacular waterfalls and not to be missed.

→ Heading W from Lake Mývatn on R1, take a L turn approx 300m after the junction with the R844 and R1. There's a car park 300m down this track. The waterfall is a short 100m walk. 5 mins, 65.6830, -17.5508 🏔📷📷

11 ALDEYJARFOSS

Upstream from Goðafoss on the Skjálfandafljót river where it crosses the Suðurárhraun lava field, is the Aldeyjarfoss waterfall plunging 20m into a canyon. An incredibly powerful waterfall, made even more dramatic by the contrast of the turbulent white water against the black basalt.

→ From the junction of R842 and R1, head S for 40km up the valley. The road changes into the F26 for the last 5km. Aldeyjarfoss is on L. 5 mins, 65.3665, -17.3369 🏔🏔

12 DETTIFOSS

Huge waterfall on the Jökulsá á Fjöllum river in the Vatnajökull National Park and thought to be the most powerful in Europe. The water cascades down from 45m over a width of 70m into the Jökulsárgljúfur canyon. From the edge, looking upstream, you can see another impressive waterfall. This is Selfoss, smaller in height at 10m but about 100m wide. Beautiful rainbows often form in the spray.

→ From Reykjahlíð village (65.6419, -16.911) head E on the R1 for 35km then turn L at the R862 junction. Travel a further 25km N on the 862 then turn R, following the track for 3km. It's a short 800m walk from the end of the track. 10 mins, 65.8151, -16.3856 🏔🐾

13 KRAFLA

The Krafla caldera is a distinctive geological feature at the junction of the Eurasian and American tectonic plates. It's a collapsed volcano that is still very active, set in a steamy ochre-coloured landscape. The 'cauldron' has a diameter of around 10km and this includes the Víti crater (see 8).

→ Head E from the village of Reykjahlíð (65.6419, -16.911) on the R1 for approx 5km. Turn L onto an unmarked road and travel 8km N. Krafla is a further 0.5km on foot.

15 mins, 65.7171, -16.7544

CULTURE & HISTORY

14 GRÍMSEY

Small island of 5 sq km lying 40km off the north coast. It is bisected by the Arctic Circle and during the summer its cliffs are covered with nesting seabirds. There are two guesthouses as well as a restaurant (only open in summer). Great for bird watching.

→ The ferry to Grimsey carries 108 passengers and leaves from the village of Dalvik (65.9721, -18.529). It runs 3 times a week (Mon/Wed/Fri) year-round and takes three hours each way. To book go to www.landflutningar.is/saefari/english

66.5423, -17.9961

15 DVERGASTEINN

Known in English as 'Dwarfs´ Rock', this unusual, triangular-shaped boulder lies in a prominent spot on the northern shore of Seyðisfjörður. According to local legend, the boulder was once on the other side of the fjord and moved to its current position when the Christian church was relocated there. The dwarfs who lived in this boulder wanted to be near the church and their rock mysteriously floated over the fjord to the church's new location. The church has been moved again since then, but so far the rock has remained in its current position.

→ From the town of Seyðisfjörður follow the R951 along the N shore of the fjord. After approx 7km you'll see a signposted track on the R. The stone is 120m down the track.

5 mins, 65.2921, -13.9298

16 HÚSAVÍK WHALE MUSEUM

As Iceland's tourism industry grew, the money it brought in enabled many whalers to give up whaling and diversify into running whale-watching trips. The town of Húsavík became the centre of these activities and in 1997 the Whale Museum was founded with the aim of educating visitors about whales and their habitat. A visit to the museum, which has huge skeletons of several different species on display, is a fascinating experience. Best done in conjunction with a whale-watching excursion.

→ Hafnarstétt, Húsavík, +354 414 2800. www.whalemuseum.is

66.0469, -17.3446

17 BUSTARFELL

Preserved turf-roofed farm in the Vopnafjörður area that is the oldest of its kind in Iceland. Now an intriguing museum of rural life from the 18th to mid-20th century. During the summer the museum hosts numerous events and the Hjáleigan café serves delicious refreshments, specialising in traditional dishes from local produce.

→ Signed on the R off the R85 heading S from Vopnafjörður. Minjasafnið Bustarfelli. Hofsárdal, Vopnafirðl, +354 471 2211. www.bustarfell.is

65.6153, -15.0998

18 DIMMUBORGIR

Mysterious area of volcanic caves and rock formations with numerous fantastical arches that children will love exploring. Reminiscent of a collapsed castle, its name translates (roughly) into English as 'dark castles'. There's a visitor centre, where you can learn more about the geology and the many myths associated with the area, and also a café.

→ Starting at the village of Reykjahlíð (65.6419, -16.911) on the R1, turn R and head 5km S on the R848, then take a L turn onto a smaller unmarked road for approx 1km. Dimmuborgir is a 700m walk from the end of the track.

20 mins, 65.5854, -16.9033

19 GALTASTAÐIR FARM

Well-preserved example of a traditional turf-roofed farmhouse from the 19th century, which was inhabited until 1967. Featuring a communal living and sleeping room, this was the most common type of dwelling in Iceland in previous centuries. Women would have spun cloth and done other handicrafts in the communal space, and at this farm there was a cattle shed directly below. A fascinating glimpse into the old way of life on Iceland.

→ Start at Egilsstaðir (65.2669, -14.3948), travel 5km N on the R1, then turn R onto the R925. Continue for 18km then turn L onto the R927. After 2.5km turn L onto an unmarked road. Galtastaðir Farm is 1.5km ahead.

65.4521, -14.4360

20 KAFFI KÚ

Café in Eyjafjarðarsveit located in the loft of a working cowshed. You can watch the cows being milked while you sip a milkshake made from fresh milk. There's also a well stocked bar and the waffles are delicious.

→ Located 10km S of Akureyri. Garði, 601 Akureyri, +354 867 3826. www.kaffiku.is
65.6032, -18.0329 ⓘ

21 MÓÐIR JÖRÐ

Stay on an organic farm in B&B or bunkhouse accommodation. Delicious 'field-to-table' vegan breakfasts are served in the greenhouse. The farm shop sells their vegetables and grain. Enjoy the good-life, Icelandic style.

→ 9km S of Egilsstaðir just off Route 1. Vallanesi, 701 Egilsstöðum, +354 471 1747. www.vallanes.is
65.1965, -14.5438 ⓘ ⓘ

22 HÓTEL LAXÁ

Fabulously located hotel on a prominent ridge with views over the Laxá river and Lake Mývatn. The hotel is designed to be as green as possible and the restaurant specialises in sustainable local produce. The Mývatn Nature Baths are close by (see 1).

→ Located 90km E of Akureyri just off Route 1. Við Olnbogaás, 660 Mývatn, +354 464 1900. www.hotellaxa.is
65.5707, -17.0865 ⓘ

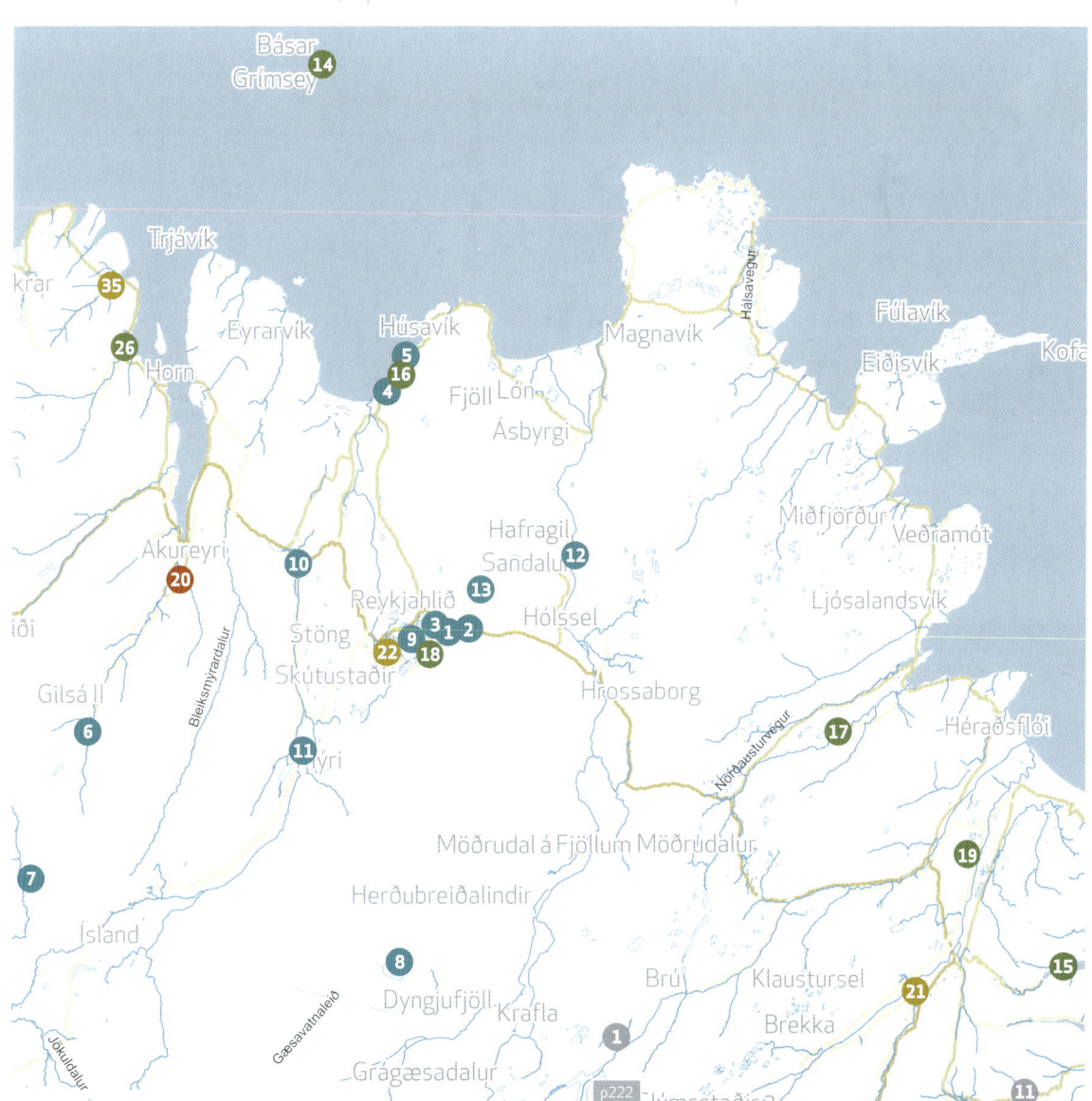

SOUTH EAST ICELAND

Our perfect week

→ **Soak** in a remote highland hot spring.

→ **Taste** ancient ice from the Jökulsárlón glacial lagoon.

→ **Find** the lighthouse on the Ingólfshöfði cape.

→ **Dare** to sample rotten shark meat at Randulff's Sea House.

→ **Shower** under a steaming waterfall in the fairytale Hveragil canyon.

→ **Hunt** for ice diamonds on a black-sand beach.

→ **Discover** why the rocks at Svartifoss inspire Icelandic architects.

→ **Eat** fresh langoustines while watching them being landed from small boats.

→ **Climb** up to the Lake of the Sisters high above Kirkjubæjarklaustur.

→ **Discover** what the local fisherman are landing by ordering the catch of the day at Hótel Framtíð.

→ **Pull** over for a roadside hot bath as you pass Djúpavogskörin.

Travelling along Route 1 on the south coast you'll be distracted by the luminous blue glow apparently given off by icebergs floating in the Jökulsárlón glacial lagoon. Calved from the Breiðamerkurjökull glacier, this ancient ice then makes its way out to sea. When large pieces wash back up onto the black volcanic sand of the beach opposite, they sparkle like cut diamonds as they refract the sunlight. A spectacular sight.

The south-east quadrant of Iceland is easily the most remote. Defined in this guide as extending from Seyðisfjörður on the east coast to the estuary of the Skaftá river in the south, it's skirted by a 475- kilometre section of Route 1. Around 300 kilometres of this runs between the sea and the stunning Vatnajökull National Park, which is the largest in Europe. The park is also home to Iceland's biggest ice cap, which feeds the numerous glaciers that reach out in different directions.

You can use summer mountain roads and hiking paths to explore the highlands up to the edge of the glaciers, but this is an incredibly remote area and appropriate care must be taken. Always make sure you let someone else know not only your intended route but also when you expect to arrive at your destination. It is possible to venture onto the ice cap itself, but you will need to employ a local guide with the relevant specialist equipment and knowledge.

Heading clockwise around Route 1 – before you reach Jökulsárlón – the road traverses Skeiðarársandur. This vast desert of grey sand stretching from the sea to the glacier is punctuated only by glacial rivers flowing down from Vatnajökull.

Just before you leave the area, the road takes you through Kirkjubæjarklaustur – a village rich in history and once home to a community of Irish monks. Establishing themselves here in the sixth century, they were the very first settlers on Iceland.

If you make the journey through this south-eastern region after visiting the volcanic areas around Lake Mývatn in the north east, it will be very obvious to you why Iceland is popularly known as the 'Land of Fire and Ice'.

HOT SPRINGS

1 LAUGARVALLADALUR

Getting to this pool, located in the remote Laugarvalladalur valley in the Icelandic highlands, involves either an off-road vehicle or a good day's hike. If you decide to hike in, this is a great spot to wild camp with fantastic views. On your way you'll pass the ruins of the old farmhouse at Laugavellir. The Laugarvallalaug pool is about a 15km walk from the dam at Kárahnjúkar – the largest of its kind in Europe and a controversial construction. It's one of a series of five dams and three reservoirs that are used to generate hydroelectric power for the Fjarðaál aluminium smelter in Reyðarfjörður. The pool itself is unique for Iceland in that it's fed by a warm waterfall that you can shower under. The stream below has been dammed with rocks, to form a pool for bathing. Very special and well worth the hike.

➜ From the R1 (E of Egilsstaðir) take the Möðrudalsleið road (65.3077, -15.3253) to the junction with the F907. Follow this road until it finishes at the Kárahnjúkar dam. From here you'll need to hike along the reservoir for 15km. A local map and compass are essential.
6 hours, 65.0060, -15.7611

2 LAUGARFELL

Reasonably large, round stone-lined pool that can accommodate approximately 15 people at a time. It's surrounded by a paved area close to the hotel, but there are no changing facilities specifically for the pool. Fed by a hot spring, the temperature is generally a very comfortable 34°C. The water is reputed to have healing properties and there are several spectacular waterfalls within walking distance.

➜ From Egilsstaðir, take the F931 SW, then turn W onto the F910 for approx 30km. The spring is located 2km off the road, near the Laugarfell Highland Hostel, 701 Laugarfell, +354 773 3323. www.highlandhostel.is
20 mins, 64.8861, -15.3520

3 DJÚPAVOGSKÖRIN

Two plastic industrial tanks (IBCs) converted into hot tubs are set in a field about 40m from the road with great views towards the sea. The water comes from a hot spring and is about 40°C.

➜ 2 km W of the village of Djúpivogur on the R1. Approx 40m S of the road. Consult a local map for the exact location.
64.6545, -14.3392

4 HOFFELL

Five spring-fed hot tubs of different shapes and temperatures are located at the base of a rocky outcrop with views of the Hoffelsjökull glacier. Change in a small hut with a shower. You're expected to make a contribution towards your visit by leaving a small payment in an honesty box. Great for aching legs after a day of hiking.

➜ From the town of Höfn (64.2497, -15.2064), travel N on the R99, then turn L onto the R1. After approx 11km, turn R onto the track which leads to the Glacier World Guest House. Hoffell is situated 200m NW of this. Glacier World, Hoffelli 2B, 781 Hornafirðl, +354 867 7416. www.glacierworld.is
64.3974, -15.3393

5 HVERAGIL

Very remote and really spectacular hot spring that runs through a very narrow lava canyon and over several small waterfalls. Hike in and then soak in the pools and shower under the waterfalls. A fairytale canyon swathed in steam and a very special experience.

➜ Extremely remote. From Egilsstaðir, take the F931 SW, then turn W onto the F910, then L onto the F902. Continue until you reach the

cabin at Sigurðarskáli (64.7473, -16.6314) (approx 55km). From here there is a trail to Hveragil, which is approx 12km over rough terrain. A local map and compass are essential and it's advisable to let someone know your intended route.

3 hours, 64.6760, -16.5594 🖼️📷🏔️⚙️

FIRE & ICE

6 JÖKULSÁRLÓN

A literal translation of this place name is 'glacial river lagoon'. Jökulsárlón is a large and very dramatic glacial lake at the head of the Breiðamerkurjökull glacier. Many years ago the glacier reached as far as the sea, but global warming has caused it to retreat and the lake is increasing in size. The ancient ice that calves into the lake looks luminous blue from the road, but is actually crystal-clear seen at close quarters. It's possible to take a boat ride on the lake and get right up to the glacier itself and some of the icebergs. Taste some ice that's over a thousand years old.

➜ From the town of Höfn (64.2497, -15.2064), travel N on the R99, turn L onto the R1, and continue for approx 70km. Jökulsárlón is to the R of the road and is easy to see.

64.0747, -16.2227 🚗📷🚶

7 DIAMOND BEACH

If the weather and sea conditions are right, mother nature may treat you to another breathtaking spectacle at the Jökulsárlón. Smaller icebergs and blocks of ice can break free from the lagoon and get pulled out to sea by the tide. The incoming tidal currents then deposit them along the beach south of the lagoon. This beach is composed of jet-black volcanic sand and when the ice washes up and the sun shines through it the result is so magical it will leave you completely speechless. And you'll understand why it's called Diamond Beach.

➜ Follow directions for Jökulsárlón (see 6). The beach is on the seaward side of the road.

10 mins, 64.0268, -16.2302 📷🌀

WATERFALLS

8 SVARTIFOSS

The 'Black Fall' can be found in the Vatnajökull National Park and is a popular spot. Framed by dark hexagonal basalt columns, the water plunges 20m straight down onto jagged rocks and is an impressive sight. The distinctive columns here inspired the design of both the Hallgrímskirkja church and the National Theatre in Reykjavík.

→ Starting at the junction of the R998 and R1 (E of Kirkjubæjarklaustur), head NW on the R998 for 3km up the valley on a winding track, past the R turn to the visitor centre. Park here and follow the well-signed trail for 1.5km.
20 mins, 64.0210, -16.9816 ⬛⬛

NATIONAL PARKS & HIKES

9 INGÓLFSHÖFÐI CAPE

An isolated cape and nature reserve connected to the mainland by a bar of black volcanic sand. It is named after Ingólfur Arnarson who was the first person to settle in Iceland from mainland Scandinavia, spending the winter here in 874-875 before moving further west. There is a substantial bird colony on the headland, which is home to thousands of seabirds including puffins and the great skua. If you explore further you will also find a lighthouse and the remains of old fishermen's huts.

→ Ride on a tractor trailer through the marshes to Ingólfshöfði. The start point is signposted off R1 just west of the HQ of the operator Local Guide (63.8814, -16.6461), +345 894 1317. www.localguide.is
63.8463, -16.6057 🖼️🐎

HISTORY & CULTURE

10 KIRKJUBÆJARKLAUSTUR

The gateway village to the basalt pavement of Kirkjugólf and the Vatnajökull National Park. Before settlers arrived from mainland Scandinavia, Irish monks lived here. In 1186 the convent of Kirkjubæjar ('church farm cloister') was established, remaining until the Reformation around 1550. In the highlands above the village you'll discover Systravatn (Lake of the Sisters) and flowing from it in two long tongues down towards the village is Systrafoss (Waterfall of the Sisters). According to legend, two nuns drowned in the lake and apparently redheads in Iceland can trace their family history back to the monks!

→ The turning into Kirkjubæjarklaustur is just N of the bridge over the Skaftá river on the R1.
63.7867, -18.0670 ✝️

LOCAL FOOD

11 RANDULFF'S SEA HOUSE

Located in Eskifjörður, this lodging and herring-processing building for fishermen from the late 1800s is now a museum and restaurant. The restaurant is on the first floor, while the second is a well-preserved

fishermen's quarters where you'll find artefacts belonging to the original tenants. It's named after Randulff, the Norwegian who built it and who left the upper part completely untouched when fishing went into decline. Until the building was purchased by a museum trust in 1980, it had lain undisturbed for over 70 years. The restaurant offers local delicacies such as shark meat, dried fish, pickled herring and reindeer, as well as fresh fish from the fjord. It's run by the proprietors of the Mjóeyri guesthouse, who also rent out small boats with outboard motors for fishing in the fjord. The fishing here is very good.

→ Mjóeyri Guesthouse: Strandgata, 735 Eskifjörður, +354 477 1247. www.mjoeyri.is
65.0603, -13.9931

12 HUMARHÖFNIN

Local food restaurant specialising in delicious langoustine landed from the boats in the harbour you can see from the window. All dishes on the menu are freshly prepared with produce sourced from the immediate Ríki Vatnajökuls region.

→ Located in the town of Höfn 5km S of Route 1 beside the harbour. Hafnarbraut, 780 Höfn, +354 478 1200. www.humarhofnin.is
64.2506, -15.2051

13 HÓTEL FRAMTÍÐ

Slow food restaurant and boutique hotel in a tiny fishing village with a population of only 450. The daily special is always the catch of the day from the adjacent harbour. Very cosy rooms. Fishing equipment can be borrowed if you'd like to try catching your own dinner.

→ Located beside the harbour in the village of Djúpivogur just off Route 1. Vogalandi 4, Markarland, 765 Djúpivogur, +354 478 8887. www.hotelframtid.com
64.6562, -14.2804

ACCOMMODATION

14 HOTEL SKAFTAFELL

A basic hotel built to withstand the severe winter weather but in a stunning location and perfect for exploring the Vatnajökull glacier area. The hotel has stunning panoramic views of both the glacier and Hvannadalshnúkur, which at 2,109m, is Iceland's highest mountain. The restaurant serves good local food.

→ Located 14km W of Hof on Route 1: Skaftafelli 2, Freysnesi, 785 Öræfi, +354 478 1945. www.hotelskaftafell.is
63.9906, -16.8922

15 SILFURBERG

Small boutique hotel located on the Þorgrímsstaðir farm in the picturesque Breiðdalur valley. The kitchen specialises in healthy and delicious local food. There's also a sauna and outdoor hot tub.

→ 54km S of Egilsstaðir on R1: Þorgrímsstaðir, 760 Breiðdalsvík, +354 475 1515. www.silfurberg.com
64.8945, -14.5058 🛏️ 🍴

16 LAUGARFELL HIGHLAND HOSTEL

A guesthouse and café located in the eastern part of the Icelandic Highlands that during the summer is accessible with a normal car and is a great starting-off point for several great hikes. There are two natural hot springs (see 2). Keep an eye out for reindeer.

→ 70km SW of Egilsstaðir: 701 Laugarfell, +354 773 3323. www.highlandhostel.is
64.8860, -15.3520 🛏️ 🍴 ♨️ ⛺

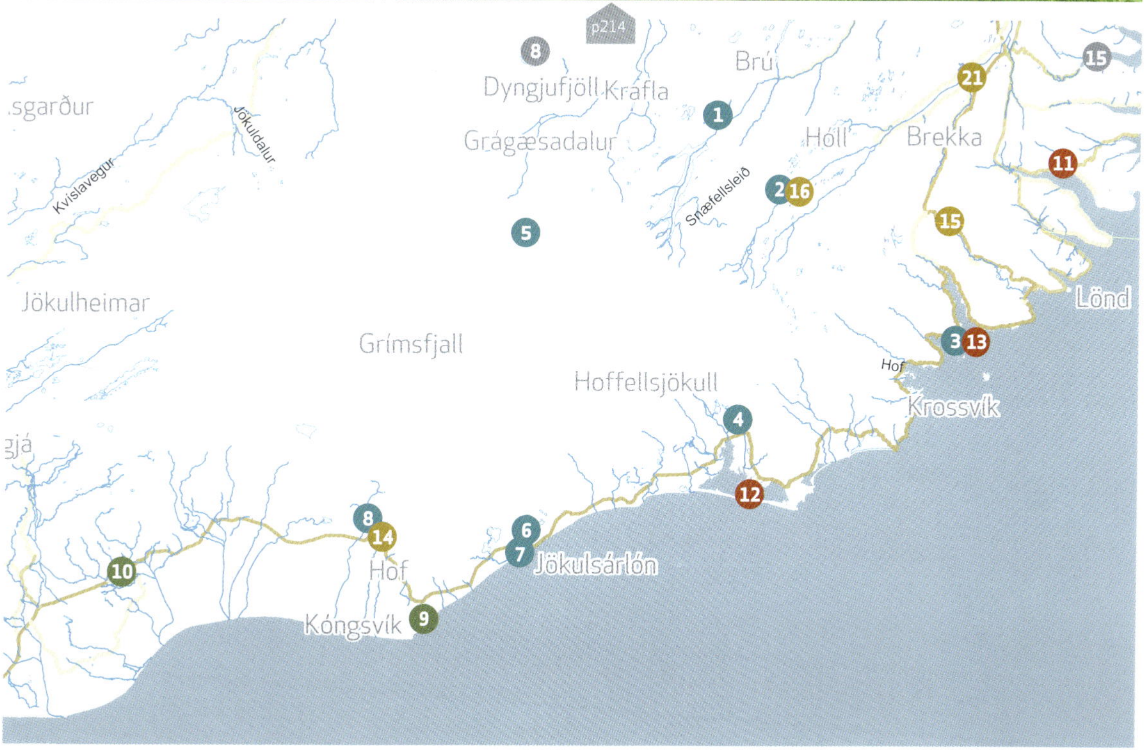

DENMARK

SEALAND COAST AROUND COPENHAGEN

Our perfect week

→ **Row** a Viking longship at the Roskilde Viking Ship Museum.

→ **Sip** craft ales from the Herslev microbrewery while camping at their secret local beach.

→ **Picnic** on the ramparts of Hamlet's castle at Elsinore.

→ **Camp** in an old fortress ringed by a moat.

→ **Swim** in a saltwater pool made from African adobe wood at Kastrup Søbad.

→ **Find** the King's Oak in a forest park and measure its girth.

→ **Cook** dinner over an open fire at the Røsnæs Nature School.

→ **Stay** in the only room at the Central Hotel & Café in Copenhagen.

→ **Experience** life as a Viking at the Land of Legends.

→ **Fish** for your dinner at Bjerge South beach.

Heading north along the east coast from the Danish capital, Copenhagen, at the town of Helsingør you can be excused for thinking you've travelled back in time. Here an impressive fairytale castle stands sentinel over the Øresund (the sound between Sweden and Denmark), which at that point is only four kilometres wide. Called Kronborg, it is perhaps better known as Elsinore in Shakespeare's *Hamlet*.

Denmark is made up of more than 400 islands, and Sealand is the largest of them. Since 2000, Sealand has been permanently connected to the Swedish mainland by the very impressive Øresund Bridge, which is almost eight kilometres long. Many people now use it to commute, crossing the sound every day to work in Malmö (at the Swedish end).

Wherever your adventures on the island take you, it will never be far from a beach. Even around Copenhagen there are great opportunities for a dip and in the Øresund, not far from the centre of the capital, are three very special saltwater swimming baths. Camp just outside the city within the ramparts of a 19th-century fortress (see 22) and start your urban explorations with a refreshing swim after following a traffic-free cycle path into town.

Everywhere you go in Denmark you will discover evidence of the Viking period. The Viking ship museum at Roskilde is well worth a visit and has some particularly fascinating archaeological finds on display. These include an excavated Viking ship that was one of several sunk in the adjacent fjord as 'block' ships to act as an underwater barricade in the 11th century. One of the most direct links to this period, though, is not a museum exhibit but a living person. Margrethe II, the current queen, is the 53rd in an unbroken line of Danish monarchs that goes right back to 980.

According to an old Norse legend, the island of Sealand was carved out of Sweden by the goddess Gefjun. Take a look at a map of Sweden and find Lake Vänern (the largest lake). It is indeed a very similar shape to Sealand.

BEACHES

1 GUDMINDRUP BEACH

Classic sandy Danish beach fringed with grassy dunes. Great for children – the bottom shelves very gently and there are no dangerous currents. Windsurfing and kitesurfing are popular here and you can rent boards and kit. During the summer months there's a manned lifeguard tower. Located on the west coast of Sealand only a couple of hours from Copenhagen.

➔ The beach runs to W of, and parallel with, the R21 as it passes through the town of Gudmindrup. Numerous access points.

10 mins, 55.908, 11.5277

2 SANDDOBBERNE BEACH

Sandy beach with a large lagoon to the rear backed by dunes, giving it the feel of a desert island. The beach and dunes are protected and part of the Odsherred Geopark, an area once weighed down by huge sheets of ice. The name Sanddobbernes refers to the low and irregular sand dunes which formed when the glaciers retreated. The lagoon warms up in the sun and is great for small children to paddle in.

➔ From Snertinge 7.5km N on the R225. Road runs parallel to the beach for about 2km and parking is between the road and the sea.

5 mins, 55.7750, 11.3808

3 BJERGE SOUTH BEACH

Another quintessentially Danish beach, bordered by dunes and very spacious. Why not bring a fishing rod and try to catch your dinner from the beach?

➔ Follow the R22 S from Kalundborg for approx 10km then turn R onto Nørrevang just before the OK filling station. This road will take you all the way to the beach.

5 mins, 55.5774, 11.1526

4 HØVE BEACH

Beautiful rough sandy beach backed by broad-leaved woodland. Bring a hammock and string it up between two trees on the shoreline. The beach is popular with nudists.

➔ Follow Route 225 through Høve to the village of Høve Strand and find numerous points of access to the beach.

5 mins, 55.8585, 11.5091

5 TISVILDELEJE BEACH

The further you walk along this beach, in the opposite direction to the town, the more beautiful it gets. To the rear are high dunes and scrub then broad-leaved woodland. Clear, clean water and a gently shelving beach make this a great place for children. The name 'Tisvilde' derives from 'Ti's vælde', and means a place dedicated to Tyr, a Norse deity associated with justice and heroic glory.

➔ Follow the R237 from Rågeleje W to where it ends at a car park by the beach. From here you can walk either way, but head off SW to leave civilisation behind.

56.0630, 12.0746

SWIMMING

6 KASTRUP SØBAD

Beautifully designed seawater baths constructed from azobe, an African hardwood that doesn't rot. Illuminated at night, the sea bath features platforms and diving towers and great views of the Øresund Bridge. Close to central Copenhagen.

➔ On the E coast of Amager 5km N of the Danish end of the Øresund Bridge at the S end of the Amager Strandpark. Amager Strandvej 301, 2770 Kastrup, +45 30 760235. www.taarnby.dk/oplev-taarnby/idraetslivet-i-taarnby/kastrup-soebad

55.6453, 12.6494

7 DRAGØR SØBAD

Old seawater swimming baths with three separate pools – a main (mixed) pool and two single-sex pools where you're allowed to swim naked. Walls on three sides offer privacy as well as protection from any wind. Situated in the old fishing village of Dragør.

➜ On the E coast of Amager. 8km S of the Danish end of the Øresund Bridge immediately SW of Dragør Fort. Batterivej 15, 2791 Dragør, +45 32 530564. www.hollaenderhallen.dk 55.5869, 12.6755

8 HELGOLAND

One of the oldest seawater swimming baths in Copenhagen, constructed in 1913 and fully renovated in 2008. While it was being restored, many regular swimmers purchased the old wooden planks as souvenirs. There's a mixed area and two single-sex areas where swimwear is optional. The water is deep so it's more suitable for adults than children.

➜ On the E coast of Amager, 7km N of the Danish end of the Øresund Bridge at the N end of the Amager Strandpark. Helgoland Badeanstalt, Øresundsstien 11, 2300 København S, +45 26 302482. www.facebook.com/Helgolandbadeanstalt/ 55.6637, 12.6401

CULTURE & HISTORY

9 ROSKILDE VIKING SHIP MUSEUM

Excellent museum documenting the history of seafaring, boatbuilding and ships in Denmark during the medieval and prehistoric periods. Among the exhibits are remains of several ships that were deliberately sunk in the Roskilde Fjord in the 11th century to form an underwater barrier against attack. Also on display is the longest Viking ship ever discovered – a colossal 36m. Floating on the fjord itself you'll see a 29.4m reconstructed Viking longship called the 'Sea Stallion'; in 2007 it sailed from Roskilde to Dublin. For the ultimate Viking experience contact the museum to find out when it would be possible to try crewing it.

➜ The museum is in the town of Roskilde, at the head of the fjord next to the water. Vindeboder 12, 4000 Roskilde, +45 46 300200. www.vikingeskibsmuseet.dk 55.6508, 12.0805

10 KRONBORG SLOT

The setting for Shakespeare's *Hamlet*, this castle in Helsingør – 'Elsinore' in English – is now a UNESCO World Heritage Site. A building was established here in the

11

1420s and expanded by Frederik II in the 16th century, only to be largely destroyed by fire in 1629 when it was subsequently rebuilt by his son. According to legend, the knight Holger the Dane is said to be sleeping underground and will return to defend the castle should Denmark ever face danger. During the Second World War 'Holger Danske' was the name used by a Danish resistance group. With its powerful fortifications and copper pinnacles, this castle will definitely make an impression on you. Great spot for a picnic.

→ The castle is in Helsingør on a promontory. Signed off the E47, N of where the ferry leaves for Helsingborg. Kronborg 2C, 3000 Helsingør, +45 49 213078. www.kronborg.dk
5 mins, 56.0390, 12.6212

11 SAGNLANDET, LAND OF LEGENDS

Archaeological open-air museum with numerous reconstructions including an Iron Age village and sacrificial bog, an 18th-century farmstead and a Viking marketplace. Many families come and live here for a week at a time to dress in period costume and recreate the past. Learn about ancient skills and handicrafts such as flintknapping, weaving and blacksmithing.

→ 10km W of Roskilde on the R21, turn L onto Orehøjvej for 3.2km then R on Ledreborg Allé. At the end of the road turn R onto Slangealleen for 1.3km to arrive at the museum. Slangealleen 2, 4320 Lejre, +45 46 480878. www.sagnlandet.dk
5 mins, 55.6160, 11.9439

12 TRELLEBORG VIKING RING FORTRESS

Best-known example of a Viking ring castle, – a type of circular fort also known as a 'trelleborg'. Often surrounded by ramparts, it had roads and gates pointing in the four cardinal directions. This one was built around AD 980 and one weekend every July a Viking market is held there. It's likely that it was built by King Harald Bluetooth who, coincidentally, inspired the name for modern wireless technology.

→ From the village of Hejninge head S on Hejningvej and take the first R to head W on Trelleborg Allé. This brings you directly to the museum by the fort. Trelleborg Allé 4, Hejninge, 4200 Slagelse, +45 58 549506. www.vikingeborgen-trelleborg.dk
5 mins, 55.3940, 11.2656

12

NATURE & WILDLIFE

13 RØSNÆS

Very rugged and beautiful peninsula where cliffs and woodland drop down to rocks and a narrow strip of white-sand beach. The trees and shrubs have been shaped by the wind, and from the cliffs there are amazing sea views. At the small nature school here they keep farm animals and run a variety of educational activities. There's a fire pit and outdoor tables, making it ideal for a picnic.

→ The Røsnæs peninsula is reached by following Røsnæsvej W from Kalundborg. For the nature school: Røsnæs Naturskole, Røsnæsvej 458, 4400 Kalundborg, +45 59 509776. www.rns.dk
15 mins, 55.7394, 10.8928

14 JÆGERSBORG DYREHAVE

Forest park not far from Copenhagen, which covers about 11sq km and is home to numerous veteran oaks and a large population of over 2,000 fallow and red deer.

→ The park is 1km E of the E47 as it passes through Hjortekær. For more information about the parks and a calendar of events, contact: Jægersborg, Dyrehaven, 2930 Klampenborg, +45 39 973900. www.ltk.dk/jaegersborg-dyrehave
15 mins, 55.8027, 12.5752

15 TYSTRUP-BAVELSE LAKES

Two lakes separated only by a short channel through a low spit of land. This channel is the river Suså, which runs through the 20m-deep pools formed by glacial meltwater during the last ice age. Great spot for birdwatching and wild swimming.

→ Head S of Sorø on the R157 and after 10km Tystrup lake is on E side of road.
10 mins, 55.3660, 11.5692

16 KONGEEGEN

The King Oak is estimated to be 1500–2000 years old and has a trunk circumference of 14m. The shape and structure of the tree has led people to believe that it once grew in an open meadow and it could be the oldest living oak in the whole of Northern Europe.

→ Find the oak in woodland very close to the NW edge of the Roskilde Fjord opposite Ølsted on the other side of the fjord. You'll need to consult a local map.
20 mins, 55.9103, 11.9892

LOCAL FOOD

17 FUGLEBJERGGAARD

Fascinating and diverse organic farm with a shop selling a range of produce. There is also a fantastic café, restaurant and cookery school – a great opportunity for tasting Scandinavian organic gastronomy at its best.

→ 55 km N of Copenhagen. Hemmingstrupvej 8, 3200 Helsinge, +45 48 393943. www.fuglebjerggaard.dk
56.0561, 12.2427

18 HERSLEV BRYGHUS

Charming micro-brewery located in beautiful surroundings in the village of Herslev at the centre of the Skjoldungelandet National Park. Taste and stock up on their delicious organic beers – try the honey and chamomile brew – and head to the local beach to camp for the night. Staff at the brewery will tell you where you can find a camping shelter and fireplace.

→ Located in the centre of the village of Herslev approx 10km NE of Roskilde: Kattingevej 16, Herslev, 4000 Roskilde, +45 46 401807. www.herslevbryghus.dk
55.6695, 11.9850

SLEEP

19 CENTRAL HOTEL & CAFÉ

Quirky and very small hotel in downtown Copenhagen that has only one room. Located above a tiny coffee shop that has seating for only five. Book well in advance if you'd like to stay here.

→ Tullinsgade is just off Gammel Kongevej, 800m W of Vesterport Station. Tullinsgade 1, 1610 Copenhagen V, +45 33 210095. www.centralhotelogcafe.dk
55.6740, 12.5515

20 HOTEL DRAGSHOLM SLOT

Originally built in 1215 but then remodelled in the Baroque style in the 17th century, Dragsholm Castle is now a hotel. One of the oldest castles in Denmark and the oldest building in use as a hotel, it is reputed to be haunted by no fewer than three ghosts. Situated in beautiful countryside and with a restaurant renowned for its gourmet dishes made from locally sourced ingredients.

→ Just off the R225 (Kalundborgvej), 8.5km N of Snertinge village. Dragsholm Allé, 4534 Hørve, +45 59 653300. www.dragsholm-slot.dk
55.7711, 11.3910

21 NAKKEHOVED ØSTRE FYR

Bed & breakfast in an old lighthouse keeper's cottage dating back to 1772. The lighthouse is one of the few preserved coal lighthouses in the world. Panoramic views out to sea and across to Sweden from the gardens.

→ On the coast immediately E of Gillette. Fyrvejen 29 B, 3250 Gilleleje, +45 21 235440. www.bblighthouse.dk

56.1192, 12.3487

22 CHARLOTTENLUND FORT CAMPING

Unusual campsite at the centre of a 19th-century fortress (complete with howitzers!) only 7km from the centre of Copenhagen. Not wild camping but cosy and perfectly situated for a 25-minute cycle ride into the heart of the capital. The quirky site has only 65 pitches and its kitchen and bathrooms are located in the old casemates. Bicycles can be hired and there's also a small café where you can buy freshly baked bread and pastries.

→ The fort is on an island surrounded by a moat in Charlottenlund just off Route 152. Strandvejen 144 B, 2920 Charlottenlund, +45 44 220065. www.campingcopenhagen.dk

55.7463, 12.5871

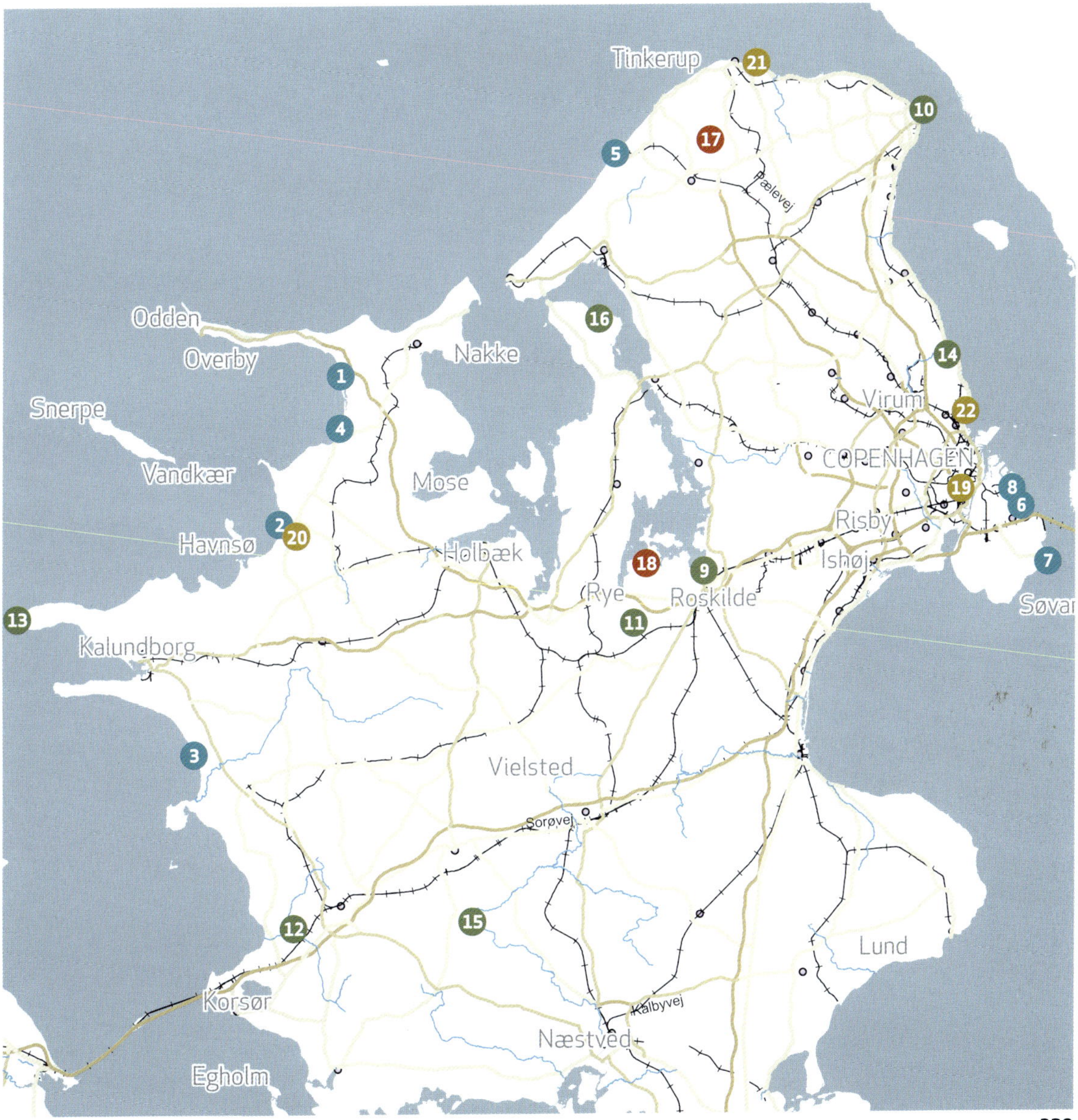

FUNEN

Our perfect week

- → **Camp** in a wildflower meadow at Sarup Teltplads.
- → **Enjoy** the view over the archipelago from the Svanninge Bakker.
- → **Watch** the kite-surfers from Flyvesandet beach.
- → **Investigate** a Bronze Age passage grave by candlelight.
- → **Watch** the sunset from Funen Head.
- → **Cook** dinner over an open fire at the Åløkkestedet nature school.
- → **Explore** the islands of the South Funen archipelago by kayak.
- → **Stay** overnight in a unique coastal shelter.
- → **Gather** juniper berries on Enebærodde to cook with the fish you've caught.
- → **Wade** out to Æbelø Island at low tide.

If you rely on roads to explore Funen then you'll miss out on some of the very best that the island has to offer. A sea kayak will take you on a halcyon adventure out to unspoiled islands and along the coast to hidden beaches. In the southern islands you can then stay overnight in a network of basic yet wonderfully unique shelters.

The third-largest of the Danish islands, Funen is connected by a bridge to Sealand and by two additional bridges to Jutland. Odense, the main city (named after the Norse god Odin) is located centrally at the head of a fjord of the same name, but Funen's remaining towns are dotted around the 1,100 km-long coastline. Idyllic sandy beaches characterise this coast and there are 96 offshore islands, most of them forming an archipelago off the south coast.

Inland treasures on the island range from thatched farmhouses with pastures and orchards to prehistoric sites, and castles. This magical landscape has a rich tradition of folk tales, and Norse mythology from the area is packed full of mythical beings. Tell children about the nisse, who was said to live in the house and barns of a farm and act as a guardian spirit. He could, however, be mean and troublesome so people left out food, such as a bowl of porridge, to appease him.

It's easy to see where the world-famous Dane, Hans Christian Andersen, got the inspiration for his enduring stories. He grew up here, and throughout your explorations on Funen you're likely to see his name in several locations and meet statues of many of the characters from his stories. If your plans include heading off to Copenhagen, don't forget to also visit the Little Mermaid.

Why not explore the island at a nice slow pace in a horse-drawn wagon fitted out like a traditional gypsy caravan? As you wend your way between campsites there'll be plenty of time to stop and fish or forage. Whatever your age, it's easy to create your own fairytale adventure on the island of Funen.

BEACHES & ISLANDS

1 TØRRESØ BEACH

Thin sandy beach close to the town that's good for swimming and windsurfing. Unlike most other beaches in the area, this one is next to a rocky breakwater and road rather than sand dunes. A handy spot for fishing if you want to carry equipment from your car.

➜ Immediately N of Otterup off the R162 on the N coast of Funen. Numerous access points.

5 mins, 55.5985, 10.3850

2 FLYVESANDET BEACH

Popular family beach on the north coast of Funen west of Tørresø (see 1) and north-west of the small town of Otterup. The beach shelves very gradually making it extremely shallow and safe for children. Explore the big sand dunes then watch the wind- and kite-surfers do their stuff out at sea.

➜ Follow Flyvesandsvej W from Agernæs to the end of the road by Flyvesandet Camping. The beach is adjacent to the camping area.

10 mins, 55.6220, 10.2979

3 ENEBÆRODDE

This spit of land, 6km long and from 20–750m wide, is a protected area rich in flora and fauna. Its name means 'Juniper Spit' – a reference to the abundance of juniper shrubs growing there. You may catch sight of adders and lizards and there are excellent views across Odense Fjord, which is a bird sanctuary. If you make the effort to walk across the causeway then you're very likely to find an isolated beach all to yourself.

➜ From Hasmark E of the R162, take Strandvejen to the coast, park. Follow Halshusene on foot SE along the coast and then along the causeway to Enebærodde.

1.5 hrs, 55.5218, 10.5531

4 DREJØ

An idyllic, small island in the middle of the South Funen archipelago with an area of 4.26 sq km, and measuring just 2km at the widest point. In the pretty village, the houses are half-timbered and the shoreline offers sandy beaches that are great for swimming and watching seabirds. Getting to the island involves taking a ferry from Svendborg (55.0575, 10.6144) through the scenic Svendborgsund (Svendborg Sound).

➜ Ferry M/F Højestene leaves from the main harbour in Svendborg, +45 6223 3080. www.svendborg-havn.dk/højestene.

75 mins, 54.9708, 10.4190

5 SKARØ

Another small island in the South Funen Archipelago, located at the mouth of the Svendborgsund and served by the same ferry as Drejø (see 4). Only 1.97km long, it is easily explored on foot or by bike. Largely salt marsh, it's home to numerous seabirds. Swim from one of the many unspoilt sandy beaches.

35 mins, 55.0054, 10.4651

6 SOUTH FUNEN ARCHIPELAGO BY KAYAK

Explore some of the 55 low-lying and tranquil islands that comprise the South Funen Archipelago. Novice kayakers can hug the coast in the shallow water and those with more experience can cross between islands. Kayaks and equipment can be hired from Nicus Nature, who will also give safety instruction and help you to plan a route appropriate to the conditions and your skill level. For a multi-day trip you can stop overnight along the network of coastal shelters (see 18).

➜ Nicus Nature are based near the harbour in the town of Svendborg. Kullinggade 2, 5700 Svendborg, +45 40 418982. www.nicusnature.com

55.0569, 10.6126

CULTURE & HISTORY

7 DEN FYNSKE LANDSBY

Fascinating open-air village museum with a collection of buildings from the 18th and 19th centuries. The land is managed and cultivated as it would have been during the 1850s and you'll see historic breeds of horses and cows roaming the pastures. The museum recreates a village environment from the same period and during the summer people in traditional costume go about their daily tasks, including milking and baking bread.

➜ Located in S Odense approx 2km N of exit 50 on the E20, Sejerskovvej 20, 5260 Odense S, +45 65 514601. www.museum.odense.dk
55.3665, 10.3852

8 NORDFYNS MUSEUM

Great local museum with a really interesting collection of archaeological finds from North Funen, particularly from the Viking period. There is also an exhibition of the geology of the island of Æbelø (see 13).

➜ The museum is in the town of Bogense close to the harbour. Vestergade 16, 5400 Bogense, +45 64811884, www.nordfynsmuseum.dk
55.5649, 10.0861

9 GLAVENDRUPSTENEN

This spectacular rune stone is decorated with the longest runic inscription (210 runic letters) carved on a stone in the country. Said to have been erected around AD 900 by Ragnhild, the stone commemorates her husband Alle – a local chieftain and a priest. It's part of one of the longest of all the preserved stone ships – burial sites surrounded by stones forming the outline of a ship – found in Denmark. The original site would have had double rows of stones 60m long and 12m wide. The inscription ends in a curse.

➜ The stone is in a grove of trees approx 0.5km N of the village of Glavendrup (55.5053, 10.2945) on the Stenager road. The entrance is beside the road on the L where you can park.
55.5090, 10.2973

10 MÅRHØJ JÆTTESTUE

The largest Bronze Age passage grave (communal tomb) on Funen and very well preserved. Bring a torch or even better, some candles, as it's very dark inside. Fascinating but a little spooky.

➜ From the village of Martofte on the R315 head N for 500m and take the first R. Follow this road for about 800m and you will see the mound 280m to L in the middle of a field.
5 mins, 55.5588, 10.6621

NATURE & WILDLIFE

11 SVANNINGE BAKKER

The Svanninge Hills formed at the end of the last ice age and have been inhabited since the Stone Age. Originally covered by forest, over time the inhabitants felled the trees and the thin, sandy soil that remained was not productive. Now part of a conservation project to encourage more grassland, these hills offer amazing views to the south west and across the South Funen archipelago.

➜ Immediately E of the village of Svanninge (off the R329) with several access points.
20 mins, 55.1273, 10.2504

12 HINDSHOLM PENINSULA

The Hindsholm Peninsula juts out into the Kattegat. It's an idyllic mix of rural villages, white-sand beaches, rolling hills and rugged open spaces. Fyns Hoved, or Funen Head, is the northernmost point on Funen. The many drystone walls date back to 1810 when seven farmers in the village of Nordskov agreed to divide up the land in the area so that each would have one northern and one southern strip. During the Second World War the Germans built numerous defences here to guard the entrance to the strait and you can also see these remains.

➜ Heading NE on the R315 from Kerteminde will take you through the Hindsholm Peninsula as far as the parking area for Fyns Hoved.
55.6137, 10.5948

13 ÆBELØ

Beautiful uninhabited island in the Kattegat off Funen's north coast. Part of it is a nature reserve with oak and beech forest, and there are grassy areas where you'll see fallow deer or mouflon. The island is 2.09km2 and you can wade over to it. Start from Jersore and walk 1.5km along Lindøhoved to the coast, then wade across to Æbelø Holm and then along the Brådet sandbar for 4km to Æbelø. Wear old shoes and be aware of the tides.

➜ Æbelø is off the N coast of Funen approx 8km NE of Bogense (R162).
1 hour, 55.6405, 10.1764

14 NATURE SCHOOL ÅLØKKESTEDET

Learn all about nature at this educational centre that's also open to the public. You can hire canoes to paddle on the lakes, cook food over the campfire or stay overnight in one of their hiking shelters.

➜ E of Rolfsted off R301. Hudevad Byvej 20, 5792 Årslev, +45 63 750990. www.oversoeogland.dk
55.3166, 10.5414

DRINK LOCAL

15 AQUA VITAE SYDFYN

Small distillery crafting fruit spirits from produce grown in orchards on the northern limit of the zone in which it's possible to cultivate apples, pears, cherries and plums. Buy an aperitif for your beach picnic.

→ 5km E of Svendborg; Skårupørevej 22, 5881 Skårup, +45 61 368183, www.aquavitaesydfyn.dk
55.0798, 10.6965 🍴

SLEEP WILD

16 HORSES AND PRAIRIE WAGON HIRE

Explore the lanes of Funen in a wagon towed by two horses, with different camping areas for overnight stops. No previous knowledge is required and you get all the training you need before you head off. The wagons are furnished like gypsy caravans with sleeping berths for 4 people and cooking facilities.

→ Skårup is off the R163 E of Svendborg, Holmdrup Huse 3, 5881 Skårup,
+45 62 231825, www.hestevognsferie.com
55.0733, 10.6742 🐎

17 SARUP TELTPLADS

Basic campsite in beautiful and secluded rural location with views across wildflower meadows. As well as space for 2–3 tents, there's a three-sided wooden hiking shelter, a compost toilet and access to water. In bad weather it's possible to sleep in the hayloft.

→ From Haarby head W on R323. Take first L (Kirkenmarken) and follow it for 2.2km. For the last 400m it turns R and becomes Søbrovej. Campsite is on R. Søbrovej 12, Sarup, 5683 Haarby, +45 51 328837. www.portenisarup.dk
55.2094, 10.0862 ⛺🏕️♿

18 ARCHIPELAGO SHELTERS

Network of unique hiking shelters located around the coastline of the Funen Archipelago. Each shelter has been carefully designed so that it does not distort or interfere with the landscape. In some locations there are individual shelters and in other places you'll find them in groups. Some of them can be booked in advance and others are free on a first-come-first-served basis. For a map and details of the complete network see the website. The coordinates below are for the two Elsehoved Strand beach shelters (sleeping 9 in total). To book call Ingrid & Michael Dissing on +45 20 267838.

→ From Route 163 in the village of Oure head SE on Hammesbrovej for 1.8km until the cross roads. Go straight over onto Elsehovedvej and follow for 2.5km to the beach. From the parking area follow the obvious grass path 100m N to the shelters. www.bookenshelter.dk
5mins, 55.1055, 10.7717 🚶🛏️🏕️🛶🔥

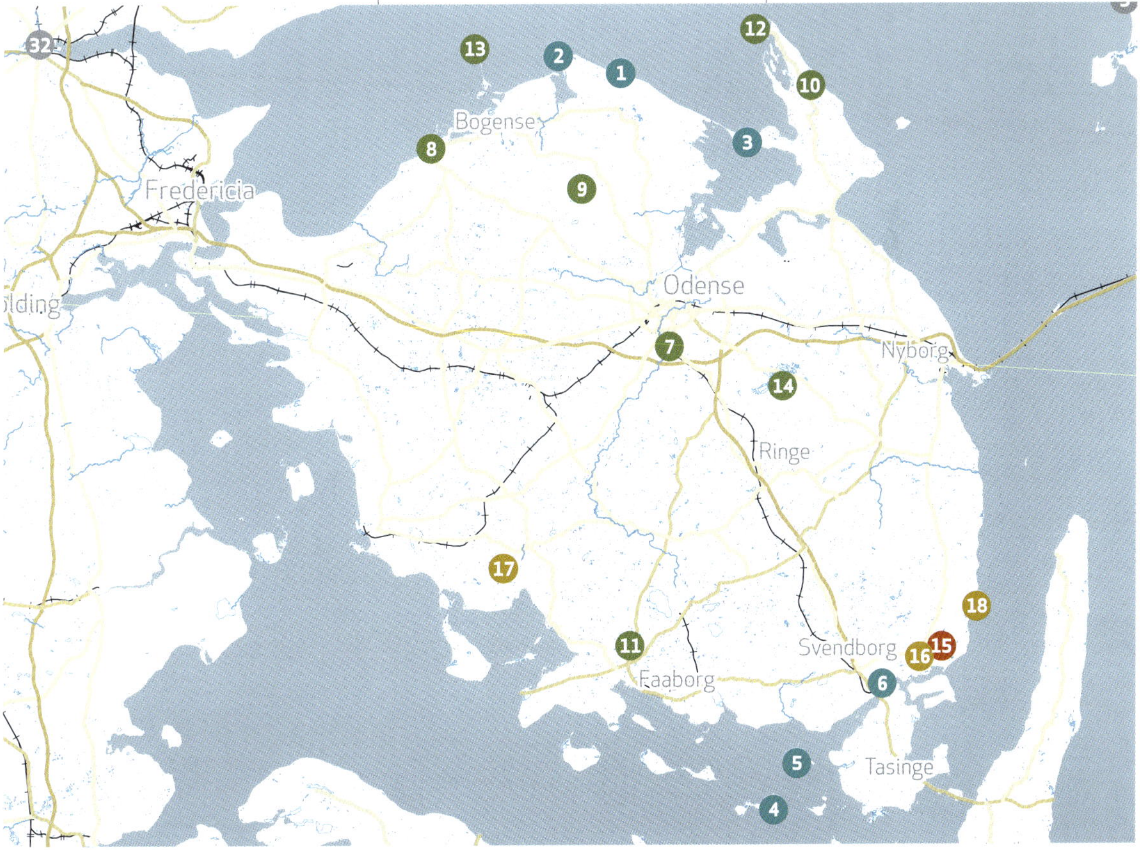

NORTH JUTLAND

Our favourite adventures

→ **Stand** with one foot in the Baltic and one in the North Sea while watching the waves battle at Grenen.

→ **Arrive** super early or sleep on the beach to watch the sun rise over the sea at Hou.

→ **Ride** the old munitions train at the Hanstholm museum.

→ **Climb** to the top of Råbjerg Mile and see the church steeple protruding from the sand.

→ **Camp** in a wildlife park where you get to say goodnight to all the animals before bed.

→ **Hunt** for fossils on the island of Fur.

→ **Meet** Tollund Man in the Silkeborg Museum.

→ **Explore** a Viking ring fortress and imagine life in a longhouse inside the walls.

→ **Picnic** in the grounds of a ruined castle at Kalø Slotsruin.

→ **Skinny** dip on a remote west coast beach at Kandestederne.

If you're on one of Jutland's many beaches on June 24th, you're likely to be invited to gather round a huge bonfire with much drinking, eating, singing and merriment. Known as Sankt Hans Aften, this evening festival celebrates St John who, according to the Christian calendar, was born six months before Jesus. The tradition is much older though, and based on an early pagan summer-solstice ritual when fires were lit to scare away witches. The bonfire you're gathered round may even be topped with an effigy of a witch.

The Danes, who have been voted the happiest people in the world by the United Nations, will describe this as a true moment of *hygge*. This is a unique word and one you will undoubtedly hear often on your travels in Denmark. Pronounced 'hoo-guh', it has no direct translation in English and refers to a special kind of cosiness – exactly what you might feel in the company of loved ones with good food and drink.

Jutland stretches from the border with Germany up to the topmost tip of Denmark where two great bodies of water meet – the Baltic and the North Sea. Here, two strong currents fight an eternal battle with waves from the Kattegat (Baltic) and Skagerrak (North Sea) straits colliding over a narrow spit of sand. Stand at the shore with a foot in each sea while you watch the spectacle.

This chapter focuses on the northern half of Jutland, where the many white sand beaches backed by sand dunes are ideal places to spend lazy summer days. Inland, there's a landscape rich in fascinating remains from the Viking period to discover.

When the wind blows and whips up some waves, get an early start at one of the northern beaches and look for a beautiful piece of amber. A local craftsperson will be able to make it into a special piece of jewellery and you'll have a unique souvenir of your adventures in Denmark.

BEACHES

1 GRENEN

At Denmark's northernmost point just off the tip of a sand spit, the strong currents of the Kattegat and the Skagerrak straits meet head on. Swimming is not allowed at this dangerous spot, but the clash of the two seas is a spectacular sight and you can paddle with a foot in each while watching the battling waves. The Danish name of this sandbar, Grenen, means 'branch' – a reference to its shape. You can either walk out to the point or catch a ride on a tractor and trailer that leaves from the parking area.

→ Follow the R40 3Km NE from the centre of Skagen (57.7248, 10.5972). Grenen is approx 1km walk from the car park.

30 mins, 57.7446, 10.6531 🖼

2 HIRSHOLMENE

Main island of a group of six lying in the Kattegat 7km north-east of Frederikshavn. A nature reserve since 1938, the islands have a significant seabird population. There's a manned lighthouse and a visitor centre with information on the island's rich plant and bird life. Visit the hidden beach of Præstebugten on the north shore with views towards the neighbouring island of Græsholm. Sheltered by a reef and with fine white sand, it's a great spot for swimming. You may be joined by seals.

→ There's a regular ferry service from Frederikshavn (57.4364, 10.5389). For timetable and booking information contact: +45 29.801438. www.seadog.dk

57.4844, 10.6230 🖼🏊

3 LØKKEN

Large sandy beach on the Skagerrak characterised by its fine white sand, dunes and fishing boats. At 10km long, finding your own space isn't difficult, or just make your way along the beach, exploring the numerous bunkers built by the Germans during the Second World War. At the end of the day the fishermen winch their boats up on the foreshore and you can often buy fresh fish. Finish your day by grilling fish on the beach while watching the sunset.

→ 40km NW of the city of Aalborg on the R55.

15 mins, 57.3710, 9.7029 🖼🏊🛶

4 BLÅVAND STRAND

Beautiful sandy North Sea beach that shelves very gradually and has very little current, making it ideal for small children. The calm conditions are created by the Horns Reef, which stretches about 40km out to sea. When the wind blows, the dunes offer shelter as do the many bunkers – relics of Hitler's Atlantic Wall. After a storm this beach is one of the best for finding amber. This fossilised tree resin floats over from the Baltic Sea and is washed ashore here by the waves. Archeological finds throughout Scandinavia often include jewellery made from amber as the Vikings wore amber amulets and traded it on their overseas expeditions. Try to find your own piece along the shoreline.

→ 30km NW of the town of Esbjerg. Follow the R431 from Bilium W to its end, just past the village of Oksby (55.5481, 8.1139).

55.5482, 8.1139 🖼🏊🚲

5 HOU BEACH

Sandy beach on the east coast lying north of the charming fishing port of Hou. Arrive very early and bring breakfast so you can sit on the beach and watch the spectacular sunrise. From the harbour catch a ferry out to the islands of Tunø and Samsø. Great swimming.

→ Hou is 10km SE of Odder on the R445 and the beach stretches N from the harbour area.

55.9270, 10.2577 🏊

6 KANDESTEDERNE

Wide sandy beach backed by high, cliff-like dunes on the west coast of the Skagen Odde peninsula. With vehicular access to over 20km of continuous beach, you can drive along and find your own secluded spot. For this reason it's a popular beach for nude bathing. Climb up into the dunes for great views out to sea.

→ On the R40 13km before Skagen, signposted L off the roundabout.
57.6622, 10.3790

7 HIRTSHALS

North Sea beach on the edge of the sea port of Hirtshals. Among the flotsam and jetsam washed up here after a storm, you'll find piles of seaweed and sea grass. Look carefully through these and you're likely to find some amber. Remember it isn't always obviously yellow so look for darker shades as well. Make an early start as you're likely to have competition.

→ Hirtshals is 60km N of the city of Aalborg on the E39. The beach runs E from the town with numerous access points. Use a local map.
57.5911, 9.9922

8 SKAGEN NORDSTRAND

Beach immediately to the west of Grenen (see 1) on the Skagerrak. Not safe for swimming owing to strong currents and waves, but a wonderful place to enjoy a local-food picnic sourced in nearby Skagen.

→ 1.5km NE of Skagen on the R40. Either park in Skagen and walk along the coast or park as for Grenen and walk back along the coast E towards Skagen.
20 mins, 57.7328, 10.6240

9 SKAGEN SØNDERSTRAND

Beach immediately to the east of Grenen (see 1) and stretching along the east coast of the Skagen Odde peninsula on the Kattegat as far as Højen. More protected than Skagerrak beach so you can safely swim here.

→ Follow Buttervej from a roundabout on the R40 in the centre of Skagen (57.7219, 10.5750) all the way to a parking area at the end of the road, or park as for Grenen (see 1) and walk round the spit for 2km.
57.7435, 10.5614

The image shows a number **8** marker in the lower left corner.

CULTURE & HISTORY

10 KALØ SLOTSRUIN

One of Denmark's largest and best-preserved ruined castles, built in 1313 by the Danish king Erik Menved. It's located on a small island in Kalø cove, connected to the mainland by a cobbled causeway. With its impressive walls and ramparts it's great fun to explore and a perfect spot for a picnic. Gustav Vasa, the future king of Sweden, was once held prisoner here.

➜ At the head of Kalø Vig (Bay) 30km NE of Aarhus; Molsvej 31, 8410 Rønde, www.kaloslot700.dk

56.2746, 10.4666

11 MUSEUMS CENTRE HANSTHOLM

Wherever you explore along the coast of Denmark you cannot help but notice the extensive defences built by the Germans during the Second World War. These were part of Hitler's Atlantic Wall and are now being washed into the sea, disappearing under the sand. At the museum at Hanstholm, located in an old coastal gun battery, you can discover more about the Danish section of these defences. Children will love riding on the old munitions train.

➜ In the coastal town of Hanstholm 90km W of Aalborg; Molevej 29, 7730 Hanstholm, +45 97 961736. www.museumscenterhanstholm.dk

57.1207, 8.6170

12 REBILD BAKKER

In 1912 a group of Danes who – like many others before them – had emigrated to the USA, purchased an area of Danish pastureland. Their gift to the Danish people was conditional on its being kept as a natural space where Danish-Americans could celebrate their shared heritage. It's now a beautiful national park where every year the Rebild organisation arranges festivities on American Independence Day.

➜ The park is immediately W of the centre of the town of Rebild, 30km S of Aalborg E of the E49. The organisation is based close to the park and has more information about events there; Rebildselskabet, Rebildvej 29, Rebild, 9520, Skørping. www.rebildfesten.dk

56.8367, 9.8353

13 HALS WHALE JAWS

Archway formed by two enormous jaw bones from a blue whale. The original pair, erected by a ship's captain from the town, were destroyed in 1953 when they were hit by

The image shows a number **12** marker and a number **11** marker.

a truck. The current bones, which must be from a whale that was over 30m long, were a gift in 1955 from the consul of Sandefjord in Norway.

→ The bones are at the west end of the town square (Torvet) in Hals, just off the R541 on the road signposted to the ferry.
56.9946, 10.3059 ⛴

14 TROLDKIRKEN – TROLL CHURCH
Stone Age dolmen set on top of a long barrow and surrounded by 47 standing stones. Local legend has it that a troll, annoyed by the ringing of church bells in the village, threw a large boulder at the church. Instead of destroying it, the boulder landed short, forming the capstone of the dolmen which became known as the Troll Church.

→ Head E out of the village of Sønderholm on Nibevej and take the first L (Troldkirkevej). The dolmen is 600m along this road on L.
57.0083, 9.7509 ✝ 📷

15 LINDHOLM HØJE
What at first glance appears to be just a rocky field is actually a graveyard used for burials from the Nordic Iron Age (5th century AD) through to c.1050 in the Viking Age. On closer inspection, patterns in the rocks

become apparent, including stones arranged in the shape of ships. There are over 700 graves here and the adjacent museum has some fascinating information about the site.

→ Lindholm is just off the R55 on the outskirts of Nørresundby, on the opposite bank of the Østerå river from Aalborg. Start at the adjacent museum: Lindholm Høje Museet, Vendilavej 11, 9400 Nørresundby, +45 99 317400 www.nordmus.dk
57.0782, 9.9101 ✝ 📷

16 SKOVSNOGEN ART SPACE
Wacky sculpture garden set in a forest. The first piece – a giant wooden snake you can crawl through – has been supplemented by a further 50 contributed by various artists. Have fun trying to find them all. Free entry with numerous events throughout the year.

→ From the village of Skarrild (55.9781, 8.8975) on the R439, head S on Sdr Ommevej for 15km and then turn L onto Døvlingvej. The entrance to the forest and parking are 140m along on N side of the road. Døvlingvej, 6933 Kibæk, +45 30 258658. www.skovsnogen.dk
55.9229, 8.9079 ⛴ 📷 🅿

17 RUBJERG KNUDE LIGHTHOUSE
Lighthouse built in 1900 on a cliff.

Subsequently, with coastal erosion at a rate of about 1m a year, the tower is now almost submerged beneath the shifting sands blown off the North Sea. See the lighthouse before it disappears completely.

→ From the village of Lønstrup (57.4738, 9.7975) W of Hjørring, head S on Strandvejen then Rubjergvej for approx 2.5km to see a sandy parking area on R side of the road. Park here and follow the track on foot for 1.3km to the lighthouse.

20 mins, 57.4489, 9.7744

18 AGGERSBORG

Largest of all the Viking Age ring fortresses in Denmark. Dating this one precisely has proved difficult because it's also the site of a previous Iron Age village. Believed to have been constructed around the time of King Harald Bluetooth and Sweyn Forkbeard (AD 980).

→ At the junction of Thorupvej and Aggersborgvej 1.7km SW of the village of Aggersund, off the R29.

56.9954, 9.2549

19 FYRKAT

Viking ring fortress from around 980AD from which traffic over the mainland route

between Aalborg and Aarhus would have been controlled. Just outside the fort is an accurate reconstruction of a Viking longhouse, and a visitor centre where you can find out more about daily life in the area in the Viking Age.

→ Start your visit at the Viking centre and make the short walk from here to the fortress. Head SW out of Hobro on Fyrkatvej and the centre is signposted on L. The fortress is a further 1km along the road on L. Viking Center Fyrkat, Fyrkatvej 37B, 9500 Hobro. +45 99 82 41 75. www.nordmus.dk

56.6232, 9.7705

20 JELLING STONES

Two massive carved rune stones from the tenth century. The first was raised by King Gorm the Old in memory of his wife Thyra, and the second by the king's son, Harold Bluetooth, in memory of his parents. The stone also celebrated Harold's conquest of Denmark and Norway, and the conversion of the Danes to Christianity. You'll also find here the two biggest burial mounds in Denmark, built over existing Bronze Age mounds. Buried beneath one of them is a huge stone ship, which at 354m long, far exceeds the size of any other similar ships.

→ The burial mounds are in the centre of Jelling (R442) at the opposite end of Stationsvej to the railway station and immediately S of the church.
55.7560, 9.4193

21 MUSEUM SILKEBORG

Former manor house, now a museum with an extensive collection of archaeological finds with a particular focus on the early Iron Age. The highlight for visitors is Tollund Man. He was discovered in a peat bog in 1950 in a state of such natural preservation that archeologists thought he was a recent murder victim. This mummified corpse of a man dating from before the Iron Age is believed to have been the victim of ritual sacrifice.

→ The museum is in the centre of Silkeborg: Hovedgårdsvej 7, 8600 Silkeborg. +45 86 821499. www.museumsilkeborg.dk
56.1690, 9.5531

NATURE & WILDLIFE

22 RÅBJERG MILE

Largest migrating sand dune in Northern Europe, which covers about 1 sq km, is 40m high and moves up to 18m per year. Whereas other dunes in the area have been stabilised, Råbjerg Mile has not and its continued movement is closely studied. It is currently in the process of consuming a church and now only the top of the steeple can be seen protruding from the sand.

→ Heading towards Skagen on the R40, turn L just before the village of Hulsig. After 3km turn L again and park. Råbjerg Mile is approx 500m walk across the sand dunes.
57.6482, 10.4060

23 FUR ISLAND

Beautiful island with an area of 22 sq km and a permanent population of less than 900 in the Limfjord at the northern tip of the Salling peninsula. Famous for its deposits of diatomite, the naturally occurring fossilised remains of diatoms (single-celled aquatic algae). Diatomite is used commercially as a filtering aid, a bulking agent and as an absorbent, for example in cat litter. Visit the island museum to get some tips on what to look for and then do some fossil-hunting at the base of the spectacular cliffs.

→ Catch the ferry to Fur at Branden, at N end of the R551. Fur Museum: Nederby 28, 7884 Fur, +45 975 93411. www.museumsalling.dk
56.8264, 9.0190

24 ROLD SKOV

The biggest and oldest forest in Denmark, rumoured to be the domain of trolls and other mysterious forest folk. There are several trails through 8,000 hectares of gnarled pines and beeches for exploring by bike or on foot.

➜ N of the village of Rold on the R535, 7.5km E of junction 33 on the E45.
For more information see: www.roldskov.info
56.7967, 9.8557

25 LILLE VILDMOSE

Raised bog and nature reserve that is the largest in Western Europe and the only one in Denmark. With a unique flora thanks to the plentiful supply of water and the nutrient-rich peat, it was part of an extensive area of heathland that stretched from Limfjorden to Rold Forest but is now a fragile habitat. The visitor centre has an interactive exhibition on how this landscape was created and the flora and fauna it supports.

➜ 1.5km S of Dokkedal on the R541. Start at the visitor centre 2.5km W of here on Birkesøvej. Lille Vildmosecentret, Birkesøvej, 9280 Storvorde. www.lifelillevildmose.dk
56.8716, 10.2218

26 THY NATIONAL PARK

The biggest and oldest national park in Denmark, and not just an important natural landscape. Remains dating from the Stone Age have been found in numerous historical sites here, and there are also coastal defences built by German troops during the Second World War. Helpful information about the various features is available at the visitor centre as well as maps for hiking or biking routes. The total area of the national park is 244 sq km.

➜ Head W from Sundby on the R571 and you'll find the Stenbjerg landing area information centre by the beach at the very end of the road: Stenbjergvej 120, 7752 Snedsted, +45 22 221666. www.nationalparkthy.dk
56.9298, 8.3382

27 HIMMELBJERGET

One of highest points in Denmark at 147m but not, according to geologists, a 'real hill' because it is not evenly rounded on all sides. This feature, called a pseudo-hill was formed at the end of the last Ice Age. At the top is a tower built to commemorate King Frederik VII signing the constitution in 1849 that established a Danish parliament and made the country a constitutional monarchy. Great views and a nice spot for a picnic.

➜ From the R52 at Rodelund head E on the R445. After 13km turn L onto the R461 and follow it N for 2.5km to the parking area at the end of the road. From here it's a 500m signposted walk to the top of the hill.
56.1056, 9.6837

28 SAMSØ LABYRINTEN

The world's largest maze (and recognised as such by Guinness), covering an enormous 6 hectares with over 50,000 bushes and trees. As you explore you're also likely to come across various species of woodland animal. Great family fun.

26

30

→ Take Issehoved N for 10km from the centre of Nordby on the island of Samsø. Issehoved 1, 8305 Samsø, +45 86 596659.
www.samsolabyrinten.com
55.9724, 10.5539

LOCAL FOOD

29 SKAGEN BRYGHUS

Northernmost Brewery in Denmark that is also a restaurant and music venue with regular events and guided tours. After a day on the beach enjoy the local food and taste the delicious beers.

→ Next to Skagen Church. Kirkevej 10, 9990 Skagen, +45 98 450050.
www.skagenbryghus.dk
57.7222, 10.5836

SLEEP WILD

30 SCANDINAVIAN DYREPARK DJURSLAND

Spend the night sleeping in a Sami lavvu tent in the middle of a wildlife park where you will hear wolves howl, bears roar and eagles calling during the night. When the day trippers have left, a guide takes you round to say goodnight to the animals and then you have the place to yourself. A fantastic adventure for families.

→ From Grenaa head SW for 23km on the R15 then turn R onto Drammelstrupvej. Continue on to the village of Pederstrup where you turn L on to Nødagervej. The first turning on R after leaving the village will take you to the animal park: Skandinavisk Dyrepark, Nødagervej 67b, 8560 Kolind, +45 86 391333.
www.skandinaviskdyrepark.dk
56.3462, 10.6589

31 BUNKEN STRAND CAMPING

Large campsite on the Kattegat with direct access to both the forest and the beach. It's in a perfect location for exploring the Skagen Odde peninsula on foot or by bike. Glamp in a Mongolian yurt at the edge of the beach or in the dunes with amazing sea views.

→ Approx 18km from Skagen just S of Hulsig off the R40. Ålbækvej 288, 9982 Ålbæk, +45 98 487180. www.bunkenstrandcamping.dk
57.6443, 10.4622

32 DEN GAMLE ARREST

Old Jailhouse where the former prison cells have been converted into quirky and simply furnished bedrooms. There's also a café and arts and crafts are sold in the dungeon.

→ Opposite cathedral in Ribe. Torvet 11, 6760 Ribe, +45 75 423700. www.dengamlearrest.dk
55.3277, 8.7620

33 HOUDAM FARM BED & BREAKFAST

Organic dairy farm offering fun and stylish B&B with local ecological food. Children will love feeding and milking the cows.

→ 5km W of Lemvig. Houdamvej 7, 7620 Lemvig, +45 97 836041. www.houdam.dk
56.5424, 8.2113

Krage

Aalborg

Dall

Fløj

Hov

Als

Anholt by

Hobro

Randers

Viborg

Holstebro

Husby

Aarhus

Eg

Odden

Silkeborg

Herning

Uhre

Horsens

Hundested

Bøvl

Vejle

Høed

Kolding

Odense

Rud

Esberg

Funen

Å

257

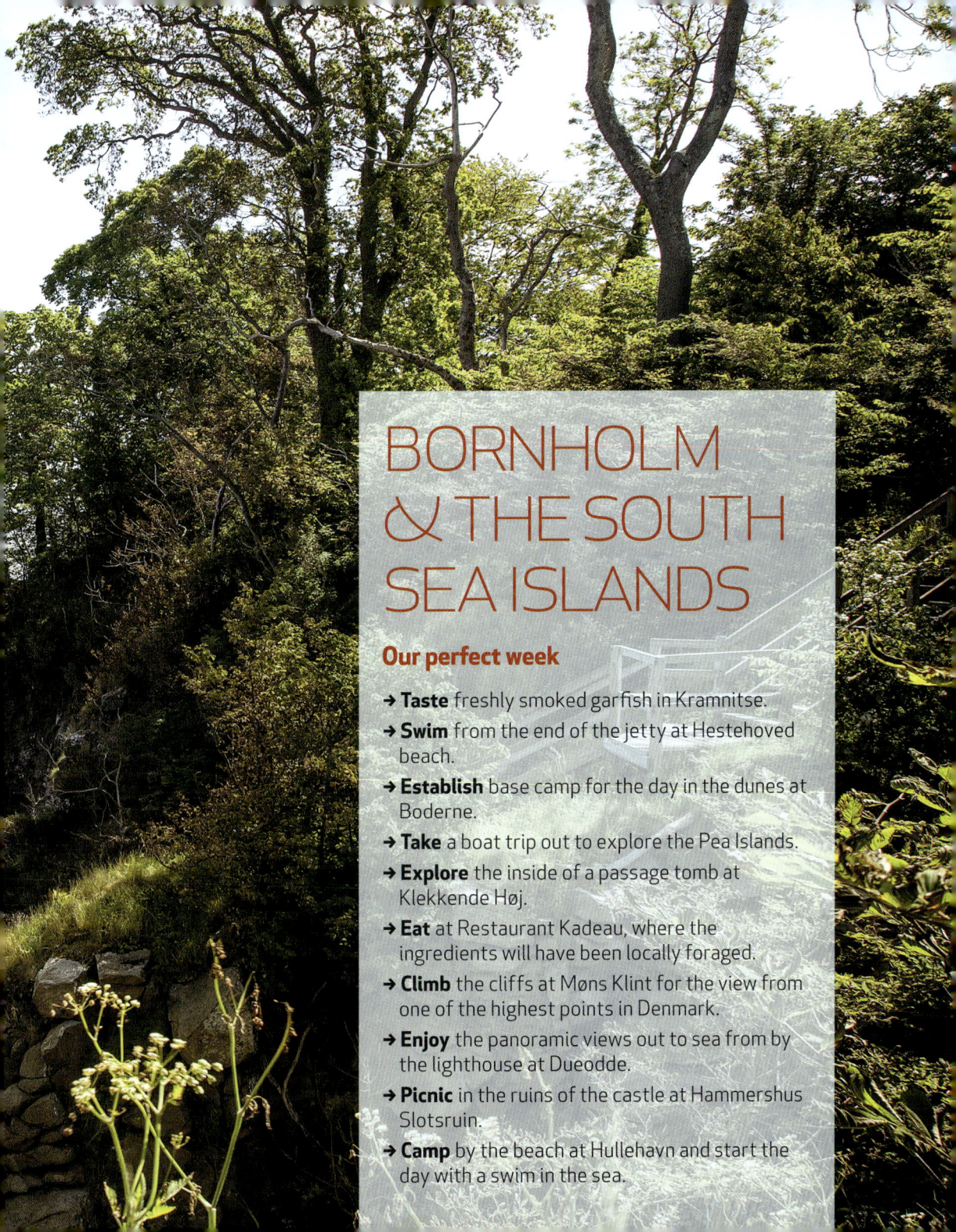

BORNHOLM & THE SOUTH SEA ISLANDS

Our perfect week

→ **Taste** freshly smoked garfish in Kramnitse.

→ **Swim** from the end of the jetty at Hestehoved beach.

→ **Establish** base camp for the day in the dunes at Boderne.

→ **Take** a boat trip out to explore the Pea Islands.

→ **Explore** the inside of a passage tomb at Klekkende Høj.

→ **Eat** at Restaurant Kadeau, where the ingredients will have been locally foraged.

→ **Climb** the cliffs at Møns Klint for the view from one of the highest points in Denmark.

→ **Enjoy** the panoramic views out to sea from by the lighthouse at Dueodde.

→ **Picnic** in the ruins of the castle at Hammershus Slotsruin.

→ **Camp** by the beach at Hullehavn and start the day with a swim in the sea.

Cycling around Bornholm you can't help but be amazed that a small island with an area of just 588 square kilometres can have such a variety of breathtaking landscapes. Following the network of roads, lanes and tracks that run almost parallel to the 158 kilometres of coastline, you'll pass many incredibly beautiful places. Walk through deep wooded valleys with waterfalls, visit granite outcrops with ruined castles, and sit on beaches with sand so fine it was once used for hourglasses.

These history-rich landscapes have also been the source of many exciting archaeological and paleontological finds. A hundred million years ago a large bird lizard known as a dromaeosaur lost a tooth on the island and in 2000 it was sensationally discovered by a young girl. Palaeontologists are still looking for more dinosaur remains.

In addition to the island of Bornholm, this chapter also includes the islands of Ærø, Langeland, Lolland, Falster and Møn. Bornholm, in the Baltic, is about 120 kilometres east of Copenhagen and only 37 kilometres south of Sweden. The best way to get there is, in fact, by ferry from the Swedish towns of Ystad or Simrishamn in Österlen (see p178). The other islands, which are all linked by bridges and are immediately south of either Sealand (see p232)or Funen (see p240), are easily reached by road.

On every one of these islands you're never far from an amazing Danish beach. Some are more protected than others, and those beaches that shelve very gradually are much safer for small children. Bornholm, in particular, is well known for its cuisine and after working up an appetite in the fresh air, make sure you try the local delicacy of smoked herring fillet on rye bread –sol over gudhjem.

Away from the coast, a visit to the museum on the island of Ærø offers a fascinating insight into the pace of life on a typical Danish island before fast ferries and enormous bridges. In Bornholm's Døndalen valley, take a break from watching the deer and buzzards to see how many of the 150 tree species that have been planted there you can identify, then follow the path to Denmark's highest waterfall.

BEACHES

1 DUEODDE, BORNHOLM

Stunningly beautiful beach with white sand so fine that it was once used for hourglasses. Behind the beach, which is a protected area, the dunes have been planted with pine trees and grasses to prevent the sand drifting in the wind. Dueodde lighthouse, which is sometimes open, overlooks the beach and has far-reaching, panoramic views. This is a good place to swim – deeper water is close to the shore between the sandbars. There are also two partially built wartime bunkers: the German soldiers were moved to Norway in 1941 before the structures were completed.

→ Dueodde beach is on the southernmost tip of Bornholm and has numerous access points.
15 mins, 54.9871, 15.0755

2 MARIELYST STRAND, FALSTER

Typical Danish sandy beach with calm shallow water and fringed by grassy sand dunes that offer protection on a windy day. During the summer the beach has lifeguard cover so it's particularly safe for small children to swim and play in the sea.

→ Located on the E coast of the island of Falster. The beach stretches S from the small town of Marielyst. Numerous access points.
10 mins, 54.6893, 11.9696

3 KRAMNITSE, LOLLAND

Long, sandy beach where seaweed and driftwood often wash up on the tideline, making it a good spot for beachcombing. The surf is also good and this is a popular beach for surfing, kite-surfing and windsurfing. If you want to stay for a while, there are several campsites around. The flat inland areas are protected from coastal flooding by a series of dykes and pumps, including the most powerful pumping station in Northern Europe. Around the harbour from 21–24 July there's a garfish festival when the unusual-looking fish are caught, smoked and eaten.

→ 8km-long stretch from Lilleholm Kanal just N of Kramnitse to Rødbyhavn on the W coast of Lolland island. Numerous access points.
10 mins, 54.7037, 11.2582

4 HESTEHOVED BEACH, LOLLAND

Lovely sand beach created on Nakskov Fjord that has particularly calm and shallow water. A great place for families with small children. The area around the beach is a Natura 2000 protected area due to its diverse bird life. For a decent swim, head to the 190m bathing jetty and strike out across the fjord.

→ Beach is 2km to the W of Nakskov and can be reached by following Strandpromenaden from the town centre to the end of the road.
5 mins, 54.8325, 11.0896

5 RISTINGE BEACH

Often cited as one of the best beaches on Langeland, with fine sand and grassy dunes. Spread out and spend the day here or just take a picnic. At the far end of the beach are 30m-high sandy cliffs where you can hunt for fossils. A great beach for swimming.

→ Located S of the small town of Ristinge with numerous access points over its 8km length.
5 mins, 54.8163, 10.6383

6 BODERNE, BORNHOLM

Sand beach backed by rugged dunes where you can find a sheltered hollow and set up base camp for a long day by the sea. Favoured by people who want a discreet spot to swim and sunbathe nude.

→ On the W coast of Bornholm and runs S for 1.6km from the harbour in the village of Boderne, where there's a car park and the best access to the beach.
10 mins, 55.0229, 14.9064

CULTURE & HISTORY

7 HAMMERSHUS SLOTSRUIN, BORNHOLM

Cliff-top remains of a once large and important medieval castle, built to defend Bornholm in 1200. After it was abandoned in 1745, the structure was used as a source of building materials for local people and gradually decayed. Now the ruined castle, in a very commanding position with fantastic views, is a fascinating place to explore. Children will love the informative exhibition in the old castle yard, including pieces of (very heavy) armour to try on. Bring a picnic.

→ The castle is 4km S of the northern tip of Bornholm on the west coast. It can be reached by following Slotslyngvej N from the R159.

5 mins, 55.2713, 14.7554 🔲🔲🔲🔲

8 ERTHOLMENE ISLANDS

Christiansø and Frederiksø, lying 20km NE of Svaneke (Bornholm), are known collectively as the 'Pea Islands' (Ertholmene). Since 1684 they have functioned as Denmark's easternmost military outpost and extensive fortifications have been built there over the centuries. Bring your binoculars for the amazing birdlife.

→ Ferry from Bornholm to Christiansø (20km)

leaves from both Allinge and Gudhjem. For timetables and booking information see: +45 56 485176. www.bornholmexpress.dk

50 mins, 55.3207, 15.1859 🔲🔲🔲🔲

9 MADSEBAKKE CARVINGS, BORNHOLM

Denmark's most extensive rock-carving site dating from the late Bronze Age. One of the rocks is embellished with 14 ships, 5 wheel crosses, 5 engravings shaped like feet, and many cup marks. Unlike the images at some sites, the carvings here are very easy to distinguish.

→ From Sandvig at the far N of Bornholm, head S on Strandvejen for approx 1.2km. Just after the Statoil petrol station, turn R into Stadionsvej and follow it to the end. Continue along the path on foot for a further 150m and find Madsebakke on L.

15 mins, 55.2819, 14.7888 🔲

10 GRØNSALEN, MØN

The largest long barrow in Denmark, a whopping 100m long and 10m wide and surrounded by 134 standing stones. Believed to date back to the Neolithic period on account of its shape. According to folklore, Grøn Jæger, legendary hunter and king, is said to be buried here alongside his wife, Fane.

Very impressive owing to its sheer size.

→ From the village of Store Damme in the SW of the island of Møn, head S on Fanefjord Kirkevej. After approx 2km there's a marked parking area on the R. Park and then walk about 100m up the track on the opposite side of the road. The barrow is at the end on R.

10 mins, 54.8964, 12.1519 ⬛✝

11 KLEKKENDE HØJ, MØN

Fascinating megalithic tomb thought to be around 4,500 years old. Of the more than 100 that can be found on the island, this is by far the best preserved with two parallel stone-lined passages leading into a large earth mound. It has been fitted with an electric light so you can go inside and take a look. A rare opportunity to enter a burial site from Neolithic times.

→ From the village of Røddinge (N of Askeby) in the SW of the island of Møn, head S on Røddingevej for approx 1km then turn L on to Klekkendevej. After approx 40m and just before a copse on L follow a path S across the field for approx 250m to the burial chamber.

5 mins, 54.9362, 12.1642 ⬛▫

12 ÆRØSKØBING BYMUSEUM, ÆRØ

Learn about life on a small Danish island through interesting displays of domestic, maritime and agricultural artefacts. The museum features a special collection of regional costumes and children will be intrigued by the assortment of old toys.

→ The museum is in the centre of Ærøskøbing on the E coast of the island of Ærø. For information on ferries to Ærø from Fynshav (Jutland), Svendborg (Funen) and Faaborg (Funen), go to www.aeroe-ferry.dk. Ærøskøbing Bymuseum, Brogade 3, 5970 Ærøskøbing, +45 62 522950. www.arremus.dk

54.8889, 10.4123 ⬛▫

NATURE & WILDLIFE

13 MØNS KLINT

Impressive high chalk cliffs characterise this island, which is a unique habitat for numerous rare plants. On the slopes behind the cliffs the landscape is a mix of woodland, ponds and pasture, while the beach below is a great place for fossil hunting. From the geological museum you can explore the path over the cliffs or along the beach. One of the highest points in Denmark with fantastic views.

→ Start at the GeoCenter, on the R287 E of Magleby on the island of Møn. The cliffs are immediately N of here and can be reached by walking along the beach. GeoCenter Møns Klint, Stengårdsvej 8, 4791 Borre, +45 55 863600. www.moensklint.dk

15 mins, 54.9841, 12.5437 ▫⬛

14 THE HAMMER, BORNHOLM

The northern tip of the island, known as 'The Hammer', is the only place in Denmark (apart from the Ertholmene islands, see 8) where you'll find sheer granite cliffs and crags. From the cliffs there are wonderful views out over the Baltic and along the coast. There's also a large freshwater lake that you can swim in.

→ Walk along the Hammer and enjoy a cliff-top picnic. For a circular walk round the N tip of Bornholm, start at Sandvig, heading N and follow the coastal path. Continue down the W coast to the Hammerhus castle ruins before heading back E across the island to Sandvig. The total distance is approx 14km.

3 hrs, 55.2989, 14.7732 ⬛▫⬛▫⬛

15 DØNDALEN, BORNHOLM

Picturesque valley just inland from the island's northern coast and home to Denmark's biggest waterfall, Døndaleåen. Tumbling from a height of 20m over rocks

17

18

and down into the bottom of the valley below, it is a spectacular sight. The wooded valley is particularly beautiful in springtime when carpeted with wood anemones and wild garlic. Numerous archaeological discoveries have been made here including burial mounds, cremation sites and a sword in a wooden sheath. The woodland itself, a mixture of over 150 deciduous trees including several rare wild service trees (Sorbus torminalis), was planted by a local farmer in 1916. The highest point in the valley at Amtmandssten can be reached via a flight of steps – a good location for spotting deer or buzzards. Listen out for the song of the nightingale.

→ About halfway along the R158 between Tejn and Gudhjem find a signed car park (55.2267, 14.8845). Stop here and choose from several signposted footpaths through woodland along the valley.
55.2272, 14.8846

16 EKKODALEN, BORNHOLM

At 12km, this is the longest rift valley in Denmark. It was originally named Kodalen (*ko* means 'cow' and *dalen* is 'valley') but at some point *ek* was added and it became 'Echo Valley'. Given the great acoustics created by the cliff sides, it's very appropriate. Have fun trying to find the best spot to send an echo reverberating along the valley.

→ 4km N of Aakirkeby off Almindingsvej on the island of Bornholm, find the Ekkodalen visitor centre and café. Park here and start your exploration. Ekkodalsvejen 5, 3720 Aakirkeby, +45 56 970060. www.ekkodalshuset.dk
55.1076, 14.8988

CYCLE

17 BORNHOLM CYCLING

Explore the island of Bornholm by bike. An established 102km coastal route will take you along granite cliffs, over rolling hills of bright yellow rapeseed and beside white sand beaches. This is an adventure suitable for the whole family and a variety of bicycles are available for hire on the island.

→ Bicycle hire: Bornholms Cykeludlejning, Nordre Kystvej 5, 3700 Rønne, +45 56 951359. www.bornholms-cykeludlejning.dk. For details of the 'Round Bornholm' event and a route map you can use for your own trip, see: www.cykelbornholmrundt.dk
55.1021, 14.6916

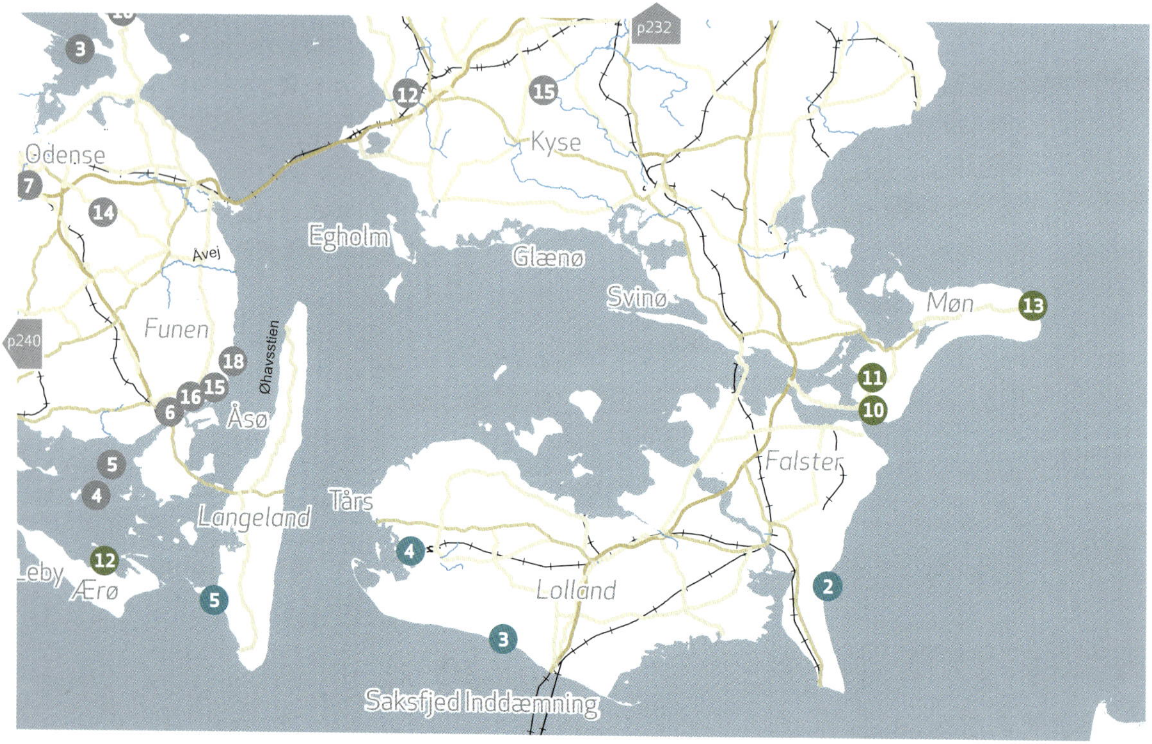

18 HASLE RØGERI (SMOKERY), BORNHOLM

Here, herring is smoked a delicious golden-brown colour over an open fire for Bornholm's speciality Sol over Gudhjem. It consists of smoked herring fillet served on rye bread, topped with radish, dill, a pinch of salt and a raw egg yolk. Smoking fish is traditional here and many of the old fishing cottages on Bornholm have chimneys with unusual pyramid-shaped bases.

➔ Approx 11km north of Rønne on the W coast of Bornholm. Søndre Bæk 20, 3790 Hasle, +45 56 962002. www.hasleroegeri.dk
55.1798, 14.7032

19 RESTAURANT KADEAU, BORNHOLM

Very special restaurant situated in a quiet location on Bornholm's west coast. Ingredients, from fish to fruit, are locally sourced and foraged. Expect dishes featuring herbs and berries as well as fish prepared using traditional techniques of smoking and pickling.

➔ Approx 7.5km NW of the southernmost point on Bornholm. Baunevej 18, 3720 Aakirkeby, +45 56 978250. www.kadeau.dk
55.0046, 14.9691

20 STAMMERSHALLE BADEHOTEL

Traditional Danish bathing hotel built next to the sea on Bornholm's rocky coast in 1911. Guests came here to enjoy the health benefits of sea-water bathing. The restaurant serves local dishes and is highly recommended. Take a swim before dinner.

➔ 2.5km S of Tejn on the E coast of Bornholm. Søndre Strandvej 128, 3760 Gudhjem, +45 56 484210. www.stammershalle-badehotel.dk
55.2394, 14.8660

21 GREEN SOLUTION HOUSE, BORNHOLM

Eco hotel that has adopted all the latest green technologies as well as pioneering a variety of new ones. Only recycled or biodegradable materials have been used in its construction, including glass and bricks from the previous hotel on the site. Waste water is cleaned using algae which is then converted to gas to generate electricity. The kitchen also uses ingredients from sustainable sources, serving classic dishes with a modern twist based on local and organic produce.

➔ On the coast road on the S side of Rønne, Bornholm. Strandvejen 79, 3700 Rønne, +45 56 951913. www.greensolutionhouse.dk
55.0852, 14.7103

22 HULLEHAVN CAMPING, BORNHOLM

Wooded campsite on the east coast of the island. The camping area runs down to the sea where there is a rocky plateau with sandy inlets. Have a dip before supper or sit and watch the sunset. Great swimming with a diving board on the rocks by the beach.

➔ On the E coast of Bornholm just S of Svaneke: Sydskovvej 9, 3740 Svaneke, +45 56 496363. www.hullehavn.dk
55.1308, 15.1507

21

Further information

Norway

Books & maps

Norway – The Northern Playground by W. Cecil Slingsby. Story of the first ascents by the British climber who is considered to be the father of Norwegian mountaineering.

Nordeca (Nordeca.com) publish a wide variety of Norwegian maps, including the Turkart series for outdoor activities. Available in the UK from Stanfords (Stanfords.co.uk).

Explore Lofoten – a fantastic companion guide to even more places and things to do in the Lofoten Islands by Kristin Folsland Olsen. Available from Folsand.no/words

Websites

Miljodirektoratet.no/en/ – website of the Norwegian Environment Agency with brochures to download on national parks and the right to roam.

English.dnt.no – the Norwegian Trekking Association (DNT) has lots of advice in English on safety and accommodation in remote mountain areas.

Sweden

Books & maps

A Year in Lapland – Guest of the Reindeer Herders by Hugh Beach. Fascinating insight from a young American anthropologist who lived with the Sami in Swedish Lapland in the 1970s and then revisited at the beginning of the 21st century.

Fishing in Utopia by Andrew Brown. Account of a journalist who moved to Sweden for love in the 70s and then after a long period back in the UK returns to Sweden and reflects on the changes in contemporary Swedish society.

Calazo.se publish numerous technical guides and maps for outdoor activities in Sweden, with English-language versions of their most popular titles in the pipeline.

Lantmateriet.se are the Swedish state mapping agency and they publish numerous maps for outdoor activities. Available in the UK from Stanfords.

Websites

Swedishepa.se – website of the Swedish Environment Agency with information on national parks and the right to roam.

Fjallsakerhetsradet.se/eng/ – the Swedish Mountain Safety Council has lots of advice in English on safety and accommodation in remote mountain areas.

Iceland

Books & maps

Read anything by Halldór Laxness, as well as the Sagas of the Icelanders.

Mál og Menning publish a wide selection of Icelandic maps that are available in the UK from Stanfords.

Websites

Road.is – travel advice on the unusual driving conditions you're likely to encounter.

Safetravel.is – mountain and wilderness travel advice from Icelandic Mountain Rescue.

Ust.is/the-environment-agency-of-iceland/ – information about the national parks and the rules about wild camping and access.

Denmark

Books & maps

The Year of Living Danishly by Helen Russell. Humorous and informative observations on contemporary Danish culture from an English journalist who moved with her husband to Denmark and started a family there.

Nordic Korthandel (Nordisk Korthandel) publish numerous tourist maps of Denmark, as does the state mapping agency (Gst.dk). Maps from both publishers are available in the UK from Stanfords.

Websites

Eng.naturstyrelsen.dk/experience-nature/ – is the website of the Danish Nature Agency and has information on access as well an interactive map of wild camping areas and hiking shelters.

Scandinavian Outdoor Group

Scandinavia is well known for its excellent outdoor brands, many of whom produce to the highest sustainability and ethical standards. We are pleased to partner with the Scandinavian Outdoor Group (SOG), an alliance of more than 50 Scandinavian outdoor companies, united and working together for good.

66 North - 8848 Altitude – Aclima – Alfa – Amundsen – Bergans - Blå Band – Cintamani – Craft – Dale – Devold – Didriksons – Drytech – Ecco – Exel – Fjällräven – Haglöfs – Helsport – Hestra – Hilleberg – Houdini – Icebug - Isbjörn of Sweden – Ivanhoe – Klättermusen – Kupilka - Light My Fire – Lundhags - Mora of Sweden - Nokian - Norröna - Northern Playground - Peak Performance - Point 65 – Polyver – Primus - Reima Oy – Röjk – Sätila – Seger – Silva – SKHOOP - Skogstad Sport – Tenson – Tentipi – Thule – Trangia – Tretorn – Ulvang – Viking – Walkstool – Wildo - Woolpower

Wild Guide Scandinavia (Sweden, Norway, Denmark and Iceland)

Swim, camp, canoe and explore Europe's greatest wilderness

Words:
Ben Love

Photos:
Ben Love
and those credited

Editing:
Candida Frith-Macdonald
Anna Kruger

Design and layout:
Oliver Mann
Marcus Freeman
Tania Pascoe

Proofreading:
Georgia Laval

Distribution:
Central Books Ltd
99 Wallis Road
London, E9 5LN
Tel +44 (0)845 458 9911
orders@centralbooks.com

Published by:
Wild Things Publishing Ltd.
Freshford, Bath,
BA2 7WG, United Kingdom
hello@
wildthingspublishing.com

Author acknowledgements I would like to thank the many people throughout Scandinavia who helped me during my travels and in no particular order - Pernilla Abrahamsson & colleagues at Amesto Translations, Inka Gurung, James Venimore, Peter & Siv Persson, Toni Franz, Emma Lundgren, Roger & Clare Sell, Betty Johannesson, Katrín Magnúsdóttir, Marie Mills, Pauline Love, Ebbe Love, Lucy Barratt, Benjamin Barratt, Isabel Barrat, Nathan Carter, Jerry Engström, Annika Hansson, Michele Tameni and all those who generously shared their photos.

WILD THINGS PUBLISHING